STATE CAPITOLS

Temples of Sovereignty

STATE CAPITOLS

Temples of Sovereignty

WRITTEN, PHOTOGRAPHED, AND PRODUCED BY

FRANCIS PIO RUGGIERO

EXCELSIOR
WORLDWIDE

Nothing may be reproduced in whole or part without written permission from
Excelsior, P.O. Drawer N, Milford, PA 18337
INTERNATIONAL COPYRIGHT CONVENTIONS APPLY

Created and produced in the Commonwealth of Pennsylvania
Manufactured and bound in the State of North Carolina
UNITED STATES OF AMERICA

Library of Congress Cataloguing-in-Publication Data is available
ISBN 0-9722231-1-8

To Marcy

Constant companion on the American journey,
my faithful love on our voyage through life

CONTENTS

"The United States themselves are essentially the greatest poem. ... Here is not merely a nation but a teeming nation of nations."

-- WALT WHITMAN, from the Preface to *Leaves of Grass*, 1855

PREFACE

Ba-dump. Ba-dump. Ba-dump.

The RV skipped down the interstate highway. The tires hitting the concrete seams of the road produced a sound as steady as a clock ticking.

Ba-dump. Ba-dump. Ba-dump.

I was becoming only gradually aware of my surroundings, waking from a rocky, broken sleep that is familiar to anyone who has slept in a moving vehicle overnight.

The sun pierced the windshield as I leaned forward and adjusted the seat upward.

"Look! Look! There it is!" Marcy exclaimed, holding the steering wheel with one hand and pointing out the window with the other.

I rubbed my eyes. "Ehh ...what?" It had been seven hours since we saw the last one.

"Look!" she demanded, the anticipation in her voice stirring me like a strong cup of coffee. The thrill of seeing one for the first time is like a bird watcher who spots the near-extinct specimen.

"Do you see it? There it is!" she cried.

It then came into focus as my eyes adjusted to the early morning light. Far in the distance I could see the outlines of the city, and the many lines of road leading to it. Cars, trucks, and buses raced by, flowing with us. And there, somewhat in the center, a beam of sunlight reflected the color gold. The RV raced to that golden speckle.

Ba-dump. Ba-dump. Ba-dump.

The rhythm was quickening. The creases in the road were closer together. We were nearing the end of the interstate. And then we both saw the object we had been pursuing. We didn't speak a word. We sized up the edifice as we passed by, assessing its features.

"Wow! I really like it," Marcy said.

"I don't know yet," I cautiously replied.

Like *deja vu*, this scene played itself out over and over again -- not once, not twice, not even a dozen times. More like forty-nine and now, here in Atlanta, Georgia, we would replay the ritual for the fiftieth and final time.

Yet on each occasion a potent awe overtook us. For what we saw with our eyes and felt with our hearts was only matched by a feeling of epic accomplishment: we were seeing and photographing all of America's Capitols.

Architecture mightier than the great cathedrals of Europe. Temples not to God, but to the rights He had given to each human being.

Temples of Sovereignty.

Americans were the first to build them and establish by law the principle behind them: that each individual in society is sovereign, and not just one of them.

The experience itself -- driving to every state, meeting different people, tasting regional cuisine, and capturing the essence of each capitol on film -- was, for my wife and me, the Incredible Journey. Its conclusion returned treasure chests of memories not easily forgotten, and an understanding of America and Americans not easily described.

The trip was the most exhilarating part of the project. Our journey began in June 2000 shortly after my wife and I, married for sixteen years, learned we would be parents at year's end. The joy of expectant parenthood was accompanied by tremors of mortality. Odd and demanding projects (like photographing each state capitol) would soon be competing with the responsibility of fatherhood. So, my sole companion of sixteen years and I made one last stab at doing "something together" and embarked on the Incredible Journey.

Loaded in a mini-RV, we departed our home in Pennsylvania and drove, over the next six months, to each American State. Do not think for a minute the trip was continuous; work and other responsibilities prohibited that. Traveling was broken into five periods. Many of the Original States were first completed, they being the closest. Next we circled in a loop around the mid-west. The third trip was the big coast-to-coast mission and included jetting to Juneau, Alaska and Honolulu, Hawai'i. The fourth portion of the trip was buttoning down our commonwealth's Capitol as well as neighboring ones. And, lastly, the southern loop: out to Arizona and ending in Georgia.

These were exciting times for us personally and as citizens. The baby was growing larger and larger but Marcy didn't mind; she loved being out and doing something. Our expedition overlapped with the presidential elections of 2000 and we felt like we were in the thick of it. On the night before the election we happened to be in Nashville, Tennessee shooting the Capitol. We stayed in a hotel overlooking last-minute preparations for the Gore Victory Party. A week later we were outside Governor George Bush's office in the Texas Capitol as the world's media settled in to cover the controversy. Near the end of the month we were in Tallahassee on the opening of the Florida Legislature. Rumors swirled that the presidential stalemate would be settled once and for all by these men and women.

Fortunately, Marcy and I did not lose sight of our mission. A wonderful Thanksgiving Dinner at the Ritz-Carlton in Atlanta, Georgia was the official end of our journey, the Georgia Capitol being completed the day before. A little over a month later, Chiara Noelle Ruggiero was born.

The next eighteen months were short on excitement, travel, and good food and long on personal adjustment. Getting use to baby Chiara was easy; maintaining the discipline to finish *this baby* was something else.

Most of all, as it is a paean to my journalism guru Russell J. Jandoli, I wanted this book to be perfect. Every fact double checked. Each attribution verified. Photograph captions confirmed. As the states are the principal sources of the information contained herein, the accuracy of their facts and figures is presupposed. A quick phone call could verify facts recorded on-site. We made many phone calls.

The result you hold in your hands is a history book, documenting the individual birth of fifty states. It is a study in architecture, detailing the interior and exterior of fifty unique temples. It is a photography book, capturing the essence of America's mighty monuments. Nearly 700 pages and 824 photographs are featured. We drove 21,393 miles and flew 4,316 air miles.

Considering the myriad facts and photographs which had to be assembled, and knowing firsthand of man's imperfection, it is possible that an error slipped passed our eyes, in which case I ask the reader to notify me at the address below so that it may be corrected in future editions.

Francis Pio Ruggiero
Milford, Pennsylvania
May 10, 2002

STATE INDEX

INDEX BY STATE TYPE

Each American State is placed in one of five categories: 1) *The Original States*, these being the thirteen original members of the United States; 2) *The Charter States*, these being the states made from territory held by the various Original States; 3) *The Nation States*, these being states which were independent nations or republics before joining the United States; 4) *The Purchased States*, these being states made or gained through purchase or negotiation; 5) *The War States*, these being the states or territories gained in war by the United States.

ORIGINAL STATES

CHARTER STATES

[1]Minnesota's eastern half was ceded to Great Britain in 1763 by France and passed to the Original States with the Revolution's conclusion. This half was considered part of the Northwest Territories. In an effort to ensure that the Mississippi's headwaters were included, the Northwest Angle was created by American and British negotiators — a true geographical enclave, a piece of Minnesota that sits inside and surrounded by Canada, resulted because of inaccurate maps. The western part of the state was part of the Louisiana Purchase. Because St. Paul, the capital, is located in the eastern portion, Minnesota is assigned here.

NATION STATES

PURCHASED STATES

WAR STATES

SEE THE INDEX BEGINNING ON PAGE 651

[2]Kansas' southwest corner was originally part of Texas.

[3]Colorado's eastern half was part of the Louisiana Purchase; its southern portion was originally part of Texas; and the western part of the state was gained in war with Mexico (1848).

[4]Montana's extreme west was part of the Oregon Territory.

[5]Wyoming's southwestern corner was gained in the Mexican War; the western portion of the state was originally part of the Oregon Territory.

[6]North Dakota's extreme east and north passed to the Original States with the Revolution's conclusion.

[7]Oklahoma's famous pan handle was originally part of Texas.

[8]Arizona & New Mexico gained additional southern lands on the border with Mexico as a result of the Gadsden Purchase, 45,535 square miles of territory, the majority of which is now in Arizona. The United States bought it for $10 million from Santa Anna in 1853. So upset were the Mexican people, the leader was banished from Mexico the next year.

[9]New Mexico's eastern half was gained by the U.S. from Texas; its western half was won in the Mexican War.

Introduction

The unanimous Declaration of the thirteen united States of America.

"... WE hold these Truths to be self-evident, that all Men are created equal, that they are endowed by their Creator with certain unalienable Rights, that among these are Life, Liberty, and the Pursuit of Happiness -- That to secure these Rights, Governments are instituted among Men, deriving their just Powers from the Consent of the Governed, that whenever any Form of Government becomes destructive of these Ends, it is the Right of the People to alter or abolish it, and to institute new Government, laying its Foundation on such Principles, and organizing its Powers in such Form, as to them shall seem most likely to effect their Safety and Happiness."

-- Declaration of Independence, July 4, 1776, with a facsimile of its formal title. By this document the states through their delegations in the Continental Congress pledged "to each other our Lives, our Fortunes, and our sacred Honor" in the cause of American Independence.

By law, each American maintains dual citizenship: one is a citizen of the state he or she lives in and is a citizen of the United States. That is because each of the United States maintains itself as a separate body politic from the others. And it is why an American State has a Capitol in the first place. The United States of America is a federal nation of constituent states. Legally it is not a consolidated nation-state like Canada, Great Britain, and France where powers not given to the provinces are reserved to the national government. In the United States there are no provinces and the exact opposite arrangement exists: all powers not given to the federal government by the U.S. Constitution are reserved to each state or the people thereof.

In fact, the United States more closely resembles the structure of the European Union than any of its member nations. In both the U.S. and E.U. the constituent parts pre-existed the formation of the union and are maintained independently within it.

Here's another way to understand these facts: no American village, town, county, region, or district has a Capitol. Only each American State and the United States. Your state can rearrange, merge, and divide all of its political subdivisions. Your village, city, town, county, etc. was chartered by your state and it has ultimate authority over these parts.

But the American States are not chartered by the United States and they are not its political subdivisions. In fact these states -- more precisely, the people forming the body politic in each -- chartered the United States and voluntarily restricted their own state's powers to empower it.

A state cannot be unwillingly rearranged, merged, or divided by any authority. Each state is indivisible except Texas, which alone retains the right to divide itself into five states within the United States.

Virginia was the first to call the building its political assembly met in the *Capitoll*. It officially named it this in 1699. Since that time to the present several hundred have been built throughout America and have been the scene of many great historical events. In these various capitols (or facilities borrowed for the purpose) each of the Original States authorized the Declaration of Independence. From here the delegates to the Constitutional Convention received their individual instructions. And by state law conventions of the people met to accept the federal constitution.

It was in a State Capitol where women were given the vote; where slavery was abolished; where public education was begun. Not for the whole of America, mind you, but for the people of that single state.

The first child labor laws, unemployment insurance benefits, minimum wage, and workman compensation laws were made in State Capitols.

The first Declaration of Independence, Bill of Rights, and Constitution were made in a State Capitol for that state's citizens alone, before delegations from all of the states accomplished it for the United States in general.

If your native state -- or the one you were living in during grade school -- accomplished any of the above, surely you were taught as much. But as far as knowing about the unique accomplishments of every other state, these tended to be lumped together under the rubric "United States history."

In other words, even the best student knows a lot about his or her own state and the United

States and little of any other as a distinct entity. This is a problem for one who wants to comprehend American history. For all of the principal issues and events interwoven in the fabric of our history involves, in varying degrees, the actions of individual states and their citizens.

Worse, the telling of history suffers from generalization and the tendency to focus on explaining "the one," to the exclusion or independent consideration of the many constituent parts. Modern histories tend to explain the creation and development of the United States nation (the one) and not the separate growth and development of the states, its constituent parts. In fact, the accomplishments of one state or the failure of another is made common to all.

For Americans this is not troubling because of their strong bonds with one another, common legal systems based on individual sovereignty, and a shared, glorious history. Yet something is to be gained by looking at American history as a patchwork quilt of fifty histories, and not just one. Perhaps a more balanced perspective on the great issues which have confronted us and a truer picture of reality await. By offering a more particular understanding, history becomes less general.

Thus civil rights and wrongs are related to the legally-designated community of their origin and do not sully the reputation of others. For instance, instead of saying that Americans destroyed the original inhabitants and their culture, we can say that while the Rhode Islanders established peaceful and interdependent relationships with native tribes, the Georgians deported tens of thousands of Cherokee to the Indian Country.

Being particular when it comes to different bodies politic or states is mandatory in understanding who did what. Under what authority was something done? This is the question that must be answered when speaking of human affairs. It would be inappropriate to say Europeans were responsible for the Holocaust when this was Germany's crime. How, then, can Americans be held responsible or be given credit for the distinct failures and achievements of the separate states? The answer is, they can be only when it is the action of the whole. Only when the United States as a single entity passes a law, conquers an enemy, protects its citizens, etc. should it be given the credit or the blame. And there is plenty of accomplishment, happy times, and victory to match any of the wrongs and defeats of so great and noble a nation.

Yet successes and failures of a state's people are theirs alone when under the auspices of, and within, the state the events occur. Two such attainments each American State can claim as its own, then, are the constituting of its body politic and the building of a Capitol to house its deliberations. Providing the facts which relate to the creation of these is the goal of this book.

This work does not intend to assign praise or blame, only identify the particular locales and participants in the great, the good, the bad, and the ugly aspects of our American heritage. And to better understand each state, the United States, and the country we call America.

The goal is accomplished by documenting and photographing the capitols while exploring each state's *raison d'etre*. The method used is more the style of a journalist than a historian, though one could argue both professions are but branches of the same tree.

The two differ in this: the journalist seeks to present objective fact for its sake alone; the historian attempts to explain the facts and their inter-relationships.

To execute this project in the mode the author has been trained is expedient. It is also easier and safer to carefully assemble and present facts than worry about passing judgement on them. The latter is fraught with corruption, manipulation, subjectivity, and error. The facts herein are easily verified. Conclusions to be drawn from them are left with the reader.

One benefit derived from examining the parts is a better understanding of the whole. As the author has no mission beyond presenting an accurate account of each state's creation, larger issues unfold naturally. By sparing the reader the fat of opinion or purpose, this history becomes more palatable. And through the ingestion of verifiable facts one comes to a truer understanding one's past.

METHODOLOGY

The ordering of this project was a concern. How were the states to be arranged? Alphabetically, it seemed, was not appropriate in aiding the reader's understanding of the time and place of a state. Geography was rejected as well because this, too, seemed arbitrary and without meaning. In the end a system that organizes states by group and by date was devised. American States are considered equals by the terms of the U.S. Constitution, but they are not equal in their origins.

Finding a methodology to account for their similarities led to these five groups:

ORIGINAL STATES

These include the thirteen British colonies who joined together to win the American Revolution and achieved the status of "free, sovereign and independent States" by the Treaty of Paris, 1783.

CHARTER STATES

These include all those states carved out of the territory held by various Original States which was granted to the United States under the Articles of Confederation.

NATION STATES

These include those states which formerly were independent of the United States and were republics or nations unto themselves.

PURCHASED STATES

These include all of those states created out of purchased territory, or territory which was gained through negotiation.

WAR STATES

These include all of those regions or states gained in war by the United States.

With these groups established, the next concern was incorporating some sort of dating system. This seemed vital. What is history but an account of the past? And what is the past without some chronological reference? A history without dates as anchors is a ship of knowledge unmoored from comprehension.

What date should sequence the chapters? Should it be when a state joined the United States? Or the date it formed its body politic?

The date when the body politic was established is the one used for ordering the states. Would not your birth be the operative date in considering the beginning of you, not the day you were married?

When citizens constituted a body politic was determined to be with its:

1) first legislative gathering;

2) first constitutional gathering; or,

3) formal establishment of a territorial legislature elected by the territory's people as a precursor to their joining the United States.

The first of these shall be considered the constituting of a state's body politic in this work.

Efforts that order the American States by when they joined the Union obliterate each state's distinct relevance -- it's almost like saying a state didn't matter until it consented to belong.

But what about entities which pre-existed the Union, as in the case of the Original States?

And what of those states that used to be nations? Or those that had been provinces for centuries under the control of the French and Spanish?

To understand the United States of America requires some particularization. And from learning these distinctions, a more comprehensive knowledge of why we are, who we are must follow.

Deference is given to those historical facts which come to us through official documents and declarations. For instance, we know when the first legislature of a state met because there is an official record of that meeting. Likewise, when ascertaining the reasons people formed a state, the official statement in the state constitution is used. Otherwise, great effort was made to include only those easily verifiable facts.

Readers should consider the various quotations which introduce each of the main chapters together, for nothing less than the chain of sovereignty running through the American States is documented, using only official sources. Great care has been taken to quote exactly from the original documents, with the aid of various state and federal authorities.

No people on this planet are as devoted to the study and application of law as Americans. What else could be expected from a society and legal system based on the sovereignty of the individual?

It means that all of the great and small issues involving sovereignty have been debated, argued, ruled on, contested, and fought over ever since the first person stepped on the continent and became an American.

It means there is a fantastic, deep well of related accomplishments over the centuries by individuals, states, and the nation they formed. The mission here is to assemble as many of these facts as possible, and present them

objectively; not to support an idea, but to spark ideas.

It is recommended the reader have at the ready the Declaration of Independence, Articles of Confederation, Northwest Ordinance of 1787, and the U.S. Constitution for further study.

These documents are a great read, sharp, and to the point. They were written by men who had no equal in their day. Each was made to be read, understood, and followed by the people who lived under the laws which resulted from them.

May we also encourage firsthand learning at the various capitols. Let this book serve as your guide as you walk through the marbled halls, or at least inspire you to visit your own.

These temples are not museums. They are alive. They are yet sustained by the rituals and miracles performed within: the act of making war and peace with ideas, not bullets. Of protecting the one, and the many.

Not a single American Capitol would be found lacking when compared against any other nation's capitol. Even kings or dictators would find most of the edifices suitably palatial. Sufficient is the dignity conveyed through the reds and golds of the crests and the crimson drapes, the elevated Speaker Chair, the flags and fasces, eagles, and mace -- the very symbols of power. Sufficient are these to suggest to the visitor the mighty and awesome powers which are unleashed or harnessed here.

Massive structures at once monumental, yet eminently functional. Halls and pillars, chandeliers and rotundas, domes and statues: these a king would find familiar.

But an elite ruler could never get used to the other chairs about him in the Great Hall. Chairs filled not with subjects, but with the delegates of the other sovereigns.

The ones called Americans.

Temples of Sovereignty

"We, therefore, the Representatives of the united States of America, in General Congress, Assembled, appealing to the Supreme Judge of the World for the Rectitude of our Intentions, do, in the Name, and by Authority of the good people of these Colonies, solemnly Publish and Declare, That these United Colonies are, and of Right ought to be, Free and Independent States; that they are absolved from all Allegiance to the British Crown, and that all political Connection between them and the State of Great-Britain, is and ought to be totally absolved; and that as Free and Independent States, they have full Power to levy War, conclude Peace, contract Alliances, establish Commerce, and to do all other Acts and Things which Independent States may of right do."

-- Declaration of Independence, July 4, 1776, jointly issued by the states meeting in Congress after each state sanctioned the separation and instructed its delegates to vote accordingly.

S overeignty means "subject to no one." The holder of this power in old times was called "king," "queen," or "lord." The "sovereign" held power over life and property in the community. His or her word was final; the other people in the community were "subject to" his or her command. Emperors and subjects -- this was the way of the world until groups of liberty-loving people washed the mud from their eyes and saw themselves in a society as it was naturally intended. They were not made to be subjects of another. Each one of them was of flesh and bones. Of mind and soul. Not one of them was endowed by the Creator any less in these regards. People may not be equal in talents, strengths, or weaknesses but before the law they are equally human beings.

The people who made manifest these truths were Americans. And it was quite an accomplishment. Sovereignty is not an easy concept to comprehend for people who never wore a robe or crown, or held a scepter.

To be sovereign, one is in the business of determination. To be sovereign, one is empowered to sacrifice the interests, rights, and liberties of one for another. To have final say on all laws and activities; to speak for the one community. To command the necessary power and force to carry these judgements forward; to see through the determination. This is sovereignty.

In a world without kings and queens, where does a community draw its rights to exercise governmental power and maintain order? What is the fount, but the consent of each person in the community to abide by the determinations of all? In return for this consent and as its first responsibility, the one community warrants to each member absolute protection of all those freedoms and liberties retained by each individual.

The consent of those governed is more than a legal principle. It is a natural law. Only with it will the governed obey the laws. A society in which laws are regularly broken, where the individual acts with impunity to the rulings of the many, is not legitimate. When large numbers of the body politic no longer follow the mandates of the law, it is the law which must be illegal and not individual violators.

That is why, to be effective, to be truthful, to be just, and most importantly, to be democratic, the sovereign power to make those laws which touch on the most intimate concerns of the individual, must be located as close to the individual and his community as possible, yet just far enough away to render justice.

In this, sovereignty is like the sun and the body politic like the planets. Feel too strongly its power, and the community of individuals burns up. Feel not enough of its unifying rays, the community never bonds. But strike the proper balance of power and freedom -- this is the living body politic.

Sovereignty is the body politic in action. An individual who possesses complete liberty and freedom is sovereign; in joining together with other individuals and agreeing on the terms of union, the body politic is constituted. In return for the benefits derived, the individual voluntarily accepts certain constraints on his or her liberties to empower the body politic -- the superintending authority removed from the passions of the rival peoples, communities, or ideas of which it is composed.

In the earliest times, all of the people in a territory or district were subjects of a sovereign and together with this ruler, a body politic was created -- a whole lot of bodies, but little politic. Citizens are equal members in a body politic; subjects are unequal when one or a select group is over all.

With the settlement of Jamestown in Virginia in 1607 began the creation of distinct political entities in North America. Though still British subjects, the isolation of the American colonies from the motherland required development of independent bodies politic. The British kings recognized this and granted the colonies self-rule in their various charters.

A true body politic is defined as a distinct community established under the authority of the separate individuals composing it, authorized to carry out the functions of government by, for, and of those members exclusively.

The Original States of Virginia, Maryland, Massachusetts, Connecticut, Pennsylvania, Rhode Island and Providence Plantations, Delaware, New York, New Hampshire, South Carolina, North Carolina, Georgia, and New Jersey each constituted itself a separate body politic, some before and some at the start of the American Revolution.

Earlier, each entity was established by the King under separate and distinct charters. Each colony developed independently of the other colonies during America's first one hundred years of European settlement.

Initially they were but corporations, each owing allegiance to the British King. Separated from England by the Atlantic Ocean in the east, and encountering native cultures to the west, the colonists bent the environment to aid in their survival and prosperity. Each domain required local control to ensure survival and to improve its circumstances.

Yet, one does not need authorization from a king thousands of miles away to form a militia for defense; to form a system of laws and justice; to regulate the interactions of people in their separate capacities as individuals,

families, and communities. This happens naturally, as does the development of the philosophical explanation for these realities -- the concept that individuals and communities possess sovereignty and other rights. The body politic balances the liberty and freedom of the community and the liberty and freedom of the individual.

The words *nation*, *state*, *republic*, *commonwealth* are convertible terms with "body politic"and "sovereignty in action." It is in the degree of powers the individual retains, what is delegated, and to whom by which we determine the extent of the body politic's power.

Sovereignty's source is each individual, its aspects collected together or "constituted" when each pledges to abide by the one (the lawmaking power) in return for respect of the individuality of all. Find a constitution among people specifying how laws are to be made and exercised, and you have, to some extent, a body politic. And where there is a body politic, there is sovereignty.

In that body politic which has the fewest members, individuals possess the most power, because they can quickly correct deficiencies. That body politic of body politics, with many individuals and communities as members, must possess the least power, if the rights and privileges of the parts are to be protected.

Certainly the largest, constituted body politic must have as its first purpose (that to which it is to be held accountable) the protection of the rights and privileges of the smaller bodies politic and the people who compose them. Without such safeguards, sovereignty becomes a commodity. Privileges once granted in solemn conventions of the people now become traded in the marketplace of the body politic -- the legislature and, more recently, the courts.

Sovereignty is the alpha and omega of civil society. Behind all constitutions, governments, states, nations, and the wars and oppressions which result from their interaction, is the question of sovereignty. To create systems in which separate sovereignties can operate perfectly within their sphere; ones in which the delegations of sovereignty are clearly and voluntarily made -- this is to perfect the art of government and insure justice for the many individuals and communities.

The Americans who threw off royal authority and created their own free and independent states knew something about this subject. The Declaration of Independence is but a dissertation on sovereignty, detailing why the states felt compelled to assume their lawful position in the world of nations. The American Revolution was the result.

Wars are the handmaiden of sovereignty. There can only be war where sovereignty is disputed. Every war Americans have been in -- the Revolution, Civil War, World War I, World War II, Korea, Vietnam -- involved parties who refused to be subject to the other.

Thus the opposite must hold: through the establishment, codification, and protection of sovereign communities can peace be secured. Denying the sovereign rights of individuals and communities must eventually lead to war.

Violence (man against man), war (state against state) are evidence of sovereignty denied and sovereignty asserted. When one man commits an act of violence on another, he is asserting the principle of being "subject to no one." A state or nation does no less when it makes war. But the assertion of such will or power over another person, state, or nation must concomitantly threaten the sovereignty of the other. In all such transactions, one must ask: Is there justice for all?

The body politic is formed rather easily. It begins with one individual. An individual alone is a body politic unto himself. And a body politic of many individuals, alone, is like one individual.

In making the one body politic, the individual members or their delegates agree on a basic law by which all other laws will be made, and the limitations of the law making power. This agreement is known as a constitution. From it all actions of the body politic must be derived to be legal. So, we can say the beginning of a body politic is with the meeting of the people's representative's in assembly, or with the drafting of a formal agreement to make law for, and in the name of, the one community.

Each American State achieved its status as a separate body politic in its own way. With the start of the Revolution, each of the Original States had established a constitution, many including a Declaration of Rights. Some styled their body politic a republic, others a commonwealth, and others a state.

Each one asserted sovereignty over its domain and continues to do so -- more than two centuries after the Declaration of Independence was written.

The notion is simple and serves as the basis of all American law. Yet it is not well comprehended: as the individual is sovereign so together the people in their body politic are sovereign. This means they have reserved powers of a mystical nature only they, each one of them, can delineate. Powers inherent and at once undefined, awaiting a determination by each of them as to what is to be accepted and what is to be rejected. The right and power to determine how the community is to conduct its affairs.

So by what authority does each American State make law and order its society? From the people constituting the state's body politic. And what restrictions does the body politic accept on its powers? Only those it has outlined in its constitution or delegated to another entity.

THE ISLAND STATE

As Americans have never been nobles, and in fact have systematically rejected all forms of rank and nobility, it is difficult to imagine what it feels like to be a king or queen. Yet it is absolutely essential that the reality of individual sovereignty be felt; that each of us understand the nature of our society and our own official and private roles in it as citizens.

Sovereignty implies the One: one individual, one community, one state, one nation, one world. But one that is formed with the voluntary combination of many. In America the United States *is* the constituted federal nation, but *these* United States are constituted unto themselves.

The First Person living alone on an island determines his actions: when and what to eat, the roads and houses to be built, the social and economic customs to be practiced. The First Person is subject to no one. But with no one to share the island and perpetuate this life on the island, all would perish with his or her death.

So to bring meaning, purpose, and progress, a mate is needed. Another person with whom the First Person shall create a family. Because of this natural necessity, the First Person, though a single entity, must join with another, and it is in this union that the first community is born.

The family is the First Society. The people within the family order their lives, interact with each other, provide for the basic necessities, learn, read, study, worship, play, and dream under their own rules, as they determine them -- *subject to no one.*

In this way we understand sovereignty in action. Ideally the parents exercise a just rule upon which the most heartfelt benevolence, love, and compassion is spread. Justice is immediate and fair. The union of these people -- this First Society -- is sovereign within its domain. But should a parent leave the other, or should a parent be not respectful, fair, and loving but rather, cruel and abusive, then the disunion of these two on the island must be facilitated.

Will the breakup be fair and equitable?

If there is no other person, family, or community on the island, it cannot be. For an impartial, superintending authority must be present for this reason: by being a party to an action, one is automatically disqualified from judging the rightfulness of the outcome.

A lord or king holds the absolute power to judge those things he has an interest in. He claims a right to decide what is best for all. But the sovereign individual does not have such rights of interference with others. The individual is one of many in the body politic. So to the state goes this power to legislate on, and judge of, the interactions of its members.

The borders of individual sovereignty are thus drawn where another becomes opposed. Two people joining together as a family consent to terms of union. But where consent is withdrawn or never granted, there is required a superintending authority to insure justice.

People need each other, yet harmony is not always possible. Collision between individuals is to be expected. So people need disinterested third parties to settle disputes which arise between them. This is why they create the body politic.

It is the natural outcome of humans living together in a family, and families living together with other families that the need of sharing certain community burdens -- like justice and defense -- becomes manifest to all. For a society to be legitimate, then, in all instances where one objects to the trespass of another, the involved parties will receive justice.

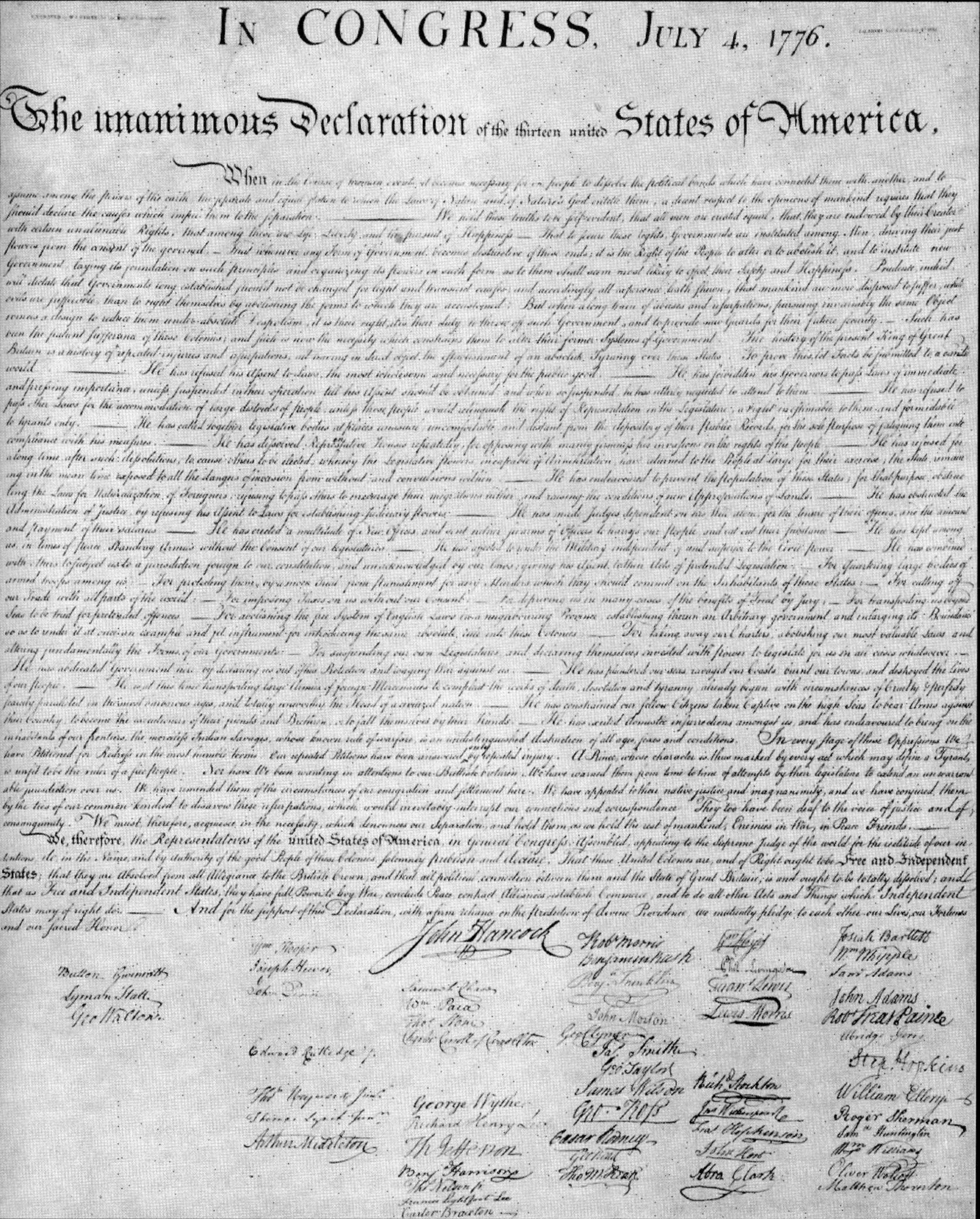

Proceedings Of The Continental Congress Recorded By Thomas Jefferson

"In Congress, Friday, June 7, 1776. The delegates from Virginia moved, in obedience to instructions from their constituents, that the Congress should declare that these United Colonies are, and of right ought to be, free and independent states ... and a confederation be formed to bind the colonies more closely together ...

Saturday, June 8, 1776. ... It was argued ... That some of them (the colonies) had expressly forbidden their delegates to consent to such a declaration, and others had given no instructions, and consequently no powers to give such consent; That, if the delegates of any particular colony had no power to declare such colony independent, certain they were, the others could not declare it for them; the colonies being as yet perfectly independent of each other; That, if such a declaration should now be agreed to, these delegates must retire, and possibly their colonies might secede from the Union.

That the question was not whether, by a declaration of independence, we should make ourselves what we are not; but whether we should declare a fact which already exists; That, as to the people or Parliament of England, we had always been independent of them, their restraints on our trade deriving efficacy from our acquiescence only, and not from any rights they possessed of imposing them; and that, so far, our connection had been federal only, and was now dissolved by the commencement of hostilities ..."

-- Within a month of these debates, each of the states had authorized their delegation to vote for independence. A resolution approving independence passed July 2, 1776 and the Declaration of Independence was issued by the Continental Congress, July 4, 1776.

Articles of Confederation

And Perpetual Union

Between The States

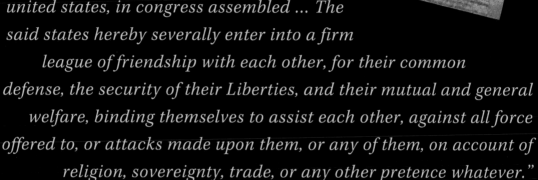

"Each State retains its sovereignty, freedom
and independence, and every Power,
Jurisdiction and right, which is not by this
confederation expressly delegated to the
united states, in congress assembled ... The
said states hereby severally enter into a firm
league of friendship with each other, for their common
defense, the security of their Liberties, and their mutual and general
welfare, binding themselves to assist each other, against all force
offered to, or attacks made upon them, or any of them, on account of
religion, sovereignty, trade, or any other pretence whatever."

-- *Articles of Confederation and Perpetual Union Between The States,*
effective March 1, 1781 with the ratification of each state. The
Continental Congress appointed a committee to draft the Articles on
June 11, 1776 and they were submitted to the states November 15, 1777.

"The fundamental principle of the Revolution was, that the colonies were co-ordinate
members with each other, and with Great Britain, of an empire united by a common
executive sovereign, but not united by any common legislative sovereign. The
legislative power was maintained to be as complete in each American Parliament, as
in the British Parliament. And the royal prerogative was in force, in each colony, by
virtue of its acknowledging the King for its executive magistrate, as it was in Great
Britain, by virtue of a like acknowledgement there. A denial of these principles by
Great Britain, and the assertion of them by America, produced the Revolution."

-- James Madison, the Father of the U.S. Constitution, explaining the
American Revolution in his *Report on the Virginia Resolutions, 1798.* He
was elected the fourth President and served 1809-1817.

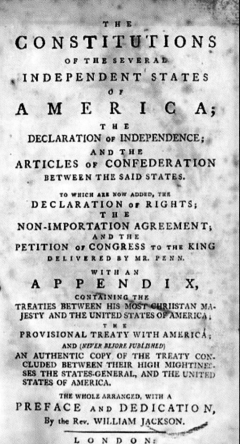

THE
CONSTITUTIONS
OF THE SEVERAL
INDEPENDENT STATES
OF
A M E R I C A;
THE
DECLARATION OF INDEPENDENCE;
AND THE
ARTICLES OF CONFEDERATION
BETWEEN THE SAID STATES.

TO WHICH ARE NOW ADDED, THE
DECLARATION OF RIGHTS;
THE
NON-IMPORTATION AGREEMENT;
AND THE
PETITION OF CONGRESS TO THE KING
DELIVERED BY MR. PENN.

WITH AN
A P P E N D I X,
CONTAINING THE
TREATIES BETWEEN HIS MOST CHRISTIAN MA-
JESTY AND THE UNITED STATES OF AMERICA;
THE
PROVISIONAL TREATY WITH AMERICA;
AND (NEVER BEFORE PUBLISHED)
AN AUTHENTIC COPY OF THE TREATY CON-
CLUDED BETWEEN THEIR HIGH MIGHTINES-
SES THE STATES-GENERAL, AND THE UNITED
STATES OF AMERICA.

THE WHOLE ARRANGED, WITH A
PREFACE AND DEDICATION,
By the Rev. WILLIAM JACKSON.

L O N D O N:
Printed for J. STOCKDALE, in Piccadilly. 1783.

"CONGRESS having agreed upon a plan of confederacy for securing the freedom, sovereignty, and independence of the United States, authentic copies are now transmitted for the consideration of the respective legislatures.

"... Permit us, then, earnestly to recommend these Articles to the immediate and dispassionate attention of the legislatures of the respective states. Let them be candidly reviewed under a sense of the difficulty of combining in one general system the various sentiments of a continent divided into so many sovereign and independent communities ...

"... In short, this salutary measure can no longer be deferred. It seems essential to our very existence as a free people; and, without it, we may soon by constrained to bid adieu to independence, to liberty, and safety ..."

-- Excerpts from the *Official Letter Accompanying The Act Of Confederation*, In Congress, Yorktown, November 17, 1777.

"I find, by the public papers, that your Commercial Convention failed in point of Representation. If it should produce a full meeting in May, and a broader reformation, it will still be well. To make us one nation, as to foreign concerns, and keep us distinct in domestic ones, gives the outline of the proper division of powers between the general and particular governments. But, to enable the Federal head to exercise the powers, given it, to best advantage, it should be organized, as the particular ones are, into Legislative, Executive and Judiciary."

-- Thomas Jefferson writing to James Madison from Paris, December 16, 1786 following the Annapolis Convention. Less than a year later, a federal constitution was drafted and submitted to the state conventions.

The imaginary island that once had only the First Person now has many people and many families. It is apparent that some basic rules are needed on the island that all must consent to. How will these laws and rules be made? How will good ones be made better and bad ones removed? Who will administer these laws? Who will judge of their fairness?

These fundamental questions need to be answered before all others, and a basic law which operates above all others must be established. So the various individuals meet and draft that basic law. They constitute themselves as one and create a system by which the one shall operate.

The limits of the one are carefully delineated; the rights of the many are reserved. And so each person (in reality an island unto him or her self) now joins with the others to make an island unto themselves. With all agreeing to the basic principles of their constitution, the body politic is formed.

This Island State, where each person, their families, and their communities bond to make laws and administer justice, exercises the powers of sovereignty only to the extent the members have allowed.

All of the most important laws that directly affect their lives they, or their representatives, make. Should a bad law be passed, it is quickly fixed because the representatives are one with the people and feel the laws' consequences directly.

But should many bad laws be made, a defect could exist in the machinery that makes the laws. In these cases everyone on the island must reconvene and correct that which produced such results.

So it is with each American State. The basic code or constitution is drafted in constitutional convention and agreed to by a majority of a state's citizens. The result is a government with certain powers and limitations, outlined in this formal agreement.

Sovereignty implies and requires boundaries, both geographical and metaphysical. With every step towards the conglomeration of sovereignty -- from the individual and family to the community, the communities to the state, the states to the nation, the nations to each other -- borders are needed to protect the rights of the sovereign individual and the various bodies politic individuals create.

As sovereignty originates with the individual, it cannot be used by the body politic to interfere in the individual's rightful domain. Establishing this domain's borders is simple: where another sovereignty is not contacted, where the cause and effect operate alone, on, or within the individual -- this is each person's separate domain.

And it cannot be rightly interfered with.

According to the Declaration of Independence, human beings "are endowed by their Creator with certain unalienable Rights, that among these are Life, Liberty, and the Pursuit of Happiness ..."

Pursuing one's happiness in a manner determined solely by that person is an attribute of individual sovereignty.

So, too, does this principle speak to the state. Where another sovereignty is not contacted, where the cause and effect operate alone, on, or within the body politic -- this is each state's separate domain, and it cannot be rightly interfered with.

A constitution of the individual is needed, not to standardize each person to a code, but to setoff those attributes which the individual alone shall order. To establish the rights of personhood, which is, first and foremost, freedom from interference from another. The right to think, speak, worship, protest, write, associate, live as one sees fit -- *subject to no one.*

The right to defend oneself and one's community. The right to be secure in one's home from trespassers, including the government. The right to possess property and to use it as one sees fit, provided its use does not interfere with the rights of another. The right to justice as determined by a jury of one's peers. The right to be fairly treated when in custody.

Individual sovereignty is protected in declaration of individual rights established at the time of the forming of the body politic. It is no coincidence that each American State includes a listing of individual rights within its constitution for its citizens alone.

Whereas the constitution of the state or nation defines the powers of the body politic in action, such declarations of rights draw a border around the individual which the community cannot pass. In so doing is the implicit recognition that the ordering of the individual's personhood is a unique act, that he or she alone controls.

The most important right individual sovereigns hold is the right to define additional rights. People change, societies change, economies change, etc. -- individual and community rights do not change, but the need to more clearly define them does. The longer a society exists, the more it evolves, and the rights of the people are more clearly understood.

For instance, people have a right to a clean, healthy environment. When initial declarations of rights were written, this right was taken for granted, there being nothing to the contrary to suggest its enumeration. Centuries later, after industrial and economic revolutions, the need to define such rights may come to the fore.

And yet, this right and every other one unwritten is provided for in each citizen's state constitution and in the federal constitution. All of the people's rights exist there in reservation, almost written and awaiting proclamation. In this way are individuals to understand the infiniteness of their sovereignty.

The individual gives up much to form the state; still each person is subject to no one, except as each consented when creating it. Such was the case of the American States at the time of their revolution. Remarkably, the throwing off of royal authority did not mean anarchy and chaos. In fact, just the opposite was true. Without an unjust system of government, the people of each state accepted the determinations of the just body politic.

So simple was the transference in power, that states like Connecticut and Rhode Island, which held extensive rights of self-government as colonies, kept their colonial charter as their state constitution, substituting the authority of the people where the word "King" existed before.

Though sovereignty is indivisible, its delegation is divisible. The individual obviously cannot be divided and neither can the individual's sovereignty. Yet individuals may apportion the attributes of sovereignty to as many different authorities as they see fit.

As people build relationships outside their body politic, new ones are created.

Like the First Person united with others to form the First Family, and the First Family united with the other families to form the community, and the communities joined with communities to form the Island State, now the islands join together to form one nation or republic of islands. The reasons for this union are the same as every other one before it: justice and defense.

The people of the Island State came to know of other islands, and other people who, like them, had constituted themselves a body politic. These other islands had developed and matured differently, yet like the Island State, shared in the basic principles of liberty and freedom. Now the people of the various islands interacted with each other for economic, social, and religious purposes.

Who was to be the judge in the relations and disputes between the neighboring islands? What superintending authority existed to establish rules and laws between the islands and judge dispassionately of them? In matters of security, would not a common defense of the individual islands be wise, given the hostile forces that threatened each one of them?

And so in uniting the specific functions of society -- defense, money, a forum for the settlement of inter-island disputes, joint management of common waters and property -- a new body politic was created from the conglomeration of many states. A constitution was drawn, and certain powers formerly held by the individual states were granted to the new body politic by the people of each body politic.

Yet this federal government had specific, delegated powers, designed to perpetuate the individual body politics. Guaranteeing the smaller parts survival and defending them became the chief responsibilities of the new one.

So played the story of the American States and their implementation of the United States Constitution in 1789.

The One To Many, The Many To One -- this is the unending cycle of sovereignty. Once a body politic is established, it engages other bodies politic as part of its duties. Once people from one family engage another, the community is born.

The rise of continental and global communities is like the earlier ones. If an Island State in disagreement with another needs a superintending authority to act as an unbiased judge, what about when nation disagrees with nation? Should strength alone determine what is fair? Or is strength shackled fairer yet?

As all sovereignty radiates equally from each individual within the body politic, what natural limits are there on its emanation? Certainly this: an individual's sovereignty cannot be used against him. No person can relinquish their sovereignty, nor direct it against himself.

When individuals create a body politic for common purposes, often what is created grows beyond those initial purposes and assumes other powers, duties, or privileges not well understood at its formation. With consolidation into the United One, each unit in the sovereignty chain -- individual, family, community, state, nation -- must be all the more jealous to protect each other's prerogatives.

Sovereignty cannot be transferred. Its attributes can be delegated from individuals to the state, but always recalled. Power derives from the people; as they alone possess it, so they retain the right to recall it or alter its application.

By remaining in and abiding by the body politic, the individual voluntarily consents to its legal decisions, even if he or she disagrees with them. In this way we understand the individual is sovereign and the people are sovereign, because everything is done according to their collective wishes. Hence, they are subject to no one.

As states and nations are constituted from emanations of individual sovereignty, we must look to the individual in family and community to establish norms of behavior. In this the science of sovereignty is grounded. How individuals relate in their smallest communities, in peace and happiness, is the example states and nations must follow when dealing with each other. Bodies politic must do unto others as they would want done to them.

THE TEMPLES

It is no coincidence that the place where the sacred power of sovereignty is uncloaked and set loose is in a building that resembles a temple. Indeed, the act of ordering society in councils of individuals chosen for that purpose demands appropriate alters for the rite. But the American contribution to the world of monumental architecture, the Capitol, is more closely connected to religion than is commonly appreciated.

The Original States were primarily settled by Protestants who, by their religion, rejected central control of the individual's spiritual relationship with God. In revolting against the Roman Catholic Church, Protestants declared that man did not need an earthly intermediary when dealing with God. In turn, local church matters were to be settled by local church leaders in council.

So why would people who rejected centralized authorities in matters of the spirit take to centralized authorities in matters of the flesh? They didn't. Civil decisions were to be made in local council as well.

A large meeting space would be needed to accommodate representatives of the colony's body politic. It's no wonder that churches were first used as these meeting places, they being the only structures big enough for the function. Often the very leaders of the church also assumed leadership roles in the colony.

It is interesting to note that in the predominantly Catholic Spanish and French colonies in the Americas, not one developed representative government. Instead, each -- including Louisiana, Florida, and New Mexico -- existed for centuries under authoritarian regimes, run by governors appointed by kings without a citizen's council or legislature.

Not so the English colonies: all allowed for some form of representative government.

In fact, the Pilgrims aboard the Mayflower made it their first order of business before landing in 1620 to draft the *Mayflower*

Compact to "combine ourselves together into a civil body politic" and establish a means for making laws. The oldest, written constitution in continuous use of any nation or state remains that of the Commonwealth of Massachusetts, adopted in 1780. The first legislative assembly to meet in America was the Virginia House of Burgesses, in 1619. They convened in the Jamestown Episcopal Church.

Now consider that the oldest Capitol building of the American States is the Palace of the Governors in Santa Fe, New Mexico. It was built in 1609 and occupied by Spanish and Mexican Governors who ruled for the central authority, no real check by the citizens on their absolute power. The people endured some 300 hundred years in this reduced state before assuming full sovereign control of the State of New Mexico with the writing of the state constitution and its principal creation, the New Mexico Legislature.

The very word "capitol" has its roots in religion and the sovereignty of the state. The *Capitolium* is the name of the Temple of Jupiter on the *Capitoline*, the most important of the seven hills upon which Rome was built. There the great deities of the Roman state were worshipped -- Jupiter, Juno, and Minerva. On the northern end of the mount, the citadel of Rome. On the southern end, Tarpeian Rock where criminals were thrown to their death.

No better example of state power existed in the minds of the Americans. The connection with Rome was natural for the future states; after all, each was descended from Great Britain which was, at one time, a Roman province. Rome symbolized order and justice to the Americans; the Romans had the power to carry out the will of the body politic, an entity first recognized and studied by the Greeks.

Thus the classical architecture of the Greek and Roman temple found a home in America.

Map of North America
Made In 1774
by Samuel Dunn, Mathematician, London

United States Constitution

"We the People *of the United States, in Order to form a more perfect Union, establish Justice, insure domestic Tranquillity, provide for the common defence, promote the general Welfare, and secure the Blessings of Liberty to ourselves and our Posterity, do ordain and establish this Constitution for the United States of America. ... The Ratification of the Conventions of nine States shall be sufficient for the Establishment of this Constitution between the States so ratifying the same.*

Done in Convention, by the Unanimous Consent of the States present, the 17th day of September, in the year of our Lord, 1787, and of the Independence of the United States of America the Twelfth ..."

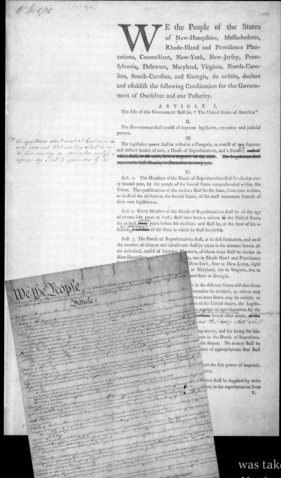

-- The first paragraph (Preamble) of the U.S. Constitution and the last. Drafted in the summer of 1787 and issued September 17, it was brought into effect March 4, 1789 after nine state conventions ratified it.

-- On the preceding page is a 1774 map by Samuel Dunn titled, "North America, As Divided amongst the European Powers."

-- Left, the U.S. Constitution after final changes were voted and approved by the Committee of the Whole. The inset is the finished version. The Committee of Style gave the preamble its pronounced *We The People* and opted not to reprint the list of states as was earlier approved. That list was taken exactly from the Articles of Confederation. Not knowing which states would or would not accept the new Constitution was highlighted by the fact that the third state listed (Rhode Island) didn't even send delegates to the convention. Using "We the People of the United States" solved any potential conflicts later for those states which did not join the union; at the same time, it more clearly expressed the formation of a distinct body politic.

Articles of Amendment to the U.S. Constitution

"THE Conventions of a number of the States, having at the time of their adopting the Constitution, expressed a desire, in order to prevent misconstruction or abuse of its powers, that further declaratory and restrictive clauses should be added: ...

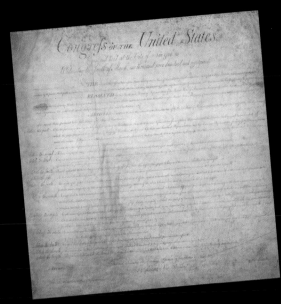

"Amendment IX. The enumeration in the Constitution of certain rights shall not be construed to deny or disparage others retained by the people."

"Amendment X. The powers not delegated to the United States by the Constitution, nor prohibited by it to the States, are reserved to the States respectively, or to the people."

"Amendment XI. The Judicial power of the United States shall not be construed to extend to any suit in law or equity, commenced or prosecuted against one of the United States by Citizens of another State, or by Citizens or Subjects of any Foreign State."

-- The states separately approved "Articles In Addition To, And Amendment Of The Constitution of the United States of America" and they became operative in 1791. These first ten amendments are informally referred to as the "Bill of Rights." They were added as a direct result of some of the states incorporating within their ratifications of the U.S. Constitution various declarations of rights. Typical was Massachusetts, which preceded its ratification with these words: "... *And as it is the opinion of this Convention, that certain amendments and alterations in the said Constitution would remove the fears, and quiet the apprehensions, of many of the good people of this Commonwealth ... the Convention do therefore recommend that the following alterations and provisions be introduced into the said Constitution: I. That it explicitly declare that all powers not expressly delegated by the aforesaid Constitution are reserved to the several States, to be by them exercised.*" The Eleventh Amendment was added five years later (see page 547).

TEMPLES OF SOVEREIGNTY

Sovereignty is power at once defined
and awaiting definition
Possessed by individuals,
Made one in the body politic
Yet sovereign powers remain with the individual, Reserved
Powers hidden, but radiant, potent, alive
Summoned in temples made for the rite:
"A will to enact, and a power to execute"
Its simple rule

BRING ME MEN TO MATCH MY MOUNTAINS

PHOTO CAPTIONS/CREDITS: Page 1 of this section is *The Samuel Dunn Map of North America in 1774* from the National Archives; Page 2, the Committee of the Whole's Constitution and the final version, from the National Archives; Page 3, the Bill of Rights, from the National Archives; Page 4, citizens protesting at the Connecticut Capitol (top); on the last day the Confederate Battle Flag flew on the South Carolina Capitol, this citizen made his feelings known (top right). Above, the State Library Building adjacent to the California Capitol.

The words above were assembled while photographing the South Carolina Capitol. Constitutional scholar John Taylor wrote of sovereignty in 1828: "A will to enact, and a power to execute, constitute its essence. Take away either, and it expires."

The columns, pedestals, entablatures, and pediments made to inspire reverence for the laws of God and Caesar, now inspired awe at the lawmaking powers of elected men and women no less suited to the task.

The first use of the word "capitol" to designate the actual building in which the body politic meets was in 1699 in Virginia, when the House of Burgesses so designated its new home. But the continent's first grand Capitol, known as the *State-House*, was begun in Philadelphia in 1739. It would become the greatest structure in the American colonies in the 18th century. With its church-like steeple rising above all other structures in North America's largest city at the time, it announced to all who entered Philadelphia that this edifice was the center of Pennsylvania. The brick building would become the Capitol of the Commonwealth of Pennsylvania. We know it today as Independence Hall, where the American States declared their independence in 1776.

That first grand Capitol had but one main legislative chamber, serving Pennsylvania's unicameral assembly until, in 1790, the commonwealth's students of the science of sovereignty decided to further harness the people's power and split the legislative powers into two branches. The simple reason all American States, except for Nebraska, have bicameral (two chambers) legislative systems is to restrain the most powerful element of government: that of the lawmakers, known collectively as the legislature. It is for them that the temples of sovereignty are built.

School children are taught that the American States and the United States have governments in which the legislative, executive, and judicial functions are separate and distinct from the others. In the everyday workings of the state and federal governments, this is true. But ultimately, the legislature commands the final and superintending authority over all other parts of government.

The U.S. Congress, for example, has near-complete power in establishing the jurisdiction of the U.S. Supreme Court. The very power the Supreme Court exercises in voiding state laws, for instance, was granted by the Congress in the Judiciary Act of 1789 and not by the U.S. Constitution. In that national charter most of the appellate power of the Supreme Court is subject to the regulation of Congress.

Likewise, each state possesses a powerful, unique legislature which is empowered according to that state's constitution. With proper majorities, lawmakers can enact laws over the veto of the governor. Depending on the state, the legislature's powers to call for constitutional referendums, amendments, and conventions make it a potent agent on behalf of the people. And in some states, the citizens can act directly to make law above and beyond the legislature itself.

This fundamental, sovereign power -- to make law and provide for its enforcement -- is entrusted not to one man or woman, nor a bench of men and women. It is given to the representatives drawn from and chosen by the people themselves, the constituent parts of the body politic.

INSIDE THE TEMPLE

What beyond the municipal goes on in this monument to sovereignty known as the State Capitol? After all, there is another Capitol in America that serves as the center of the body politic known as the United States. What of a sovereign nature could possibly be conducted in the former, when the mighty power that sits in the latter is fully considered?

The answer is plenty. Legally the American States are not political subdivisions of the United States; they are constituent parts. The states united under the terms of the U.S.

Constitution in 1789. In that document specific powers are delegated to the federal government and all others were retained by the pre-existing states separately, or by the people in each state.

And the powers and privileges are considerable.

Each state controls its society as it alone sees fit, provided it does not violate the rights of its citizens and follows the guidelines established in state and federal constitutions. In this regard, the powers of the state are unlimited. Most notably, rights and privileges asserted by any state's body politic that exceed federal standards are explicitly protected by the U.S. Constitution itself (9th Amendment).

How a state licenses the professions (doctors, nurses, lawyers, accountants, teachers, etc.) is completely within its sole discretion. The power to exclusively control and regulate the state's internal police is unquestioned, provided citizen rights are not violated. The President and Congress, for instance, have no authority over state and local police.

The power to maintain an armed citizenry, appoint military officers, train and call forth its militia are absolute. So is the right to order up federal troops to put down internal revolts. In protecting the health and safety of its citizens, the powers of the state are boundless when not used for ulterior purposes.

As the Original States existed independently of other before cementing bonds of union, so did they maintain in principle and reality the right of each state to exist as a member of the Union while maintaining its own freedom and independence.

Except for those areas in which the federal government is given exclusive power or each state is denied the right of action, each state is free to pursue its own agendas and serve the interests of its citizens, without interference from any other state separately or together as the United States.

Simply stated, American citizens -- both in their capacity as citizens of their state and as a citizen of the United States -- are *subject to no one*, but those laws made by their governments under the terms of their two constitutions.

The federal government is empowered through specific grants of authority given to it by the citizens acting within their state body politic. These national powers are limited to fundamental areas like foreign policy, defense, the regulation of interstate trade, postal service, and the coining of money.

The powers of the state, embracing all of the individual, family, and community interactions, are much more extensive and do not look to the federal constitution for sanction. State powers and state constitutions are established by its citizens alone, subject only to those constitutional prohibitions the people of the states originally agreed to in making the federal charter.

The ancient powers over life and limb, the powers to establish the criminal and civil code and judge of its worthiness, the supreme power of eminent domain -- together with the will and means to order society and execute the decisions, laws, and regulations made -- these are the sovereign powers of the American State.

As well, each state has broad economic powers. Property laws and privileges are uniquely created by the state body politic. Corporations receive their charter, their very right to exist, only from a state. Corporate law, contract law, tort law, sales laws -- these are the purview of each state to decide as it sees fit.

Together with its powers to regulate utilities and intra-state commerce, the state wields considerable authority over its natural resources and environment.

So, too, does each state have the power to set interest-rate limits on bank debt, regulate negotiable instruments, and legislate in every other financial area affecting state citizens.

Some states demand allegiance from their citizens; treason laws remain in various state constitutions. Moreover, the definition of treason in the federal constitution incorporates state allegiance when it declares, "Treason against the United States, shall consist only in levying War against them ..." and requires each state to honor the treason laws of the others.

The closest thing to citizenship papers which Americans possess is the birth certificate issued by their state, which also issues the burial permit. In the basic matters of life and death the individual turns to the state.

That other famous piece of individual identification -- the ubiquitous state driver's license -- cannot go unmentioned. The U.S. Constitution was written more than a hundred years before the automobile arrived, yet it comprehends a mobile society. "The citizens of each State shall be entitled to all Privileges and Immunities of Citizens in the several States," it declares.

When one travels in another state by automobile, it is through the state driver's license that your legal identity is certified, there being no other way to assert state and national citizenship short of a passport or state birth certificate.

Each state historically has been responsible for the public education of its citizens. Its role in this area is not limited to kindergarten, grade school, and high school. Many states provide state university systems with subsidies to its citizens who attend them. Moreover, every school -- public or private -- is chartered by the state education board.

In the areas of politics the state exclusively orders itself for all state and federal purposes.

All political parties, elections, and voting districts are under state control, including federal congressional districts. Voter qualifications are also the purview of the state, though race and age discrimination as well as poll taxes are prohibited by federal constitutional amendment.

All of these powers are granted, in varying degrees, by the state's citizens through their state constitution alone.

But it is in the powers assigned to the states in the U.S. Constitution to control the federal system which speak to the reservoir of sovereignty each state possesses to this day. These critical powers maintain ultimate state authority and influence over the national system. They include: 1) the election of the U.S. President through the state-controlled Electoral College; 2) the power to amend the U.S. Constitution; 3) the right to authorize a constitutional convention, remake the federal system, and approve its revisions. (The last time the states invoked the third power, a convention drafted the U.S. Constitution.)

Though the United States of America constitutes one body politic, it is not one consolidated body politic like in each state. It is a federation of bodies politic that make the united one.

Consider this: the only time Americans vote together as a single unit, for the same slate of candidates, is in the presidential election. Every other time they vote, it is as members of their state body politic electing its state and federal representatives.

And even in the presidential contest, votes are tabulated and won by state and not the whole continental mass. The person elected President isn't the one who receives the most popular votes. It is the one who wins the most state electoral votes. And in the event of an electoral tie? A vote is taken in the House of

Representatives -- one vote per state delegation, the same voting formula used in the Continental Congress.

Furthermore, the people's right to vote for President in each of the United States is not given by the U.S. Constitution or the U.S. Congress. It is each American State which grants its citizens the right to vote for President.

States are constituent parts of a federal system where state delegations of representatives and senators are drawn from the people of each state only, and not from the mass of Americans. Fewer than 500,000 Wyomingans have the same say in the U.S. Senate -- where treaties are approved, federal judges are confirmed, and all laws must pass -- as 32 million Californians. In a democracy, that seems outrageously unfair. In a republic, it is the status quo.

But the greatest state power over the federal government is not exercised in joint council in Washington. That power is exercised in each State Capitol, separate from the others. It is the power to amend the federal constitution -- or, as the Declaration of Independence puts it, the "Right of the People to alter or to abolish" their government.

"The Congress," begins the Fifth Article in the U.S. Constitution, "whenever two thirds of both Houses shall deem it necessary, shall propose Amendments to this Constitution, or, on the Application of the Legislatures of two thirds of the several States, shall call a Convention for proposing Amendments, which in either Case, shall be valid to all Intents and Purposes, as Part of this Constitution, when ratified by the Legislatures of three fourths of the several States, or by Conventions in three fourths thereof, as the one or the other Mode of Ratification may be proposed by the Congress; Provided ... that no State, without its Consent, shall be deprived of its equal Suffrage in the Senate."

Thus since 1776 have state ratifications sanctioned the exercise of constitutional power by the United States government.

With such safeguards in place, is it any wonder that the states have multiplied and prospered, each one retaining a share of its freedom and independence into the 21st century?

Each of the United States alone would earn the title of nation when compared to the other sovereignties with such an appellation. Together, they constitute the greatest social, economic, and military empire in the history of the world.

Such attainments cannot be a coincidence.

The seeds of sovereignty were planted by the first people who landed in America and ultimately these roots of liberty tangled with the weeds of elitism and monarchy. A land of many individual sovereigns denies the fable of one sovereign; a clash of ideals was inevitable in America.

And when that clash came, the people in each state fought for their state's independence in particular, and American independence in general. Together, as one continental force and as separate forces, they beat the United Kingdom. But they remained separate sovereignties throughout the conflict. This meant each one separately had to be defeated.

The Americans became one in purpose, but remained the many in defense. This, more than anything else, produced victory in the American Revolution. Had the states been united politically with one Capitol, the British would have easily captured it and quickly ended such pretensions. But since there were thirteen capitols in thirteen sovereignties, the challenge was made that many times more difficult.

Their separateness saved them; their independence from each other guaranteed their union. Thirteen constitutions and thirteen militias, with tens of thousands of patriotic men, women, and children willing to do whatever was necessary to resist subjugation -- with all of this, no nation, not even the mightiest in the world, which England was at the time, could defeat the Americans.

The British King recognized the freedom, independence, and sovereignty of each state in the Treaty of Peace of 1783 because it was against each one of them he had been fighting, while only one fought him.

The seeds of sovereignty had grown into one tree of liberty. Now, with their independence won, the states bonded themselves together under the U.S. Constitution.

That the majority of people of the Original State, fresh from achieving independence, would understand the need for a federal, superintending authority to harness their freedom and sovereignty, and protect their independence, hints at some sort of intervention from the ethereal plains.

That they rejected a plan for a national, centralized authority in the constitutional convention and opted for maintaining a federal system based on autonomous states, kept their country true to the spirit of the Revolution.

And that spirit lives to this day. Except where limited by the federal constitution, each state and the people therein have an exclusive right and duty to advance their state's happiness and general welfare as they alone see fit.

"It is obviously impracticable, in the Federal Government of these States, to secure all rights of Independent Sovereignty to each and yet provide for the interest and safety of all," asserts the official letter submitted with the proposed U.S. Constitution to the American States. "Individuals entering into society must give up a share of liberty to preserve the rest. The magnitude of the sacrifice must depend as well on situation and circumstances as on the object to be obtained. It is at all times difficult to draw with precision the line between those rights which must be surrendered, and those which may be reserved. And, on the present occasion, this difficulty was increased by a difference, among the several States, as to their situation, extent, habits, and particular interests."

The letter, signed by George Washington, was the final act of the Constitutional Convention meeting in Philadelphia in 1787. It concludes:

"That it will not meet the full and entire approbation of every State is not, perhaps, to be expected. But each will doubtless consider that, had her interest alone been consulted, the consequences might have been particularly disagreeable and injurious to others. That it is liable to as few exceptions as could reasonably have been expected, we hope and believe; that it may promote the lasting welfare of that country so dear to us all, and secure her freedom and happiness, is our most ardent wish."

All the evidence of their success can be seen in the State Capitols, Temples of Sovereignty.

VIRGINIA 1619

MARYLAND 1637

CONNECTICUT 1639

MASSACHUSETTS 1641

RHODE ISLAND AND
PROVIDENCE PLANTATION 1663

NORTH CAROLINA 1665

NEW HAMPSHIRE 1679

NEW YORK 1683

PENNSYLVANIA 1683

SOUTH CAROLINA 1693

NEW JERSEY 1702

GEORGIA 1755

DELAWARE 1776

Original States

"His Britannic Majesty acknowledges the said United States, viz. New Hampshire, Massachusetts Bay, Rhode Island, and Providence Plantations, Connecticut, New York, New Jersey, Pennsylvania, Delaware, Maryland, Virginia, North Carolina, South Carolina, and Georgia, to be free, sovereign and independent States; that he treats with them as such, and for himself, his heirs and successors, relinquishes all claims to the Government, proprietory and territorial rights of the same, and every part thereof."

-- From the 1783 Treaty of Paris with Great Britain which officially ended the American Revolution. The assertion of being "Free and Independent States" made in the Declaration of Independence, July 4, 1776, was recognized with this treaty.

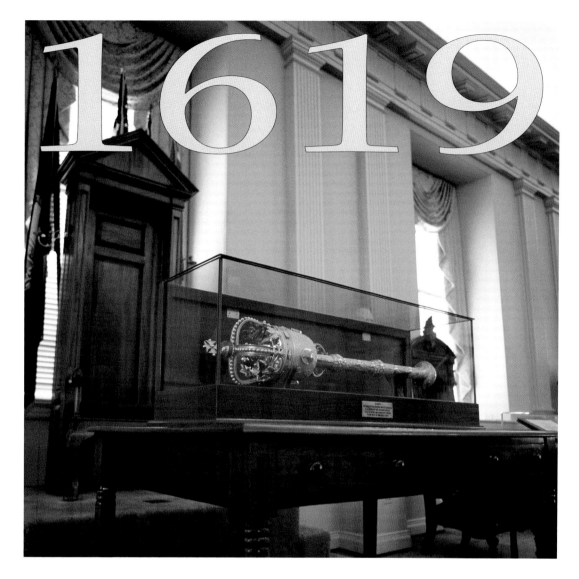

Official Name: .... Commonwealth of Virginia

Motto: .... Sic Semper Tyrannis

Citizen: .... Virginian

Capital City: .... Richmond, VA

Established: 1619

Joined Union: 1788

Left Union: 1861

Readmitted: 1870

Anthem: .... "Carry Me Back to Old Virginia"

Name: .... Named in honor of the "Virgin Queen," Queen Elizabeth I of England

Nickname: .... Old Dominion

License Plate Slogan: .... N/A

Total Area: .... 42,236 sq mi (35)

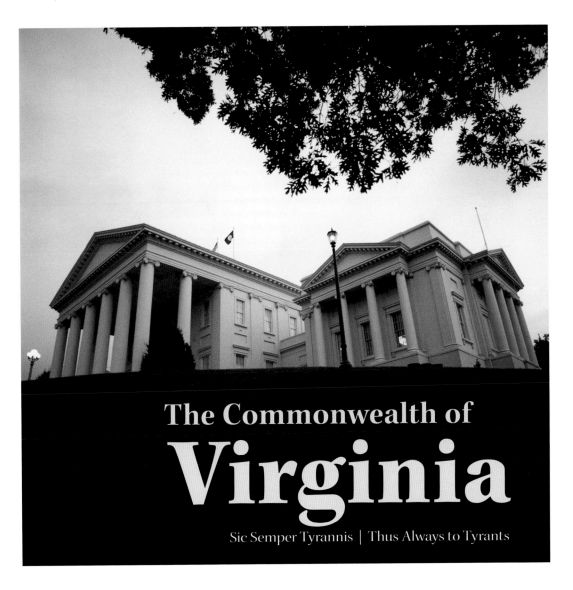

The Commonwealth of
Virginia

Sic Semper Tyrannis | Thus Always to Tyrants

Virginia is the Mother of States. From her territory were carved the better parts of Kentucky, Ohio, Michigan, Illinois, Indiana, Wisconsin, and West Virginia. Portions were chartered to her; others were won by the state's militia under the command of Brigadier General George Rogers Clark. Virginia is the Mother of Presidents. From her soil have come eight U.S. Presidents, represented in the eighteenth, nineteenth, and twentieth centuries. But before there were states and presidents, there was the Old Dominion. The Virginia legacy began at Jamestown in 1607, the first permanent English settlement in America. Twelve years later, the General Assembly held its first session in 1619 (as the House of Burgesses) in a Jamestown church. It was the first representative assembly in the New World.

VIRGINIA

So vast was Virginia in the early 1600's, in both concept and reality, that it was used concurrently with the word "America" by the English. To Virginia did the Pilgrims sail aboard the *Mayflower*. The Mayflower Compact, written just off Plymouth, Massachusetts in 1620, states it is "the first colony in the Northern parts of Virginia."

Virginia is the Mother of Rebellion. The first revolution against the British in the colonies happened in Virginia one hundred years before the American Revolution. In 1676 Nathaniel Bacon led an uprising against the colonial government, urging popular rule in the legislature and protections for citizens on the frontier. He chased the colonial governor

from Jamestown and burned the city to the ground. Succumbing to fever while beginning reforms, he died, but not before a new legislature known as "Bacon's Assembly" was empowered and the vote extended to all freemen.

Virginia's more famous, and just as rebellious, George Washington led the forces that would chase British authority away forever from American shores and achieve the goal of the Declaration of Independence: freedom and independence

for the various states. He then helped to establish a new, federal republic -- the United States of America.

Eerily, some two hundred years after Bacon, still another Virginian would lead a rebellion. When Virginia's efforts in 1861 to reconcile South Carolina's secession with the United States failed and Lincoln called for troops, he asked General Robert E. Lee to head Union forces. Lee (himself no fan of slavery or secession) declined, retired from the U.S. Army instead, pledging only to raise his sword again in defense of his state. Opposing a union of states maintained by force, Virginia left the United States and Lee was pressed into service. That war ended with Lee's surrender at Appomattox. Washington's ended at Yorktown. Both are in Virginia.

Always, Virginians made reference to first principles to justify their actions. The Declaration of Independence of July 4, 1776, written by Thomas Jefferson, declares: "We hold these Truths to be self-evident, that all Men are created equal, that they are endowed by their Creator with certain unalienable Rights, that among these are Life, Liberty, and the Pursuit of Happiness."

ABOVE RIGHT: The famous equestrian statue of Washington was begun in 1850 and completed in 1869. It stands on the Capitol grounds. The statue is designed as a "glorification, not of one individual but of an idea," states the government program, with allegorical figures representing various themes. Washington is surrounded by six other Virginians: Andrew Lewis (Colonial Times); Thomas Jefferson (Independence); Patrick Henry (Revolution, *shown above left*); Thomas Nelson (Finance); George Mason (Bill of Rights); and John Marshall (Justice).

PREVIOUS PAGES: An Edwardian-style mace, purchased by the Jamestown Foundation, is displayed in the old House of Delegates Chamber -- a symbol of the royal sovereignty that ruled over Virginia. The Virginians inherited that power with the overthrow of King George III. *Right*, a perspective of the Capitol.

One month before, on June 12, 1776, Virginia issued its Bill of Rights courtesy of the pen of George Mason, declaring: "That all men are by nature equally free and independent, and have certain inherent rights, of which, when they enter into a state of society, they cannot, by any compact, deprive or divest their posterity, namely, the enjoyment of life and liberty, with the means of acquiring and possessing property, and pursuing and obtaining happiness and safety."

This Bill of Rights has protected Virginians for 200 years and remains one of the strongest and most original elucidations on individual sovereignty created by any people in the world. Its guarantees, as well as those of other states, became the basis for the first ten amendments to the U.S. Constitution, though Virginia's protections are more extensive. It provides for freedom of the press; freedom of religion; the right to bear arms; the right to democratic assembly; limited search and seizure; rights to a speedy jury trial; freedom from excessive bail and from self-incrimination. In addition, Virginians are guaranteed the right to abolish existing government when enough so agree, as well as other rights.

With such a remarkable and enduring legacy, one would expect nothing less than a fountain of history bubbling up from the center of Virginia's Capitol.

The Rotunda features numerous busts of famous Virginians and friends, surrounding the life-size Jean Antoine Houdon sculpture of Washington. Houdon's marble bust of the Marquis de Lafayette, which was also carved from life, gazes upon Washington as do the seven Virginia-born presidents: Thomas Jefferson, James Madison, James Monroe, William Henry Harrison, John Tyler, Zachary Taylor,

and Woodrow Wilson. Jefferson's bust is a copy by Attilo Piccirilli of an original made by Houdon.

Jamestown was the first capital of Virginia until 1699, when it was moved to Williamsburg. In 1780 the Virginia General Assembly moved the seat of government to Richmond. In 1785 Thomas Jefferson, American Minister to France, was asked by state officials "to consult an able Architect on a plan fit for a Capitol" which would "unite economy with elegance and utility." Jefferson had in mind the Maison Carree building in Nimes, France as a model for the new Capitol. That building was a Roman temple built during 100 A.D. Jefferson hired Charles-Louis Clerisseau, a noted French architect at the time, to aid in the project. The cornerstone was laid August 18, 1785 for the Classical Revival temple, and building began under the direction of Samuel Dobie. Three years later, the first session was held in it.

The original building was of handmade brick walls, up to five feet in thickness. The famous portico of the building was not finished until 1790. The original building is the present day's central portion of the Capitol. When first built, the House of Delegates and General Court Chambers were located on the first floor and the Senate and Executive Chambers were on the second. During the mid-1800's, the Senate Chamber and General Court switched positions. Flanking wings were added in 1904 and 1906. Steps were added to the south portico to make a main entrance, giving the building its current appearance. The east wing was given to the House of Delegates, the west wing to the Senate.

With its roots dating to 1619, the General Assembly ranks as one of the oldest continuously meeting legislatures in the world. The House of Delegates is comprised of 100 members, elected every two years. The Senate has forty members, elected every four years. Annual sessions are held for sixty days in even-numbered years, thirty days in odd.

Acquiring a piece of Virginia's lineage was the intent behind the building of a tomb for George Washington in the basement of the U.S. Capitol. Upon its completion, the federal authorities asked the Washington family for his remains. They refused, holding true John Greenleaf Whittier's words:

Our first and best! -- his ashes lie;
Beneath his own Virginian sky.

OPPOSITE: Perspective of the Virginia Capitol.

TOP: Encircling the House of Delegates Chamber are tablets listing every session and Speaker of that body. It starts with the first session held in 1619.

PREVIOUS PAGE: Virginia Capitol Rotunda. "Virginia's most treasured work of art, a magnificent, life-size statue of George Washington, stands in the Rotunda," states the official government program. This is the only sculpture of Washington executed from life and was commissioned by the General Assembly in 1784. Thomas Jefferson, in Paris, was asked to secure a sculptor. He hired Jean Antoine Houdon, who traveled to Mount Vernon and took meticulous measurements of Washington's body and made a plaster bust of his head. The statue is carved in fine Carrara marble from Tuscany. "That is the man, himself," Lafayette is reported to have said. "I can almost realize he is going to move." Houdon's masterpiece was exhibited in the Louvre in Paris before being shipped in 1796.

TOP & RIGHT: The old and new come together in the House of Delegates Chamber. Modern electronic voting screens flank the center tablet, which commemorates Bacon's Rebellion of 1676. This was the first major Virginian rebellion against British authority. The House of Delegates opens each day's session with a salute to the commonwealth's flag. "I salute the flag of Virginia," it begins, "with reverence and patriotic devotion to the Mother of States and Statesmen which it represents -- the Old Dominion, where liberty and independence were born."

TOP: The Virginia Capitol was not damaged during the War Between the States. But disaster did strike the Capitol on April 27, 1870. The Supreme Court of Appeals, which met on the third floor, was standing-room-only for a case being heard. Suddenly the floor of the chamber collapsed, killing 62 people and injuring 251 others.

The old hall of the House of Delegates, which is in the rear of the Capitol, is now a museum. Just off the Rotunda, the chamber served the commonwealth from 1788-1906 and was the scene of numerous important events. Here, Aaron Burr was tried for treason before John Marshall, Chief Justice of the United States. (He was acquitted.) The Virginia Secession Convention met here in 1861 and the chamber also served as a meeting place of the Confederate Congress. And, the conventions which drew up Virginia's constitutions of 1830, 1850-51, 1868-69, and 1901-02 met in these chambers.

TOP: Virginia Senate Chambers. Between the flags is a tablet commemorating the Virginians who signed the Declaration of Independence: George Wythe, Richard Henry Lee, Thomas Jefferson, Benjamin Harrison, Thomas Nelson, Francis Lightfoot Lee, and Carter Braxton.

While these men fashioned a joint declaration with delegates from the other states, George Mason was busy drafting the Virginia Bill of Rights. It was proclaimed a month before the Declaration of Independence. It declares: "That all power is vested in, and consequently derived from, the people ... That government is, or ought to be, instituted for the common benefit, protection, and security of the people, nation, or community ... and that, when any government shall be found inadequate or contrary to these purposes, a majority of the community hath an indubitable, inalienable, and indefeasible right to reform, alter, or abolish it ... That all power of suspending laws, or the execution of laws, by any authority, without consent of the representatives of the people, is injurious to their rights, and ought not to be exercised ... That a well-regulated militia, composed of the body of the people, trained to arms, is the proper, natural, and safe defence of a free State; that standing armies, in time of peace, should be avoided, as dangerous to liberty ... That the people have a right to uniform government; and, therefore, that no government separate from, or independent of the government of Virginia, ought to be erected or established within the limits thereof ..."

TOP & TOP RIGHT: The front portico and main entrance of the State Capitol.

ABOVE: The Virginia flag which flew above the Capitol in 1865. When Richmond fell to the northern armies, Major Stevens hid the flag and prevented its capture. He returned it to state authorities years later.

BOTTOM RIGHT: A brick path gently declines down Virginia's capitoline, leading to a corner garden on the grounds.

TOP RIGHT: Another perspective of the Rotunda.

OPPOSITE: In Houdon's statue, Washington is holding a cane and a sword is placed to his left -- representing in physical form the philosophy Washington expressed to the General Assembly: the supremacy of the civil power over the military.

LEFT: Next to the Washington statue in prominence is that of General Robert E. Lee, a bronze made by Rudulph Evans. It is placed on the exact spot where Lee accepted command of the Army of Northern Virginia. Earlier, Lee refused President Lincoln's offer to command Union forces. Upon accepting the commission from Virginia, Lee said: "Profoundly impressed with the solemnity of the occasion, for which I must say I was not prepared, I accept the position assigned me by your partiality. I would have much preferred had your choice fallen on an abler man. Trusting in Almighty God, an approving conscience, and the aid of my fellow-citizens, I devote myself to the service of my native State, in whose behalf alone will ever again draw my sword."

In the old House of Delegates numerous statues of great Virginians fill the hall, gazing upon the large bronze of Robert E. Lee. Included are American Revolution heroes Richard Henry Lee, George Mason, Patrick Henry, and George Wythe; Confederate leaders Stonewall Jackson, J.E.B. Stuart, Joseph E. Johnston, and Fitzhugh Lee. Other busts include Matthew Fontain Maury, the Pathfinder of the Seas; Cyrus McCormick, creator of the grain reaper; and Sam Houston, the first president of the Texas Republic. The only non-Virginians in the room are the busts of the President and Vice President of the Confederate States of America, Jefferson Davis and Alexander H. Stephens.

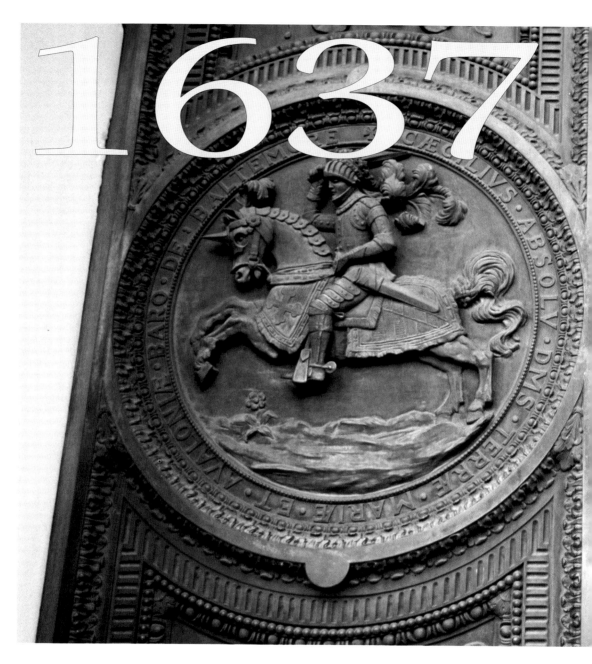

Official Name: . . . . State of Maryland
Motto: . . Fatti Maschii Parole Femine; Scuto Bonae
Voluntatis Tuae Coronasti Nos
Citizen: . . . . Marylander
Capital City: . . . . Annapolis, MD
Established: 1637
Joined Union: 1788

Anthem: . . . . "Maryland! My Maryland!"
Name: . . . . Named in honor of Queen Mary (officially,
Queen Henrietta Maria), the wife of King Charles I of
England, by Lord Baltimore
Nickname: . . . . Free State; Old Line State
License Plate Slogan: . . . . N/A
Total Area: . . . . 12,297 sq mi (42)

The State of Maryland

Fatti Maschii Parole Femine | Manly Deeds, Womanly Words
Scuto Bonae Voluntatis Tuae Coronasti Nos | With Favor Wilt Thou Compass Us as with a Shield

Intended as a refuge for Roman Catholics fleeing Protestant persecution in England, Maryland was unique in North America as a palatinate (a province beholden to a medieval lord having sovereign power in the territory). George Calvert, the first Lord Baltimore, was invested with almost complete sovereignty over Maryland in 1632, and settlement began in 1634. Up until the revolution, the familiar Catholic-Protestant tensions

MARYLAND

of Europe infiltrated politics in the state. Maryland was named after Henrietta Maria, queen-consort to King Charles I, and lifelong advocate of the Catholics. Still, Marylanders insisted on tolerance to all religions and, in 1649, Lord Baltimore (himself Catholic) initiated the Act of Toleration, the first complete establishment of religious freedom in North America.

In 1637 the first popular assembly of Marylanders met, much to the disapproval of the lord proprietor. As he alone had the right to initiate legislation and act as judge over it, he denied these rights to the citizens. But they persisted, asserting a natural right to self-government. Ultimately, the insistence of the people prevailed and these powers to make laws were shared until Maryland established her independence with a constitution in 1776. Now, the people of Maryland were palatines!

The old and the new, in religion and politics, thus meet in and mold Maryland. The Capitol's architecture suggests nothing less. The Maryland State

PREVIOUS PAGES: The rear doors of the State House feature the obverse and reverse of the Great Seal of Maryland.

ABOVE: *Washington Resigning His Commission*, by Edwin White.

TOP RIGHT: The State House's entrance foyer.

OPPOSITE: A view of the State House from the street. Maryland's Capitol is the oldest in continuous use in America.

House is the oldest state capitol in continuous use. Construction was started in 1772 and completed in 1779, following the design of Joseph Horatio Anderson. The start of the American Revolution interrupted construction, yet the building was completed prior to the war's conclusion.

The Capitol's dome and interior departed from earlier styles, creating a palace where Marylanders collectively ruled as sovereign. It is the largest wooden dome in the United States, yet it is not a complete dome as in Massachusetts or Rhode Island. Instead, it is part dome, part steeple. Designed by Joseph Clark, it replaced the original cupola and was completed in 1788. Inside, the Marylanders introduced a new concept in the ancient practice of lawmaking: spectator galleries.

Very quickly, this monument to Maryland's independence would be borrowed by the Continental Congress at the end of the Revolution. Congress convened in the State House's old Senate Chamber from November 26, 1783 to August 14, 1784, and

though its stay in Annapolis was brief, two major events occurred during this time.

General George Washington resigned his commission as commander-in-chief of the Continental Army on December 23, 1783, delivering a stirring farewell speech. The exact spot where he gave this address is marked by a bronze plaque. Above the grand staircase is the oft-reproduced original painting, *Washington Resigning His Commission,* by Edwin White.

That Washington, at the height of his popularity, having defeated the mightiest nation on earth, would resign his military powers to return to private life and not use his station for personal gain and domination ranks as one of the signature events in American history.

But not the greatest. On January 14, 1784, the Congress ratified the Treaty of Paris, in which the British King recognized the independence of Maryland and her sister states and accepted each as "free, sovereign and independent."

Today, in the very building where the Revolution was officially concluded, Maryland legislators go about their duties. The House of Delegates has 141 members, three from each of the state's 47 legislative districts. The Senate has 47 members, one per district.

ABOVE: Looking up into the Rotunda from the second floor.

OPPOSITE: The State House with its unique dome-steeple has become a timeless symbol of Maryland, yet for over a hundred years the state's northern border was not fully known. Members of the powerful Calvert family, after years of controversy, agreed with the Penn family to appoint surveyors and finally define the borders of Maryland and Pennsylvania. In 1763 the English astronomers Charles Mason and Jeremiah Dixon began work fixing the boundaries. Among their most important resources: the original map of Virginia made by explorer John Smith in 1608. "Mason and Dixon's Line" became the unofficial demarcation between the northern and southern states.

TOP: The new Senate Chamber features two statues honoring famous Marylanders in the front of the room. To the left is John Hanson, the first President of the United States under the Articles of Confederation in 1781. To the right is Charles Carroll of Carrollton, one of the State of Maryland's signers of the Declaration of Independence.

The portraits on the side walls depict all of Maryland's signers of that document, as well as Governor William Paca, Legislator Thomas Stone, Samuel Chase, Associate Justice of the U.S. Supreme Court, and Charles Carroll, State and Federal Senator. The chamber is decorated in red and white, the Crossland family colors which appear on the Maryland flag.

OPPOSITE: The House of Delegates Chamber. The interior of the original State House is made of wood and plaster. The newer section, designed by Baldwin and Pennington in 1902 and 1905, features an Italian marble that is colored rust and black, selected to match the Maryland flag of gold and black.

LEFT & BOTTOM: The issues of slavery and racism (and the triumph of justice) come together uniquely on the Maryland State House grounds in the form of separate monuments to two Marylanders. Both were judges. One was white, one was black. U.S. Supreme Court Chief Justice Roger Brooke Taney (left), an outstanding jurist whose reputation would have been unmarred but for a racist ruling, sits in front of the entrance to the Capitol. In 1857 the case of Dred Scott came before the U.S. Supreme Court. Mr. Scott had been a slave when he was taken into what is now Minnesota, a free territory that was part of Missouri. He married and had two children, living the life of a free man. When his former master returned to claim him, Scott sued in federal court claiming he was now free. He lost. Judge Taney said Mr. Scott, because of his skin color, was "altogether unfit to associate with the white race" and "had no rights which the white man was bound to respect." Thus, the federal government's Fugitive Slave Law was upheld.

Nearly 100 years later, a black lawyer argued before the U.S. Supreme Court that racial segregation in public schools was unconstitutional. He won. In his victory in *Brown vs. Board of Education*, Thurgood Marshall (bottom) made a name for himself that would eventually lead to his appointment to the U.S. Court of Appeals in 1961 and confirmation as Associate Justice of the U.S. Supreme Court (1967-1991). An elaborate monument to this outstanding Marylander sits on the opposite side of the State House grounds.

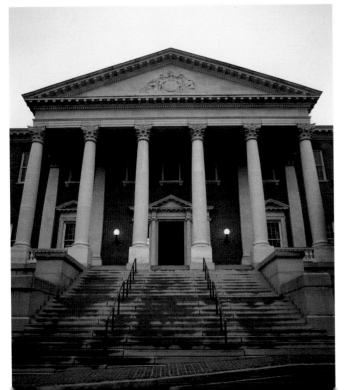

LEFT: The back entrance of the State House.

TOP LEFT: Entrance to the Senate Chamber, home to the upper branch of the Maryland Legislature. Marylanders take their right to self-government seriously and have asserted that right since 1776. Following the War Between the States, the Maryland Constitutional Convention reaffirmed rights won in the American Revolution with this clause in its Declaration of Rights: "That the people of this State have the sole and exclusive right of regulating the internal government and police thereof, as a free, sovereign, and independent State." Made to clarify the position of Maryland in the Union after the war, the clause is almost identical to one that appeared in the Maryland Constitution of 1776.

TOP RIGHT: The grand staircase leading to the Governor's office and galleries. White's *Washington Resigning His Commission* hangs in the stairwell.

Official Name: . . . . State of Connecticut	Anthem: . . . . "Yankee Doodle"
Motto: . . . . Qui Transtulit Sustinet	Name: . From the native term *quinnehtukqut* meaning "besides the long tidal river"
Citizen: . . . . Nutmegger	
Capital City: . . . . Hartford, CT	Nickname: . . . . Constitution State; Nutmeg State
Established: 1639	License Plate Slogan: . . . . Constitution State
Joined Union: 1788	Total Area: . . . . 5,544 sq mi (48)

The State of
Connecticut

Qui Transtulit Sustinet | He Who Is Transplanted Still Sustains

CONNECTICUT

In August, 1856 a terrible storm pounded the capital city of Hartford in the little State of Connecticut and, in its wake, numerous trees were toppled. One in particular -- a 1,000-year-old oak -- sent the state's citizens into mourning. For this was more than ancient timber: this tree, known as Charter Oak, had served the people of Connecticut in a most unusual way some 169 years earlier.

Connecticut was settled by people from Massachusetts, and in 1638 the towns of Wethersfield, Hartford, and Windsor bonded together under the first written constitution of a self-governing people in America and the world: *The Fundamental Orders of Connecticut.* The orders authorized a powerful General Court (legislature) and greatly restricted the power of the governor.

"And well knowing where a people are gathered togather the word of God requires that to mayntayne the peace and vnion of such a people there should be orderly and decent Gouerment established according to God, to order and dispose of the affayres of the people at all seasons as occation shall require," the preamble declares, "doe therefore assotiate and conioyne our selues to be as one Publike State or Comonwelth ..."

Even though sovereignty was with the King of England, the *Fundamental Orders* established the compact style of legitimate government -- the people agreeing, by a contract known as a constitution, to unify under a common government which they individually approved. The preamble asserts that the people "hereafter, enter into Combination and Confederation together ..."

In 1643, Connecticut and New Haven joined with Massachusetts Bay and New Plymouth to form the New England Confederation. However, in 1662 Connecticut Governor John Winthrop obtained a liberal charter from the British King Charles II recognizing Connecticut as a separate entity.

Besides uniting Connecticut and New Haven into one colony, the charter guaranteed local self-government without interference from the King or Parliament. This charter, which would end up tucked away inside an old oak tree, served as Connecticut's constitution until 1818.

But King James II wanted Connecticut to be part of the greater New England Confederacy and not separate, so he ordered Sir Edmund Andros in 1687 to retrieve its charter. When Andros showed up at night with soldiers in Hartford demanding the cherished document, Connecticut officials pretended to oblige and went to their council chamber, candles in hand, to locate it.

Suddenly, the room went dark. When the candles were relit, the charter had disappeared! Andros was told it was missing, and despite a frantic search, the charter was not found.

ABOVE: The likeness of Governor John Winthrop gazes upon those entering the Capitol. *Right,* the state flag amid the clouds.

PREVIOUS PAGES: The Soldiers and Sailors Memorial Arch designed by George Keller. It was dedicated in 1886. His ashes are buried in the east tower. Made of native brownstone from Portland, the Arch features a terra cotta frieze depicting scenes from the War Between the States. *Right,* the Connecticut Capitol.

OPPOSITE: The House of Representatives Chamber.

What happened? When the candles were blown out, one of the Connecticut officials quickly grabbed the charter and snuck out the back door with it. Then, in a desperate attempt to find a place where the soldiers would not find it, he jammed it up the hollow trunk of an old oak tree.

The charter remained there until 1693, when it became clear no one would ever again interfere with Connecticut's right to an independent existence.

Charter Oak's demise during the storm of 1856 touched a nerve in the state. To honor and maintain this symbol of their freedom, the fallen tree was converted into ceremonial chairs to be used in the state's legislative chambers. How appropriate, then, that shortly after the toppling of Charter Oak, a new Capitol was built which would house them.

Connecticut had two capital cities, Hartford and New Haven, a result of these two colonies having existed independently of each other prior to unification. The building of the new Capitol in Hartford would make it the sole capital of the state.

The Capitol was designed by Richard M. Upjohn, a noted cathedral architect, who used the High Victorian Gothic style. It was completed in 1878, eight

years after construction began. The building's exterior marble came from East Canaan, CT and the granite from Westerly, Rhode Island. The exterior features elaborate carvings that detail key aspects of Connecticut's rich past. Inside, the chambers were not balanced, but asymmetrical *a la* Massachusetts and Vermont.

Today, the Capitol serves as the enduring symbol of Connecticut's self-government and independence. Its golden dome rises high above the building atop a tower. And, within, the Lt. Governor sits in one of the Charter Oak chairs, which was carved from the famous tree.

ABOVE: The Connecticut Senate Chamber. The Charter Oak chairs are between the flags and not visible in this photograph.

OPPOSITE: Perspectives of the Connecticut Capitol and dome; the Soldiers and Sailors Arch frieze.

ABOVE: The Capitol's central tower.

OPPOSITE: The model of the *Genius of Connecticut* statue that used to top the dome. The *Genius* was made in 1877 by Randolph Rogers, stood 17′8″, and weighed over three tons. Removed for being a hazard (she wobbled when the wind blew), *Genius* was melted down during World War II to make armaments. Fortunately the original plaster model was saved and, after restoration, displayed in the lobby.

"And that this Republic is, and shall forever be and remain, a free, sovereign and independent State, by the Name of the STATE OF CONNECTICUT."

-- Constitution of Connecticut, 1776

Official Name: . . . Commonwealth of Massachusetts

Motto: . . Ense Petit Placidam Sub Libertate Quietem

Citizen: . . . . Bay Stater

Capital City: . . . . Boston, MA

Established: 1641

Joined Union: 1788

Anthem: . . . . "All Hail To Massachusetts"

Name: . . . From the Massachusetts Indians, the term means "large hill place"

Nickname: . . . . Bay State; Old Bay State

License Plate Slogan: . . . . The Spirit of America

Total Area: . . . . 9,241 sq mi (45)

The Commonwealth of
Massachusetts

Ense Petit Placidam Sub Libertate Quietem |
By the Sword We Seek Peace, but Peace Only under Liberty

MASSACHUSETTS

Though a capitol is the most visible symbol of sovereignty, it is the state's constitution which has the most practical impact on citizens' lives. Constitutions define and limit government lawmaking authority. And in making constitutions and laws, no state -- and few nations -- is the equal of Massachusetts.

The Mayflower Compact, a proto-constitution, was drafted in 1620 on a boat off the shores of what would become Plymouth to "covenant and combine ourselves together into a civil body politic, for our better ordering and preservation." Twenty-one years later, the Massachusetts *Body of Liberties* -- the first code of laws in New England -- was adopted. And, in 1643, Massachusetts men took the lead in forming "The United Colonies of New England," a confederation with neighboring New Plymouth, Connecticut, and New Haven.

These pilgrims' descendants would go on to establish the Commonwealth of Massachusetts and in 1780 draft, along with a Declaration of Rights, what remains to this day *the oldest written constitution in effect* in the world (it has been amended over one hundred times).

Its constitution, like its citizens then and now, would have a major impact on the development of the American Republic. And the place history was and continues to be made from is the Massachusetts State House, termed the "hub of the solar system" by Oliver Wendell Holmes (a precursor to the statement that Boston is "the Hub").

Built on John Hancock's cow pasture, the State House had its cornerstone laid on July 4, 1795 by Governor Samuel Adams and Paul Revere, Grand Master of the Masons, the 19th anniversary of the Declaration of Independence. A great spectacle was made when the cornerstone was brought to the building site: a parade, led by fifteen horses (one for each state in the Union), included Native Americans, patriots, farmers, and politicians. The State House was completed January 11, 1798 at a cost of $133,333.33.

Massachusetts-born Charles Bulfinch, considered one of the first American architects, was chosen to design the new seat of government. His unique gold dome would remain the dominant image of the Boston skyline until the age of the skyscraper. Mr.

PREVIOUS PAGES: The Massachusetts Senate Chamber; *Right,* the State House at night.

RIGHT & OPPOSITE: The Commonwealth flag flies outside, and the towns' flags hang inside.

The State House's Hall of Flags is where all Massachusetts soldiers are memorialized. A circular room surrounded by columns of Sienna marble, it features 400 original flags carried to battle by Massachusetts soldiers from the Civil War to Vietnam. (In fact, the flags are transparencies: the originals are in climate-controlled vaults.) The hall's murals show the Pilgrims on the Mayflower; The Return of Colors at the end of the Civil War to the custody of the Commonwealth; John Eliot preaching to the natives; and the Revolutionary War's Battle of Concord Bridge.

The relics of a heroic past are not only kept inside the State House, though. Plymouth Rock is the name given to the boulder allegedly used by the Mayflower's Pilgrims when they landed. Until the Revolution, the actual "Plymouth Rock" wasn't much of an attraction. Then, to rouse patriotic feeling, it was dug up and brought to the town square where it enjoyed widespread attention. So much, in fact, that great amounts of it were chipped off as souvenirs. In 1920 it returned to its home at water's edge, a granite portico built to protect it.

According to the Secretary of the Commonwealth: "All Massachusetts citizens have the right of free petition and may have bills introduced by a legislator." To that end, there are 160 state representatives; each serves a term of two years and represents a population of about 35,000 people. There are 40 State Senators, each representing approximately 140,000 people. A term is two years.

A commonwealth in which the legal arts are so valued has, naturally, produced some of America's leading legal minds. John Adams was one of these men. Known for promoting the resolution declaring the colonies free, sovereign, and independent states in 1776, he helped craft the Treaty of Paris in which the British King acknowledged this fact.

But it is in the Massachusetts Constitution where Adams and other leaders elucidated and secured these rights. "The end of the institution ... of government is to secure the existence of the body-politic," the centuries-old document asserts. "The body-politic is formed by a voluntary association of individuals; it is a social compact by which the whole people covenants with each citizen and each citizen with the whole people that all shall be governed by certain laws for the common good ..."

Bulfinch later contributed to the plans for the Capitol in Washington, DC and designed Maine's Capitol as well as other structures.

Numerous additions and changes have been made over the years. Unlike other capitols where the legislative chambers balance each other, the Federalist-style State House placed the General Court (House of Representatives) in the center, just below the gold dome. This architectural statement reflected a political reality: the rise of popular majority rule. Originally, Massachusetts had a true commonwealth system where representation in the General Court was based on towns. The Essex Junto, a group of Essex County Federalists, changed that to popular majority rule, thus increasing the power and influence of Boston in the state.

The State House is rich in tradition. In 1784 a merchant named John Rowe donated a wooden cod fish that hangs in the rear of the House of Representatives Chamber above the public gallery. It is considered a good luck symbol and must hang above the House Chamber for the session to be held. Another tradition involves the opening of the building's front doors. The center front doors of the State House are opened only on three occasions: when a Governor leaves the State House for the last time at the end of his term; when a Massachusetts regimental flag is returned to the permanent collection; and on official visits of the U.S. President or a foreign head of state.

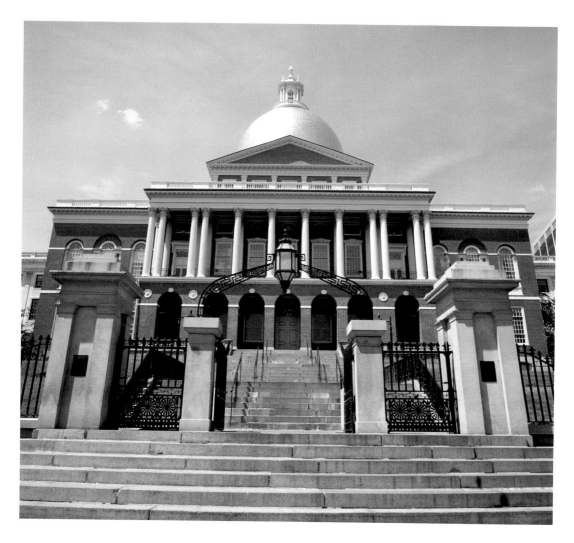

TOP: The Massachusetts State House's gold dome is the first dome to top a capitol building in America, and has served as inspiration to the national and other state capitols. According to state documents, it is the official location of Boston to cartographers. A sign on the Mass. Turnpike that says "75 miles to Boston" technically means seventy-five miles to the gold dome.

The name of Massachusetts' capital city is condensed from St. Botolph's Town, a community in England from which many Puritans came. St. Botolph was an Anglo-Saxon monk.

Massachusetts was the last state to stop the government's support of an official state church (1833). And the first place in America to impose an income tax (in New Plymouth, 1643).

OPPOSITE: Built in 1895, the House of Representatives Chamber features *Milestones on the Road to Freedom in Massachusetts* murals by Albert Herter. The chamber's paneling is of Honduran mahogany. At one time (1812) there were 749 members of the House. Today it has 160 members.

An oath of allegiance was added to the constitution in 1822 for members and other commonwealth officials. It states: "I do solemnly swear that I will bear true faith and allegiance to the commonwealth of Massachusetts, and will support the constitution thereof: So help me God."

TOP: The Senate Chamber today was the original House of Representatives Chamber. Directly above it is the gold dome. In 1838 Angelina Grimke spoke before the Senate. The abolitionist thus became the first woman to address an American legislative body. Busts of Washington and Lincoln are behind the Senate President's desk. At one time the Washington bust was believed to be that of Samuel Adams until the day LaFayette saw it and declared: "That is the Washington I knew!"

LEFT: Monument to John F. Kennedy. Other statues on the State House grounds include Senator Daniel Webster, General Joseph Hooker, and educator Horace Mann. Also on the grounds are commemorations to the religious martyrs Ann Hutchinson and Mary Dyer.

OPPOSITE: "God Save The Commonwealth of Massachusetts," the eagle proclaims in the front of the Senate Chamber.

OPPOSITE: The State House at dusk.

TOP: A ceiling mural of the Original States' official seals with the Massachusetts seal in the middle. The first settlers who landed at Plymouth made the *Mayflower Compact* because their grant was not valid and they needed some basis to conduct their community. So they created a compact among themselves, and it served as their constitution until 1691 when Plymouth unified with Massachusetts. The full text reads: "In The Name of God, Amen. We whose names are underwritten, the loyal subjects of our dread sovereign Lord, King James, by the grace of God, of Great Britain, France and Ireland king, defender of the faith, etc., having undertaken, for the glory of God, and advancement of the Christian faith, and honor of our king and country, a voyage to plant the first colony in the Northern parts of Virginia, do by these presents solemnly and mutally in the presence of God, and one of another, covenant and combine ourselves together into a civil body politic, for our better ordering and preservation and furtherance of the ends aforesaid; and by virtue hereof to enact, constitute, and frame such just and equal laws, ordinances, acts, constitutions, and offices, from time to time, as shall be thought most meet and convenient for the general good of the colony, unto which we promise all due submission and obedience. In witness whereof we have hereunder subscribed our names at Cape-Cod the 11 of November, in the year of the reign of our sovereign lord, King James, of England, France and Ireland the eighteenth, and of Scotland the fifty-fourth. Anno Domine 1620"

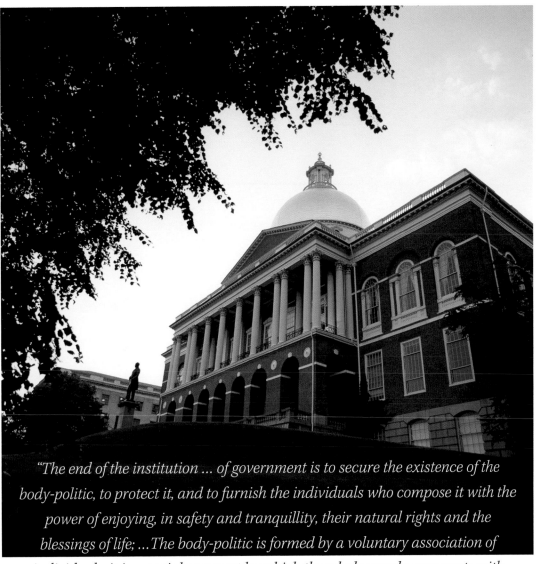

"The end of the institution ... of government is to secure the existence of the body-politic, to protect it, and to furnish the individuals who compose it with the power of enjoying, in safety and tranquillity, their natural rights and the blessings of life; ... The body-politic is formed by a voluntary association of individuals; it is a social compact by which the whole people covenants with each citizen and each citizen with the whole people that all shall be governed by certain laws for the common good ... The people of this commonwealth have the sole and exclusive right of governing themselves as a free, sovereign, and independent State, and do, and forever hereafter shall, exercise and enjoy every power, jurisdiction, and right which is not, or may not hereafter be, by them expressly delegated to the United States of America in Congress assembled."

-- The Constitution of the Commonwealth of Massachusetts

The State of
Rhode Island and
Providence Plantations

Hope

1663

Official Name: . . . . State of Rhode Island and Providence Plantations
Motto: . . . . Hope
Citizen: . . . . Rhode Islander
Capital City: . . . . Providence, RI
Established: 1663
Joined Union: 1790
Anthem: . . . . "Rhode Island"

Name: . . . . . . Aquidneck Island (on which Newport stands) is said to have resembled the Isle of Rhodes in the Mediterranean by early explorers; others have suggested the name comes from the Dutch *roodt eylandt*, meaning "red island"
Nickname: . . . . Little Rhody
License Plate Slogan: . . . . Ocean State
Total Area: . . . . 1,231 sq mi (50)

RHODE ISLAND

Religious liberty was born in Rhode Island. Whereas other states, like Massachusetts, were settled by people seeking to establish their own religious community, Rhode Island and Providence Plantations founded a community of citizens respectful to every individual's religious yearnings.

Roger Williams, fleeing from religious persecution in Salem, MA, founded Providence Plantations in 1636 as a refuge for those seeking religious liberty. Soon the state was a magnet for the oppressed: the first Jews in America made Rhode Island their home. The Touro Synagogue, built in 1763, was the first permanent synagogue in America and is still used today. Williams was the first in America to argue that the individual's conscience could not be controlled by the state, and the first to secure the right as fundamental law. Individuals were allowed to conduct their religious activities as they -- not the community -- saw fit.

His little state gained its charter in 1643, and four years later the General Assembly drafted a constitution calling for the separation of church and state. Finally, on July 8, 1663, King Charles II granted a charter guaranteeing freedom of religion -- a document that served as Rhode Island's constitution until the early 1840's.

How appropriate it is, then, that his state's Capitol be built like a Temple and be topped with a statue named "The Independent Man." Sitting on a hill in Providence, its white Georgia marble shining in the sun, the Capitol stands as one of the finest examples of Italian Renaissance architecture in the world.

Designed by the New York firm of McKim, Mead and White, the building broke ground in 1895 and was completed in 1904. The cornerstone was laid in 1896. It was built by the Norcross Brothers

Construction Co., Worcester, MA. It cost $400,607.01 to buy the land, which overlooks the city of Providence. The final cost of the building, including furnishings, was $3,018,416.33. It has been estimated that to duplicate the same building in 1998 would cost $500,000,000.

The first permanent Capitol building was the Colony House, built in 1739 by tavern-keeper and carpenter Richard Mundy. From its balcony was read the Declaration of Independence.

The Rhode Island State House is the fourth largest self-supporting, marble-covered dome in the world (the others are St. Peter's in Vatican City, the Minnesota State Capitol in St. Paul, MN, and the Taj Mahal in India). And on its top is the gold symbol of the state: The Independent Man. Designed by sculptor George Brewster, it was placed there on December 18, 1899.

"The Independent Man is a symbol for the independent spirit which led Roger Williams to settle here," according to the Rhode Island Secretary of State's pamphlet.

"He represents freedom. He reminds Rhode Islanders that it is important to stand strong for beliefs which are morally right and which will benefit all citizens. He represents men and women, young and old, times past and times present. He stands watch over our State Capitol as a protector of all Rhode Island citizens."

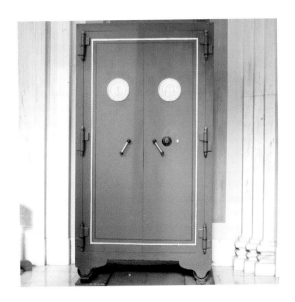

violent act of the Revolutionary War, which was the burning of the British ship *Gaspee* by Rhode Islanders in their harbor.

These documents, like the golden figure overlooking the city, symbolize the independent nature of the state. Its actions give it form: Rhode Island existed outside the United States for nearly two years, insisting on amendments to the Constitution that protected state rights before it would join.

Today, the same General Assembly that drafted the first laws guaranteeing freedom of religion over 350 years ago meets inside the Capitol. It consists of two houses -- the Senate with 50 members and the House of Representatives with 100 members -- both serving two-year terms.

Inside the Capitol, the Secretary of State keeps watch over "valuable State treasures" lodged in a vault that is opened daily to the public. The treasures are three important documents in the development of Rhode Island: 1) The Royal Charter of 1663, which guaranteed Rhode Islanders self-government and freedom of religion; 2) Rhode Island's copy of the Declaration of Independence (each of the 13 original states received an official copy); 3) The Gaspee Commission, an order from King George III demanding punishment for the first

ABOVE: The seal of the state lies directly under the dome.

LEFT: The state vault is opened every day for public inspection of its "treasures," including the Royal Charter of 1663.

PREVIOUS PAGES: The Rhode Island Capitol as seen from the train station. Rhode Island measures a mere 48 miles from north to south and 37 miles from east to west; yet, it has over 400 miles of shoreline. Providence and Newport both were considered the official capital city of Rhode Island until 1900, with the construction of the new Capitol in Providence.

OPPOSITE PAGE: The state flag atop the Capitol. In the center is the motto "Hope." According to the Secretary of State, the motto comes from a famous quote of the state's founder, Roger Williams. He told the early settlers to have "Hope in the Divine."

OPPOSITE: The sun reflects off the Capitol's Georgia marble.

ABOVE: Looking up into the Rotunda an encircling mural depicts the founding of Providence Plantations. For nearly two centuries, including sixty-seven years after gaining independence from Great Britain, Rhode Island maintained its Charter of 1663 as its constitution. This document empowered the people "to hold forth a livelie experiment, that a most flouishing civill state may stand and best bee maintained ..." It declared that "true pietye rightly grounded upon gospell principles, will give the best and greatest security to sovereignetye ..."

The Charter of 1663 ordained the people of Rhode Island to be a "body politique or corporate," but limited the right to vote to those men who owned more than $133 in real estate or received at least $7 in annual rental income, and to their sons. This excluded most of the men in Providence and other towns and meant a lack of representation in the General Assembly. By 1840 a movement against the Charter began, led by Harvard-educated Thomas Dorr. Excluded from Rhode Island's government, Dorr organized a convention of the people, drafted a new constitution

extending the vote to all men 21 years or older who met a residency requirement, and won approval for the new constitution in a plebiscite. A revolutionary government was elected with Dorr as governor. Now Rhode Island had two governments. The original one indicted Dorr and his followers and charged them with treason. Failing in an attempt to take the state's arsenal, Dorr sought refuge in Connecticut and was given it by that state's governor, who refused Rhode Island's extradition requests.

The Charter governor wrote to President John Tyler and asked for "assistance to which this State is entitled ..." Tyler balked, noting there was no violent struggle to put down. But he did recognize the Charter government because "it was enough for the Executive to know that she was recognized as a sovereign State by Great Britain by the treaty of 1783," he wrote in a letter to Congress. Later, with the aid of federal troops, Dorr's compatriots were arrested at the border. Little bloodshed resulted. Dorr surrendered, was found guilty of treason against the state, and given a life sentence. But his efforts produced results. Rhode Island adopted a new constitution in 1842 which granted native-born men the franchise. Dorr served a year in jail and, in 1851, his state citizenship was restored.

ABOVE: Looking into the eye of the dome one sees murals in the corners representing the important functions of the state: Commerce, Education, Justice, and Literature.

OPPOSITE: The Capitol's Rotunda is reminiscent of St. Peter's Basilica in Rome.

FOLLOWING PAGES: The Independent Man tops the dome. Below the statue on the Capitol's south face is this inscription taken from the Royal Charter of 1663: "To hold forth a lively experiment that a most flourishing civil state may stand and best be maintained with full liberty in religious concernments." *Right*, the House of Representatives Chamber.

ABOVE: This cannon used in the Civil War received a direct hit, and the ball remains where it was lodged. Behind it are some of the state's battle flags from that great war.

TOP RIGHT: Elevators with the state seal on the doors.

RIGHT: A perspective from the front lawn of the State Capitol's dome and tourelles (four smaller domes surrounding the main one) show influences from St. Paul's Cathedral in London.

OPPOSITE: The Senate Chamber as seen from the entry doors.

RIGHT: In the State Room is the famous Gilbert Stuart painting of George Washington -- one of two commissioned by the state. Nearby is the state's piece of moon rock and the small Rhode Island flag which was brought to the moon by the first astronauts.

ABOVE: State Room ceiling and chandelier.

TOP: Upper level of the State Library located in the Capitol.

OPPOSITE: A perspective of the Capitol at night.

"Providence Plantations founded by Roger Williams, 1636;
Providence, Portsmouth, Newport incorporated by Parliament, 1643;
Rhode Island-Providence Plantations obtained Royal Charter, 1663;
In general Assembly declared a Sovereign State, May 4, 1776."

-- Inscription On Capitol's North Portico

Official Name: . . . . State of North Carolina

Motto: . . . . Esse Quam Videri

Citizen: . . . . North Carolinian

Capital City: . . . . Raleigh, NC

Established: 1665

Joined Union: 1789

Left Union: 1861

Readmitted: 1868

Anthem: . . . . "The Old North State"

Name: . . . The original region Carolina was named in honor of King Charles IX of France and, later, King Charles I and King Charles II of England

Nickname: . . . . Tarheel State; Old North State

License Plate Slogan: . . . . First In Flight

Total Area: . . . . 52,672 sq mi (29)

The State of
North Carolina

Esse Quam Videri | To Be Rather Than To Seem

NORTH CAROLINA

No one's quite sure when the term "Tar Heel" came to represent a citizen of North Carolina or why. That the state was a key producer of pine tree tar, pitch, and turpentine for ship-builders had something to do with it. These adhesive products were tough to remove from workers' hands and feet -- much like the glue which stuck freedom, sovereignty, and North Carolinians together.

In 1771, four years before the first shots at Lexington and Concord, the Regulator movement in the western counties of the state commenced hostilities against the authorities. A major battle at Alamance Creek resulted in defeat for the rebels; seven of the leaders were hanged for treason. Though beaten in the field, the movement continued to grow. One of those western counties, Mecklenberg, issued its own declaration of independence May 31, 1775 as a "free and independent people, are, and of right ought to be, a sovereign and self-governing Association."

A year before, in 1774, the North Carolina Congress was organized within the domain, much to the displeasure of the royal governor. This Congress sent representatives to the Continental Congress in Philadelphia and was the first state authority to authorize its delegates there to vote for independence.

Meeting in Halifax in November, 1776, the Congress drafted and approved the Constitution of North Carolina, which included a Declaration of Rights. A vote of the people was not held, it being in the North Carolina Congress' powers to represent the citizens' sovereign will. Thereafter, the Congress

disbanded and a General Assembly was authorized to include a Senate and House of Commons.

North Carolina refused to join the United States until a statement of rights was included in the U.S. Constitution. The state remained independent of the republic for well over a year after the Constitution began operating on the ratifying states.

When it finally did join the Union, the state passed a set of resolutions, declaring: "Each State in the Union shall respectively retain every power, jurisdiction, and right, which is not by this Constitution delegated to the Congress ... nor shall [the federal government] ... exercise any act of authority over any individual in any of the said states, but such as can be justified under some power particularly given in the Constitution ..."

This obstinance displayed in the cause of liberty is not reflected in the administration of state government. Here, North Carolinians are more flexible. The North Carolina Capitol was built between 1833-1840 and, at its completion, contained offices of all three governmental branches -- the legislative, executive and judicial. Today it is used by the executive only; the chambers have been restored to their 1850's appearance.

ABOVE: The old House Chamber, used from 1840-1963.

PREVIOUS PAGES: The North Carolina Capitol glows against a spectacular night sky. *Left*, the new Legislative Building's dramatic stairway provides direct access to the chambers' galleries.

The North Carolina General Assembly met in the Capitol from 1840 to 1963, and then moved into a new State Legislative Building. This structure is classical in character, yet modern in appearance. Visitors walk over a giant Great Seal of the State of North Carolina at the entrance, a 28-foot diameter terrazzo (mosaic floor) and, upon entering, confront a wide, red-carpeted main staircase that leads directly to visitor galleries on the third floor. Members enter the Senate and House chambers from the second floor.

Garden Courts are located at the four corners of the first floor surrounded by committee rooms and offices. Three of the four courts have pools, and all are landscaped. The sides of each chamber open into the mezzanines of the garden courts, offering members quick access to constituents or informal meetings while being close by to return to the chambers. A small chapel is south of the Rotunda.

Three pyramidal, glass roofs top the Legislative Building, one for each chamber and one in the center over the faux Rotunda. Galleries for either chamber are connected by a mezzanine. In the center is a large landscaped pool that is open to the third floor.

The architect for the building was Edward Durrell Stone; Holloway-Reeves Architects served as associates.

OPPOSITE TOP & PREVIOUS PAGE: Rising above the new Legislative Building's pyramids are two large flags positioned in front of the state seal: one of the United States and the other of North Carolina. In the state's flag are two dates which represent the independence of North Carolina. The first, May 20, 1775, is the date of the Mecklenberg Declaration; the second, April 12, 1776, is the date of the Halifax Resolves, official instructions from the North Carolina Congress to her delegation in the Continental Congress authorizing the vote for independence.

ABOVE: The North Carolina Senate in session. The Senate and the House together are descended from the North Carolina Congress, which established the Constitution of 1776. "THAT all political power is vested in and derived from the people only ..." the Constitution asserts. "That the people of this State ought to have the sole and exclusive right of regulating the internal government and police thereof ... And whereas the Continental Congress ... have therefore declared, that the Thirteen United Colonies are, of right, wholly absolved from all allegiance to the British crown ... and that the said Colonies now are, and forever shall be, free and independent States ... therefore we, the Representatives of North-Carolina, chosen and assembled in Congress, for the express purpose of framing a Constitution ... do declare, that a government for this State shall be established ..."

OPPOSITE BOTTOM: View from the third-floor common area.

TOP: The House of Representatives Chamber.

OPPOSITE TOP RIGHT: Confederate Monument in honor of North Carolinians who died in the War Between the States. About 25% of all confederate battle deaths were from the state.

OPPOSITE TOP LEFT: The Capitol Rotunda.

OPPOSITE BOTTOM LEFT: North Carolina Veterans Monument honors state veterans who fought in World War I, World War II, and Korea.

1679

Official Name: . . . . State of New Hampshire
Motto: . . . . Live Free Or Die
Citizen: . . . . New Hampshirite
Capital City: . . . . Concord, NH
Established: 1679
Joined Union: 1788

Anthem: . . . . "Old New Hampshire"
Name: . . . . . . Named after Hampshire, England
Nickname: . Granite State; White Mountain State;
Switzerland of America; Mother of Rivers
License Plate Slogan: . . . . Live Free or Die
Total Area: . . . . 9,283 sq mi (44)

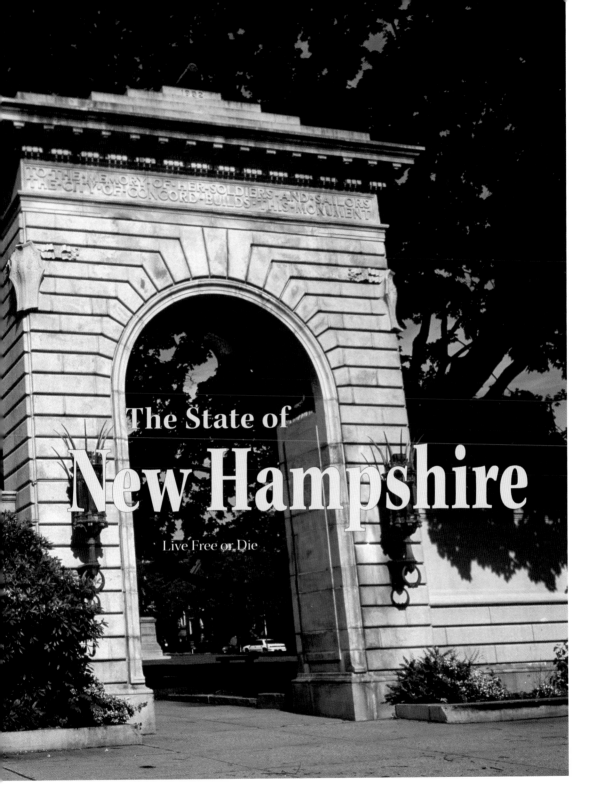

The State of
New Hampshire

Live Free or Die

NEW HAMPSHIRE

Live Free Or Die remains to this day the quintessential statement of individual sovereignty. And it is a principle which New Hampshirites have fought and died defending for three centuries. New Hampshire's motto no better fit a people, except maybe for the *E pluribus unum* of the United States. It is attributed to John Stark, Major General of the New Hampshire Militia during the Revolution -- a man who lived by his words. At Bunker Hill, General Stark led a regiment he had raised himself. Later he repelled an attempt by the British to take supplies in Bennington, hobbling the redcoats at Saratoga.

As only government, properly constituted, has the power to make laws, New Hampshirites have been careful to shackle the most powerful element of government: the legislature. The result has been a frugal operation, small state government, and fewer laws. There is no state income tax, and besides a small traveling stipend, the state does not pay its legislators for their services.

ABOVE: The hallway connecting the State House's front and back features a Civil War painting. *Right*, the Hall of Flags.

PREVIOUS PAGES: The arch at the front of the New Hampshire State House is known as Memorial Arch, erected in 1891 with this statement: "To the memory of her soldiers and sailors, the City of Concord builds this monument." Built of granite quarried locally at a cost of $20,000, it was dedicated July 4, 1892.

The legislature is at both extremes in the ratio of representatives to constituents. Only 24 senators make up the New Hampshire Senate -- the fourth smallest such body in America. One senator has 50,000 constituents and serves a two-year term with no limit. Representatives Hall holds 400 members, the largest constitutional assembly among the states of the union. In the English-speaking world, only three legislative bodies are larger: the U.S. House of Representatives, British House of Commons, and the Indian House of People.

New Hampshire's one representative for every 2,700 citizens is a world record (by contrast, there is one U.S. Congressman for about 700,000 people); so, too, is the number of representatives who are women (100), another world record. Representatives

forever hereafter shall, exercise and enjoy every power, jurisdiction, and right, pertaining thereto, which is not, or may not hereafter be by them expressly delegated to the United States of America in Congress assembled."

Like the Legislature it holds, the State House reflects the frugal nature of New Hampshire government. In 1814 the state's Capitol Commission issued a report calling for a new State House which would meet the needs of a "respectable and independent State."

The New Hampshire State House is the oldest state capitol in which the legislature uses its original chambers. The first architect was Stuart Park. The building is made of native granite, taken from the quarries in Penacook. It was enlarged in 1864 (Gridley J.F. Bryant, architect) and enlarged again in 1910 (Peabody and Stearns, architects).

Upon entering, one is immediately taken with the Hall of Flags. Over 103 New Hampshire military unit flags are on display, dating from 1819. These flags were carried by state military units in the Civil War, Spanish-American War, Mexican Border Incident, World War I, World War II, and Vietnam.

The Civil War (1861-1865) was the last major conflict in which armies organized around state and national flags on the battlefield. In New Hampshire, the bravery exhibited by New Hampshire's carriers of the colors is well documented. During the 9th New Hampshire Infantry's battle at Poplar Springs Church, Corporal James Brown was surrounded by Confederate soldiers who demanded the surrender of the New Hampshire flag he held. Rather than comply, Corporal Brown tore it to pieces. He was then killed. The staff and dangling blue fragments were later recovered by his body.

According to state documents, Captain Henry Dow of the 3rd New Hampshire sent one of his regiment's tattered flags from the Richmond, VA trenches in 1864 to his state's adjunct general with this note: "I most sincerely desire that this flag may be preserved by the State authorities, where in the future years its defenders may have the pleasure of looking upon it, remembering their service in defense of our glorious Nation's honor." In New Hampshire's Hall of Flags, their memory lives.

Live Free or Die.

are paid $200 biennially plus mileage. Terms are for two years, with no limit.

To further check government, New Hampshire's constitution provides for a Governor's Council, a body which dates to colonial times. Councilors have power of approval over the Governor's appointments, pardons and state contracts in excess of $5000. Elected every two years, Councilors are drawn from equally-populated districts and a total of five are selected every two years and compensated.

As a final bulwark against interference with the liberties of her people, New Hampshire's Constitution declares, "The people of this state have the sole and exclusive right of governing themselves as a free, sovereign, and independent state; and do, and

> *"The people of this state, have the sole and exclusive right of governing themselves as a free, sovereign, and independent state, and do, and forever hereafter shall, exercise and enjoy every power, jurisdiction and right pertaining thereto, which is not, or may not hereafter be by them expressly delegated to the United States of America, in Congress assembled."*
>
> **-- Constitution of New Hampshire, Bill of Rights**

OPPOSITE TOP: The United States and New Hampshire flags on top of the State House take their own course. "The Seal of the Republic of New Hampshire 1784" appears on the tympanum (the center of the pediment).

OPPOSITE BOTTOM: A side perspective of the State House.

TOP & PREVIOUS PAGE: The dome is made of copper, with gold leaf tiles applied which are 350-thousandths of an inch thick. The 3 3/8" square units are applied by hand. The original dome was silo-like; it was converted into a version of the 17th-century dome atop the church of the Hotel des Invalides in Paris. The eagle has stood atop the dome since 1819. The original eagle weighed 600 lbs. It was replaced in 1957 with a copper replica weighing 250 lbs. Both are 6'6" tall; 4'10" wing to wing. Carved by Lenerd Morse and then gilded, the original eagle had its head turned to the left to symbolize the eagle of war. The replica's head is turned to the right, symbolizing peace.

TOP: New Hampshire Senate Chamber.

OPPOSITE BOTTOM LEFT: Ceremonial "signing" table where important laws through the generations have been signed.

OPPOSITE TOP & BOTTOM RIGHT: Representatives Hall in which five portraits hang: 1) John P. Hale, former Speaker of the NH House and U.S. Senator; 2) Abraham Lincoln, the portrait of whom was purchased by penny contributions from New Hampshire school children in 1949 (taken down for repair); 3) George Washington, the first portrait hung in the hall, 1835; 4) Franklin Pierce, 14th President of the United States, and the only New

Hampshirite to hold that office; and 5) native Daniel Webster, who represented New Hampshire in Congress as its Senator and served as U.S. Secretary of State.

The House of Representatives was created out of the New Hampshire Congress. "WE, the members of the Congress of New Hampshire, chosen and appointed by the free suffrages of the people ... Accordingly pursuant to the trust reposed in us, WE DO RESOLVE, that this Congress assume the name, power and authority of a house of Representatives or Assembly for the Colony of New-Hampshire," states the New Hampshire Constitution of 1776.

1683

Official Name: . . . . State of New York
Motto: . . . . Excelsior
Citizen: . . . . New Yorker
Capital City: . . . . Albany, NY
Established:. 1683
Joined Union: 1788
Anthem: . . . . N/A

Name: . . . . . New Netherlands by the Dutch became
New York, in honor of the Duke of York and Albany
known later as King James II
Nickname: . . . . Empire State; Excelsior State
License Plate Slogan: . . . . Empire State
Total Area: . . . . 53,989 sq mi (27)

The State of

New York

Excelsior | Ever Upward

No better title named a state than that given to New York. It is The Empire State, for more reasons than can be listed here. Considered alone, with the wealth and resources of its people, cities, mountains, lakes, and farmland, New York would rank in the top tier of nations. But, by virtue of its first metropolis of the same name, other titles would be just as appropriate. The Capital of the World (the United Nations sits in assembly in New York City); The Financial Capital of the World (the two largest stock markets operate here); Skyscraper Capital of the World (there are more buildings over 1,000 feet high in NYC than anywhere else); Subway Capital of the Nation (more track laid than all other U.S. cities combined); People Capital of the World (most of the world's peoples are represented in distinct communities); Media Capital, etc.

NEW YORK

The Italian explorer Giovanni da Verrazzano was the first European to visit the region, reaching New York Bay in 1524. Almost a century later the Dutch sent Henry Hudson to find a passage to the Orient. He wasn't successful, but he did discover the river which bears his name and enabled the Dutch claim to New Netherlands -- a territory then including Delaware, Connecticut, New Jersey, and New York. English warships forced Dutch Governor Peter Stuyvesant to surrender in 1664 without a shot being fired. New York was named after the Duke of York and Albany (later King James II).

In 1776, at the onset of the American Revolution, the New York Congress convened in Kingston and drafted a constitution which declared, "... by the authority of the good people of this State ... no authority shall, on any pretence whatever, be exercised over the people or members of this State but such as shall be derived from and granted by them."

PREVIOUS PAGES: Perspectives of the New York Capitol front (right) and from the back and including the Empire State Plaza.

BELOW: The state seal on a building in the plaza.

OPPOSITE: The New York State Women Veteran's Memorial.

The New York Congress approved the Declaration of Independence and new state constitution on its proclamation alone, no vote from the people proffered.

But that constitution and later versions maintained vestiges of New York's old colonial system, notably tenant farming. Landlords held feudal powers under the Dutch patroon system, but these were sharply curtailed when New York gained its independence. Well into the 1800's, though, the descendants of these families owned millions of acres and asserted their manorial privileges.

When the Van Rensselaer and Livingston families attempted to collect $400,000 in back rents, all hell broke loose in Delaware and Columbia Counties. Known as the Anti-Rent Wars, the uprising saw farmers take up arms against county and state authorities to obstruct the takeover of defaulting farms. The struggle involved citizens in Albany, Columbia, Rensselaer, Schoharie, and Ulster counties. When a deputy was killed in Delaware County, Governor Silas Wright called out the militia.

In the end, this rural revolution succeeded: the New York Constitution was amended and in 1847 the farmers began receiving title to their land.

New York's lands stretch from the Atlantic Ocean to Lake Erie. From its mountains and lakes come the great Hudson, Susquehanna, Allegheny, and Delaware Rivers. And where there are no rivers for transportation, yet the need exists, New Yorkers build them, too.

PRIDE - COURAGE - HONOR

Consider the Erie Canal: it connected the Hudson River with the city of Buffalo when completed in 1825. A trip from Buffalo to New York took eight days and covered 352 miles. The Erie Canal captured the imagination of New Yorkers in the nineteenth century; the Empire State Building in the twentieth. Yet, the first grand piece of monumental architecture New York was associated with was not the Empire State Building: it was New York's Capitol. "When planning for a new Capitol in Albany began in 1866, those who championed the cause set lofty expectations for the new building," according to the *Visitors Guide to the New York State Capitol*. "This Capitol would be a source of pride for all New Yorkers. It would be a monument to our form of government."

After 25 years of construction, Governor Theodore Roosevelt declared it completed in 1899. Five architects and $25 million later, it was hailed by some as beautiful and ridiculed by others as a boondoggle. Whatever the opinion, it was very New York.

Guided by the Moorish-Gothic style, Leopold Eidlitz created the New York State Assembly Chamber -- the largest room in the Capitol. The chamber was dedicated January 1, 1879 and was called "the most monumental interior in the country" by architectural critic Henry Van Brunt.

It features large windows of clear and stained glass, thus permitting a natural lighting of the chamber. The chamber's sandstone walls hold an abundance of colors: red carpet, mahogany and

leather furniture, and greenish-blue stonework. Four pillars of granite support the vaulted ceiling. The Assembly Chamber was rebuilt in 1909 when pieces of the stone ceiling started falling and threatening assemblymen's heads. A fire claimed the State Library two years later. Numerous other changes have been made to the interior to accommodate state government.

The Senate Chamber was dedicated March 10, 1881. Its designer, Henry H. Richardson, had imprinted a style that became known as "Richardson Romanesque." Hallmarks of the style include round arches and vaults, piers instead of columns, and intricate ornamentation. The 50-foot ceilings feature carved oak. The chamber walls draw on various foreign sources: Italian Sienna marble, Scottish granite, Mexican onyx, Caribbean mahogany, Spanish red leather, and Knoxville marble.

The oversized "whispering fireplaces" in the Senate Chamber are said to serve as ideal meeting places for negotiating Senators: they can stand up within the fireplace and use the surrounding walls as a shield from uninvited ears.

Behind the Senate President's Chair is a stained-glass replica of the state seal. Adopted nearly 100 years before that other famous icon associated with New York (the Statue of Liberty), the State Seal features Lady Liberty.

"She represents freedom for the people of New York," according to an official Senate brochure. "Held high on a staff in her right hand is a peasant cap representing democratic rule by the people. Her left foot is stepping on a crown, representing the rejection of royalty."

The New York Seal has "come to be regarded as the unvarying symbol of dignity and sovereign authority of the State," wrote legal historian Henry A. Holmes. Were that seal to be placed on every product, service, and idea that emanated from New York, the state's global influence would be readily apparent as would the reason for its moniker, *Empire State*.

LEFT: A setting sun turns the New York State Cultural Education Center golden. The Center sits at the south end of the Empire State Plaza and houses the State Museum, State Library, and State Archives.

OPPOSITE TOP LEFT: The United States and New York flags fly atop the Capitol.

OPPOSITE BOTTOM LEFT: The hallway adjacent to the Senate Chamber entrance.

OPPOSITE TOP RIGHT: A scene from the William deLeftwich Dodge murals in the Governor's Reception Room.

OPPOSITE BOTTOM RIGHT: The East Lobby where the state's extensive flag collection is kept.

ABOVE: A view of the Senate Chamber from the galleries. To the right are the famous "Whispering Fireplaces" where Senators can speak in private. The New York State Legislature is comprised of the Senate and Assembly. Both the 61 Senators and the 150 Assemblymen serve a two-year term.

ABOVE: The Senate Chamber. The grandfather clock in the corner was designed by architect Henry Richardson, who also designed the room.

OPPOSITE TOP LEFT: A clock with the state seal stands outside the Senate Chamber.

OPPOSITE BOTTOM LEFT: New York's Capitol is famous for its staircases. The Assembly Staircase designed by Leopold Eidlitz (shown) uses sandstone and granite to frame its Gothic style. The Senate Staircase features carvings of animals, thus providing its second name, "The Evolutionary Staircase." And, the Great Western Staircase includes portraits of famous New Yorkers. It is known as the "Million Dollar Staircase."

OPPOSITE BOTTOM RIGHT: Assembly Chamber entrance.

OPPOSITE TOP RIGHT: The Nelson A. Rockefeller Empire State Plaza, named in honor of Governor Rockefeller who spearheaded the project in the 1960's, sits behind the Capitol. This modern piece of New York culture features government offices, the State Archives, State Museum, State Library, convention center, reflecting pool, and "The Egg" (a 980-seat theater). From the observation deck of the 42-story Corning Tower one can see the Hudson River Valley, greater Albany, and the foothills of the Adirondack and Catskill Mountains. Also on the Plaza: the Cultural Education Center, memorials to New York Police Officers, the New York's Vietnam War Memorial, Crime Victim's Memorial, and the Korean War Memorial.

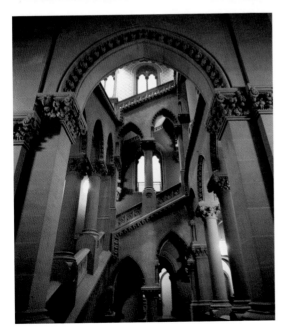

BOTTOM LEFT: Senate Chamber ceiling.

LEFT & OPPOSITE: The Governor's Reception Room features the impressive William deLeftwich Dodge murals. According to state literature, these were commissioned to complement a Flag Room which would honor New York State citizens who served in the military. Dodge began work in 1920. It would take him five years to finish. In 1929 the mural panels were installed. Dodge made the murals under the assumption that they would be forty feet from the ground floor, as plans at that time included a tower capped by a dome (like Connecticut's Capitol) that eliminated the current floor. These never came off. But so good was Dodge, the paintings do not suffer for want of distance. In the center is the *Spirit of New York* (also titled Goddess of Harmony), holding a sword in her right hand and shield in her left. The New York Seal dominates the shield. Behind her are the flags of the various nations she has been a part of.

Encircling the seal are historical scenes of military actions New Yorkers participated in, including Dutch-English, French-Dutch, Indian-French, and English-American. Inner panels honor the state's natives with individual representations of the Onondaga, Mohawk, Oneida & Seneca, and Cayuga peoples. Further out, battle depictions of the French war against the Iroquois in upstate New York, the Revolution, Gettysburg, and World War I in which New York Guard units break the Hindenburg Line in France. Naval engagements portrayed include the Battle of Lake Erie (War of 1812), Civil War Naval Engagements in general, the sinking of the Spanish fleet by the *USS New York* and *USS Brooklyn* in 1898, and World War I submarine warfare. Famous New Yorkers portrayed include Theodore Roosevelt (Rough Rider, N.Y. Governor, and U.S. President); General G.K. Warren (chief engineer of the Army of the Potomac, credited with identifying the importance of capturing Little Round Top at Gettysburg, thus ensuring Union success); General Richard Montgomery (second in command in the invasion of Quebec during the Revolution, killed in action); and the Unknown Soldier.

"This convention, therefore, in the name and authority of the good people of this State, doth ordain, determine, and declare that no authority shall, on any pretence whatever, be exercised over the people or members of this State but such as shall be derived and granted by them."

-- Constitution of New York, 1777

Official Name: .... Commonwealth of Pennsylvania
Motto: .... Virtue, Liberty, and Independence
Citizen: .... Pennsylvanian
Capital City: .... Harrisburg, PA
Established: 1683
Joined Union: 1787
Anthem: .... N/A

Name: Known as Penn's Woods (*sylvania* is Latin for "woods"), Pennsylvania was named in honor of William Penn's father, Admiral Penn, by King Charles II of England
Nickname: .... Keystone State; Quaker State
License Plate Slogan: .... Keystone State
Total Area: .... 46,058 sq mi (33)

The Commonwealth of
Pennsylvania

Virtue, Liberty, and Independence

The expansive brick building in Philadelphia with the church-like steeple will forever be known as Independence Hall, the place where the Declaration of Independence was written (1776), the Articles of Confederation negotiated (1777), and the United States Constitution drafted (1787). It served as the central meeting point for the revolutionary states of the eastern seaboard and placed Pennsylvania in the geographic, economic and social role of "Keystone," locking the liberty-minded league of peoples in place.

PENNSYLVANIA

Independence Hall would become the Capitol of a fledgling republic. But to Pennsylvanians, that building was their State House, the grandest structure in North America for the better part of the eighteenth century and the symbol of a proud and advanced commonwealth.

Plans for a new State House were first drafted in 1729 under the direction of famous trial lawyer Andrew Hamilton, who was serving as Speaker of Pennsylvania's Assembly. (Hamilton went on to represent publisher John Peter Zenger, who was imprisoned by New York authorities. Zenger was charged with libel for printing critical stories about the governor. Hamilton won acquittal, arguing Zenger could not be jailed if the charges were true. This case helped establish the foundations of a free press in America.)

PREVIOUS PAGES: The Commonwealth's Capitol; *Left*, the Supreme Court Chamber inside the building.

TOP: "In God We Trust" is chiseled at the Capitol's entrance; *Right*, the state flag flies with *Commonwealth* in the background.

OPPOSITE: *Commonwealth* is the name of the 17½ foot golden bronze statue that tops the dome. Sculpted by Roland Hinton Perry, it was installed in 1905 and refurbished in 1997. Commonwealth is "the symbolic embodiment of Pennsylvania. She represents Mercy and Justice, the principles upon which Pennsylvania was founded," according to Perry.

Hamilton felt that Pennsylvania's Assembly needed a more dignified setting for its important work. So, for the next twelve years, in between defending clients like Zenger, he made the new State House a priority, even using personal funds for its construction. But in 1741, he died suddenly.

The project did not. By 1748 the building was completed and the Assembly was meeting in its chambers. Yet something bothered that body: the new State House did not stand out from the rest of the city's architecture. Many believed that a building which is to be the embodiment of the people's will should be grander. In 1750 monies were appropriated for the solution. A monumental steeple was added to tower above the Philadelphia skyline. The large bell tower and steeple suddenly transformed

the building from meeting house to temple. And to finish the bold presentation, a new bell was purchased from John Pass and John Stow in 1753 and placed inside the tower. Twenty-three years later, the "Liberty Bell" would ring out the revolutionary news from Philadelphia.

So it was Pennsylvania's symbols which were appropriated by the newly forming American Republic. Its State House became the young nation's Capitol; its Liberty Bell, a universal symbol of freedom.

For the first fifty years after its founding, Pennsylvania did not have a State House and instead used any number of establishments for its legislative quarters. The new State House would serve its needs for the next 63 years, witnessing the drafting of the Commonwealth's first constitution in 1776 and the election of President Benjamin Franklin (the highest position in the executive council).

In 1790 Pennsylvanians drafted a new constitution which provided for a Senate. Until this time, the Commonwealth's laws were made by a

unicameral legislature, and the State House in Philadelphia was made with only one large assembly room for this purpose. In 1799 the Legislature moved to Lancaster and utilized its courthouse. In 1810, the Legislature named Harrisburg the capital city, and construction for a Capitol was begun in 1819. It was occupied in 1822.

For the ensuing 75 years the Harrisburg Capitol served Pennsylvania. In 1897 most of the historic structure was destroyed by fire. A replacement Capitol was built in its place but, as this was found to be lacking in grandeur, a new competition was established with the stipulation that the architect must be a Pennsylvanian. Philadelphia architect John Huston was selected. His plans utilized the existing structure's walls.

The cornerstone was laid May 5, 1904 and, on October 4, 1906, the new Capitol was dedicated amid much pomp and circumstance. President Theodore Roosevelt headlined the ceremony.

The Capitol's dome was modeled after Michelangelo's St. Peter's Basilica, rising 272 feet from the ground and weighing 52 million pounds. The Hall of the House, the largest room in the Capitol, is in the Italian Renaissance style. The French Renaissance style is used in the Senate.

The opulence of the Capitol brought worldwide attention. Yet a scandal erupted shortly after its completion amid charges of contractor overcharges and corruption. A state investigation led to jail time for the architect.

The Commonwealth's Capitol is a temple of sovereignty to her people. The Hall of the House holds 203 legislators, serving two-year terms, and 100 clerks who go about the daily business of the state. The Senate Chamber is no less impressive, but considerably smaller, as should be expected for a body of 50 members serving four-year terms.

William Penn, the father of Pennsylvania and the son of the man it was named after, would be most pleased were he alive today to see it. "Any government is free to the people under it where the laws rule and the people are a party to those laws," he wrote in the *Frame of Government* (1682).

For over three hundred years, Pennsylvanians have abided by their founder's words and, thus, his legacy endures.

ABOVE: Night view from the east side of the Capitol showing the newer portions of the "Capitol Complex."

TOP: The Rotunda staircase was modeled after the Paris Opera House. The Rotunda is lit by 4,000 lights.

FOLLOWING PAGE LEFT: The medallion *Law,* one of four in the Rotunda. The others are *Art, Science,* and *Religion.*

FOLLOWING PAGE RIGHT: Looking up into the eye of the Rotunda, note the lunettes adjacent to each medallion. Painted by Edwin Austin Abbey, they are titled *Spirit of Light, Science Revealing Treasures of the Earth, The Spirit of Vulcan,* and *The Spirit of Religious Liberty.*

TOP LEFT: The Seal of the Commonwealth on a portion of the original Harrisburg Capitol not destroyed by fire in 1897.

BOTTOM LEFT: The medallion *Religion* in the Rotunda.

TOP RIGHT: The Capitol dome.

BOTTOM RIGHT: G.G. Bernard's sculpture at right of entrance.

OPPOSITE: Side perspective of the Capitol's front.

"I, Benjamin Franklin, do swear that I will be true and faithful to the commonwealth of Pennsylvania: And that I will not directly or indirectly do any act or thing prejudicial or injurious to the constitution or government thereof, as established by the convention."

So said the great American statesman, scientist, and printer upon his swearing-in as President of Pennsylvania in 1785. Franklin had recently concluded (with John Adams and John Jay) the Treaty of Peace with Great Britain in which the freedom and independence of the states was recognized. He returned home to accept the presidency, where he served for three years. During this period President Franklin headed the commonwealth's delegation as it hosted the Federal Constitutional Convention of 1787 in Philadelphia.

Earlier Franklin, who was born in Massachusetts and walked to Philadelphia to meet his destiny, served as head of the Pennsylvania Constitutional Convention in 1776 in which the state's constitution was drafted and proclaimed. That same year he signed the Declaration of Independence on behalf of his state. But Franklin's distinction as the first Founding Father lies in his effort to confederate the colonies *twenty-two years before the American Revolution.* As a member of the Albany Congress of 1754, Franklin spearheaded a move to confederate and unify the colonies under British rule. Throughout the colonial period, the British government treated with each colony separately because each one was created under a different charter, for different purposes, with different rights and privileges given to each. The commissioners at the Albany Congress finally approved the Plan of Union. But when asked to ratify the plan, the colonial legislatures each rejected it for taking too much power away from the individual colonies. The Americans jealously guarded their separate privileges and independence from each other.

Benjamin Franklin died in 1790 -- one year after the United States Constitution came into operation -- and the same year the Pennsylvania Constitution was redrawn in a convention headed by Federalist James Wilson. The Scottish-born Wilson was Associate Justice of the U.S. Supreme Court at the time. Seeing no conflict of interest, he and his allies struck out from the 1776 Declaration of Rights the third right, *to wit:* "That the people of this State have the sole, exclusive and inherent right of governing and regulating the internal police of the same."

The full import of surrendering this right was realized by western Pennsylvanians four years later. When these people refused to pay a new federal excise tax on their whiskey and Judge Wilson certified noncompliance, President Washington ordered militia under the command of Virginia's Governor Lee to enforce collection. Washington himself would command troops in the skirmishes that followed this, the first instance of the new federal government enforcing its laws with force. The 1790 convention, which was dominated by members of the Federalist Party, also substituted the more powerful single-chamber legislature with two houses and abolished the presidency and executive council. In its place the office of governor was created.

OPPOSITE: The *Apotheosis of Pennsylvania*, the name of the mural on the front wall of the Hall of the House, behind the Speaker's chair. "Upon the throne sits the Genius of State," the official guide states, "below, the first steps are occupied by those individuals who played key roles throughout the history of the Commonwealth. Explorers and pioneers occupy the highest tier. Intellectual and spiritual leaders of the Colonial and Revolutionary eras are below them. To the right are leaders and workers in science and industry; to the left, Pennsylvania's military history is celebrated."

ABOVE: The Hall of the House, the chamber of the Pennsylvania House of Representatives.

TOP: The Pennsylvania Senate Chamber.

OPPOSITE TOP: The view of the House from the public gallery.

OPPOSITE BOTTOM: One of the many murals by Violet Oakley in the Courtroom of the Supreme Court in the Capitol. This one is titled *Divine Law*. Touted as the oldest court in North America, the Pennsylvania Supreme Court began in 1684 as the Provincial Court and received its current name in 1722. Besides acting as the court of last appeal, the Supreme Court has unique policy-making authority to complement incomplete legislation. And, it holds the "King's Bench" power -- a right to intervene in any legal proceeding within Pennsylvania as it alone determines necessary.

Official Name: . . . . State of South Carolina
Motto: . . . . Animus Opibusque Parati;
Dum Spiro Spero
Citizen: . . . . South Carolinian
Capital City: . . . . Columbia, SC
Established: 1693
Joined Union: 1788
Left Union: 1860

Readmitted: 1868
Anthem: . "Carolina"; "South Carolina On My Mind"
Name: . . . The original region Carolina was named in
honor of King Charles IX of France and, later, King
Charles I and King Charles II of England
Nickname:. Palmetto State; Rice State; Swamp State
License Plate Slogan:. . . Smiling Faces, Beautiful Places
Total Area: . . . . 31,189 sq mi (40)

The State of

South Carolina

Animus Opibusque Parati | Prepared in Mind and Resources
Dum Spiro Spero | While I Breathe I Hope

South Carolina's first State House was completed in 1753 and burned in 1788. That was an accident. Its replacement was burned in 1865. That was intentional, as the northern armies destroyed the capital city, Columbia, ending the War Between the States. The third and current Capitol had its cornerstone laid December 15, 1851 after the General Assembly authorized a "Fire Proof Building." The architect, Major John R. Niernsee, died before the building was completed, and not until the early 20th century was it finished. The General Assembly had appointed P.H. Hammerskold as the original project architect, but he was dismissed in 1854 for "general dereliction of duty."

SOUTH CAROLINA

In his place they named Niernsee, who determined that the building was of defective materials and must be dismantled. Niernsee went to work in a new location and, three years after starting, reported in 1860 that the structure had risen sixty-six feet above the foundation. He spent $1,240,063 to this point. When Sherman's army burned Columbia to the ground on February 17, 1865, the old State

ABOVE: The mace used by the South Carolina House of Representatives is the only one in use in America that predates the Revolutionary War. It is a symbol of the sovereign power that passed from the King to the People of South Carolina on their independence from Great Britain. Made in London in 1756 by Magdelen Feline, it was purchased by the "Commons House of Assembly of the Province of South Carolina" for 90 guineas. The mace is made of silver with gold burnishings and its panels have the coat-of-arms of South Carolina, Great Britain, and the House of Hanover. It is the custom every day, upon the opening of the session of the House of Representatives, that the Sergeant-at-Arms bear the mace ahead of the Speaker and place it in a special rack on the rostrum. The mace is borne at the head of the procession whenever the House officially visits the Senate and on other state occasions. Twice in its history the mace has disappeared. During the Revolution, the mace vanished and was not recovered until 1819. In that year Langdon Cheves of South Carolina was named President of the Bank of the United States and discovered it in a Phildelphia vault. In 1971 it was stolen from the rostrum and later recovered in Gainesville, FL.

House went up in flames. In it were Niernsee's architectural records, books, drawings -- 25 years' worth of his practice. "These," said Niernsee, along with "one of the latest and best busts of Calhoun, were utterly swept away during that terrible night -- an irreparable loss." Yet, at least one perspective drawing was saved, giving future architects an idea of what he contemplated for the Capitol.

To lose critical drawings of the Capitol was one thing; to lose a bust of John C. Calhoun was more tragic to state officials. Calhoun, the ardent state rights advocate, will remain one of South Carolina's most famous citizens. His motto -- "Liberty dearer than Union" -- summed up his philosophy.

Calhoun was most accomplished in national politics: he served as Secretary of War under President Monroe, Vice President under President John Quincy Adams, and Vice President under Andrew Jackson (one term). Calhoun opposed high tariffs on imports by the federal government and argued they were unconstitutional. Further, he said, under the U.S. Constitution each state, when it believed it necessary, could nullify a federal law if it injured that state's citizens. This policy of "nullification" was denounced by Jackson, though the old general supported the principle of state rights. South Carolina did nullify the tariffs in 1832 just before a compromise was worked out in Washington.

Calhoun spent the remainder of his life detailing his political theories, which his state would use in justifying secession from the United States ten years after his death. He argued that sovereignty existed in the people in their capacity as state citizens and was not resident *en masse* in the nation.

In striking confirmation of his tenets, the U.S. Congress pushed through the 14th Amendment to the

OPPOSITE: The Corinthian columns of the Capitol are cut from a single piece of stone, stand 43 feet high, and weigh 37 tons.

PREVIOUS PAGES: The entrance of the Capitol features fasces on each side of the door. Fasces (bundles of rods topped with an axe) are an ancient Roman symbol of power of the state over life and limb and were borne by guards in front of the Emperor. *Right*, a perspective of the Capitol from the rear.

U.S. Constitution *after* the war, creating a "United States citizen" with "privileges and immunities" concurrent with an American's state citizenship.

It would take more than fifty years for the little state to recover from the War Between the States. The price it paid in blood and treasure prohibited it from completing the Capitol. But at the turn of the century, finishing the project became a priority.

The Capitol's present dome was not contemplated by Niernsee. He designed a tower which rose 180 feet from the ground in the building's center, with arches and piers as support. Pyramidal in outline, it has been termed a "rectangular lantern." Of the actual dome, a legislative committee said, "No uglier creation could be devised." In 1900 Frank P. Millburn began service as architect. He hired McIlvain and Unkefer as contractors to build the present dome and the north and south porticos.

In 1904 the state elected Charles C. Wilson of Columbia as architect. He was the last architect to work on the building and is considered responsible for its final completion.

OPPOSITE: A view of the Rotunda and foyer area from the second floor. Galleries to the legislative chambers are accessed on this level.

ABOVE: The state seal in stained glass adorns the second floor of the foyer.

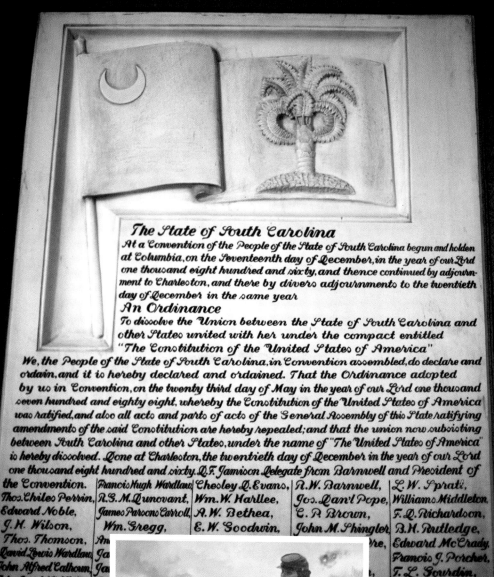

The State of South Carolina

At a Convention of the People of the State of South Carolina begun and holden at Columbia, on the Seventeenth day of December, in the year of our Lord one thousand eight hundred and sixty, and thence continued by adjournment to Charleston, and there by divers adjournments to the twentieth day of December in the same year

An Ordinance

To dissolve the Union between the State of South Carolina and other States united with her under the compact entitled "The Constitution of the United States of America"

We, the People of the State of South Carolina, in Convention assembled, do declare and ordain, and it is hereby declared and ordained. That the Ordinance adopted by us in Convention, on the twenty third day of May in the year of our Lord one thousand seven hundred and eighty eight, whereby the Constitution of the United States of America was ratified, and also all acts and parts of acts of the General Assembly of this State ratifying amendments of the said Constitution are hereby repealed; and that the union now subsisting between South Carolina and other States, under the name of "The United States of America" is hereby dissolved. Done at Charleston, the twentieth day of December in the year of our Lord one thousand eight hundred and sixty. D.F. Jamison Delegate from Barnwell and President of the Convention.

	Francis Hugh Wardlaw	Chesley D. Evans,	R.W. Barnwell,	L.W. Spratt,
Thos. Chiles Perrin,	R.S. M.Dunovant,	Wm. W. Harllee,	Jos. Dan'l Pope,	Williams Middleton,
Edward Noble,	James Parsons Carroll,	A.W. Bethea,	C. P. Brown,	F.D. Richardson,
J.H. Wilson,	Wm. Gregg,	E.W. Goodwin,	John M. Shingler	B.H. Rutledge,
Thos. Thomson,	An...		...re,	Edward McCrady,
David Lewis Wardlaw	Ja...		...n,	Francis J. Porcher,
John Alfred Calhoun,	Ja...		...n,	T. L. Gourdin,
John Izard Middleton,	Jo...		...ok,	John S. Palmer,
Benjamin E. Sessions,	Will...		...es,	John L. Nowell,
J.N. Whitner,	Hen...			John S. O'Hear,
James L. Orr,	In...			John G. Landrum

TOP: The U.S. and state flags fly atop the Capitol. "I salute the Flag of South Carolina and pledge to the Palmetto State love, loyalty, and faith," reads the *Official Salute to the Flag of South Carolina*. The Confederate battle flag flies below.

ABOVE LEFT: A marker on the Capitol grounds indicates where the old State House stood prior to Sherman's burning of Columbia in 1865.

OPPOSITE: An engraving of South Carolina's secession ordinance in marble hangs in the foyer. *Below*, the painting depicts brother helping brother during the War Between the States.

ABOVE: A bronze of John Calhoun in the foyer. A graduate of Yale in 1804, he was taught law by Connecticut Judge Tapping Reeve. Judge Reeve was a member of the Federalist Party which later organized the Hartford Convention (1814-1815), a conclave of New England state officials organized to discuss relations with the United States.

ABOVE & LEFT: The Senate Chamber. South Carolina has a Sword of State which sits in a rack on the Senate rostrum in front of the President's chair. The present sword was presented as a gift to South Carolina by Lord Halifax, former British Ambassador to the United States, in 1951. It replaced the one utilized up to that time, an 1800 cavalry model used in the War of 1812 and the War Between the States. According to historian A.S. Salley, the earliest mention found of the sword is 1704 in the journal of the Commons House of Assembly of South Carolina where authorization is made for a Sword of State "for the Rt. Hon. the Governor and all succeeding Governors for the Hon. of this Government." Salley further states: "On March 26, 1776 South Carolina adopted a Constitution independent of the government of Great Britain and elected John Rutledge, President of the State. He was inaugurated the following day... preceded by the sheriff bearing the Sword of State ...The same Sword of State has been in constant use ever since, being borne by the Sergeant-at-Arms of the Senate ..."

ABOVE: Custom wallpaper in the Senate Chamber in which the repeating pattern is the state seal. The House Chamber wallpaper also features this pattern.

ABOVE & OPPOSITE: The House of Representatives Chamber.
Note the mace on the left.

"We, the people of the State of South Carolina, in convention assembled, grateful to Almighty God for this opportunity, deliberately and peaceably, of entering into an explicit and solemn compact with each other, and forming a new constitution of civil government for ourselves and posterity, recognizing the necessity of the protection of the people in all that pertains to their freedom, safety, and tranquillity, and imploring the Great Legislator of the universe, do agree upon, ordain, and establish the following declaration of rights and form of government as the constitution of the commonwealth of South Carolina."

-- SOUTH CAROLINA CONSTITUTION, 1868

ABOVE: A monument to the Palmetto Tree on the Capitol grounds. The tree is closely associated with the state, appearing on its flag and seal.

TOP RIGHT: Ground floor of the Capitol.

BOTTOM RIGHT: Monument to South Carolina's Senator Strom Thurmond.

OPPOSITE TOP: Front view of the Capitol.

"Whereas the British Parliament, claiming of late years a right to bind the North American colonies by law in all cases whatsoever ... the said colonies, therefore, severally remonstrated against the passing, and petitioned for the repeal, of those acts, but in vain; ... And whereas the delegates of all the colonies on this continent, from Nova Scotia to Georgia, assembled in a general Congress at Philadelphia, in the most dutiful manner laid out their complaints at the foot of the throne, and humbly implored their sovereign that his royal authority and interposition might be used for their relief ... And whereas large reenforcements of troops and ships have been ordered and are daily expected in America for carrying on war against each of the united colonies ... And whereas in consequence of a plan recommended by the governors, and which seems to have been concerted between them and their ministerial masters to withdraw the usual officers and thereby loosen the bands of government and create anarchy and confusion in the colonies ... And whereas ... some mode should be established by common consent, and for the good of the people, the origin and end of all governments, for regulating the internal polity of this colony. The (South Carolina) Congress being vested with powers competent for the purpose, and having fully deliberated touching the premises, do therefore resolve ... That this congress being a full and free representation of the people of this colony, shall henceforth be deemed and called the general assembly of South Carolina ..." -- **Constitution of South Carolina, 1776**

Official Name: . . . . State of New Jersey
Motto: . . . . Liberty and Prosperity
Citizen: . . . . New Jerseyan
Capital City: . . . . Trenton, NJ
Established: 1702
Joined Union: 1787

Anthem: . . . . N/A
Name: . . . Named after Sir George Carteret's native island of Jersey, in the English Channel
Nickname: Garden State; Clam State; Jersey Blue State
License Plate Slogan: . . . . Garden State
Total Area: . . . . 8,215 sq mi (46)

The State of
New Jersey

Liberty and Prosperity

NEW JERSEY

Few patriots opposed the centralization of government and defended the principles of local control like William Paterson of New Jersey, whose work in the Federal Constitutional Convention forever lent his state's name to the cause of maintaining state sovereignty. Called the New Jersey Plan, Paterson proposed that voting in the Congress remain as it was during the Revolution (1774-1783) and Articles of Confederation period (1781- 1789): one vote per state, regardless of the state's population.

Nationalists in the convention wanted voting to be proportional to population. Ultimately a compromise was reached with Paterson and the state rights group when College of New Jersey (later, Princeton University) graduate Oliver Ellsworth of Connecticut proposed the solution: voting by state population in the U.S. House of Representatives, voting by state in the U.S. Senate. Each state would be guaranteed a seat in the House with the remainder allotted by population, and each state would get two votes in the Senate regardless of population.

New Jersey was the fourth smallest of the Original States, and in colonial times, was smaller yet as it was divided into two: East Jersey and West Jersey.

Swedish settlements on the Delaware River were conquered by the Dutch and the territory was made part of New Netherlands. The British, in turn, conquered the Dutch province and the Duke of York (later King James II) granted Nova Caesarea (or New Jersey) to Sir George Carteret, a native of the Isle of Jersey, and John Berkeley, brother of the tyrannical Virginia Governor.

The grant was for the lands between the Hudson and Delaware Rivers. Now begins New Jersey's struggles with its two large neighbors, New York and Pennsylvania. Carteret's son Philip was made governor and, in 1668, called the first colonial legislature. This met in Elizabeth amid a growing problem with New York authorities, who insisted on collecting duties from ships docking in East Jersey ports. The New Yorkers were determined to snuff out the competition. New York Governor Edmund Andros captured Carteret on a military raid into

PREVIOUS PAGES: The New Jersey State House dome at night; *Left*, the Senate Chamber.

OPPOSITE: A gold eagle greets visitors in the Rotunda.

ABOVE: View of the State House from West State Street. This portion of the Capitol was built after the Fire of 1885.

New Jersey. He was taken to a New York jail and imprisoned for the next two years.

Meanwhile, Berkeley sold his portion of New Jersey, and it eventually ended up in the hands of William Penn and his associates. This West Jersey province had its capital at Burlington; East Jersey had its capital at Perth Amboy. Penn later purchased East Jersey in an auction. But Governor Andros succeeded in 1685 to incorporate both parts of New Jersey into New York. In 1702 New Jersey was made a royal colony, yet the New York Governor ruled until 1738.

When the American Revolution erupted, restless New Jerseyans saw their opportunity to gain freedom. Meeting in Burlington, Trenton, and New Brunswick from May 26 to July 2, 1776, the New Jersey Congress drafted and proclaimed a constitution. It declared: "We, the representatives of the colony of

New Jersey, having been elected by all the counties, in the freest manner, and in congress assembled, have, after mature deliberations, agreed upon a set of charter rights and the form of a Constitution ..."

Finally, this little state was independent of the English (not to mention New Yorkers and Pennsylvanians). Small wonder that maintaining the rights of his state was so important to William Paterson.

Paterson served one term as U.S. Senator before resigning so he could serve as Governor. In that post he was elected three times, successfully reforming the state's legal code and justice system. In his honor was named one of the earliest manufacturing centers of America: Paterson, NJ.

New Jersey's State House has served as the Capitol since 1792 when the original was built by Jonathan Doane. Doane's building was a simple rectangle made of rubblestone with a bell tower. Since that time, numerous additions and renovations were completed, so that today the building (like the government it houses) no longer resembles the original.

Despite this, the Capitol is considered the third oldest in America in continuous use (Maryland 1779, Virginia 1788, and New Jersey 1792).

The continual additions to the Capitol over the last two centuries have mirrored the growth in population. Today, New Jersey is the most densely populated of the United States. And as its face has changed, so too has its Capitol. In 1845 a new dome and north facade were added under the direction of Philadelphia architect John Notman. In 1865 the Delaware River-side portico was extended, and in 1871 work was begun on new wings for the legislature. A major fire in 1885 led to reconstruction at the hands of Lewis Broome of Jersey City. Adopting the Second Empire style, he created a new dome in proportion to the growing building.

He also created a new rotunda. In 1903 the Senate wing was remade in the American Renaissance style. In 1905, twenty years after a new Assembly wing was created, work was begun on a larger wing that was to be made in the late-Victorian style. The original east wing of 1792 was replaced in 1906 with a four-story office section. In 1911-12, the front area of the east side and west side was extended. In 1991 an extensive restoration of the legislative areas of the Capitol was completed.

ABOVE: A meeting room opposite the Senate Chamber.

TOP: The front of the State House at dusk. The bronze state seal adorns the top center of the building and is illuminated at night.

ABOVE: Looking up into the Rotunda. The Fire of 1885 forced the rebuilding of the Rotunda, which today includes portraits of the state's earliest governors. In the center is a bust of Woodrow Wilson, the only New Jersey governor to become a U.S. President.

"There shall be justice until the Heavens fall," states an inscription in Latin which encircles the ceiling of the Rotunda. To guarantee justice, the New Jersey Constitution of 1844 declares: "All political power is inherent in the people. Government is instituted for the protection, security, and benefit of the people, and they have the right at all times to alter or reform the same, whenever the public good may require it."

ABOVE & LEFT: The New Jersey Legislature is comprised of two bodies: the General Assembly and the Senate. Pictured are two perspectives of the General Assembly Chamber. Two assemblymen from each of the 40 legislative districts compose the 80-member body. The chamber is lit by a chandelier from Thomas Edison's General Edison Electric Company (forerunner of GE). The great inventor worked out of laboratories in New Jersey.

RIGHT: The Senate Chamber. The Senate consists of one senator elected from each of the 40 districts.

Official Name:................... State of Georgia
Motto:.. Agriculture and Commerce, 1776; Wisdom,
Justice, Moderation
Citizen:............................... Georgian
Capital City:........................ Atlanta, GA
Established:............................... 1755
Joined Union: 1788
Left Union: 1861

Readmitted:................................ 1870
Anthem:.................. "Georgia On My Mind"
Name:... In fulfillment of charter obligations James
Oglethorpe named Georgia after King George II
Nickname:.. Empire State of the South; Peach State
License Plate Slogan:......... Georgia On My Mind
Total Area: .... 58,977 sq mi (24)

The State of
Georgia

Agriculture and Commerce, 1776 | Wisdom, Justice, Moderation

S ome American States were founded on the high principle of freedom of religion, but only Georgia was founded on a religious principle in action -- that of mercy. Mercy differs from charity in this: those who receive it actually deserve some punishment. Such was the case with debtors who languished in English jails in the 1700's. In 1729 a committee of Parliament investigated the poor conditions of debtor prisons. So troubled was the chairman of the committee by the conditions these debtors suffered under, he dedicated a good portion of his life to aiding these destitute people. His name was James Oglethorpe, the founder of Georgia.

GEORGIA

Along with twenty associates, Oglethorpe gained a charter from King George II in 1732 that vested a Board of Trustees with near-complete sovereignty.

The settlers, who numbered in the thousands and included members of persecuted Protestant sects, were forbidden from having slaves. Oglethorpe successfully defended his refuge for debtors against a Spanish attack in 1742 at Frederica, guaranteeing Georgia's survival. By then, ironically, Oglethorpe was heavily in debt for having made loans to so

PREVIOUS PAGES: Looking up into the Rotunda; *Right*, a perspective of the Capitol's front near the Richard Russell statue.

ABOVE: A portrait of James Oglethorpe, Georgia's founder, hangs in the Rotunda.

many colonists. Returning to England in 1743, he served as a Major General in a campaign against the Jacobites but was court-martialed for not pursuing and finishing off the retreating enemy. He showed mercy instead. The court acquitted him.

Much like William Penn in Pennsylvania and Roger Williams in Rhode Island, Oglethorpe treated the natives and immigrating population fairly and enjoyed relative peace during his administration. But there were stirrings against Oglethorpe and British rule. In fact, the publication of *A True and Historical Narrative of Georgia* in 1740 is the first printed protest against British policy.

By 1750, the winds of change were blowing. The first assembly of the Georgia Legislature was held January 15, 1751 in Savannah, but one year later, Oglethorpe resigned his charter and Georgia became a royal province. The first General Assembly sat in 1755 and continued to make laws up to 1775 when, with the outbreak of the Revolution, a Council of Safety was established and a Provincial Congress was called. In 1776 a provisional constitution was enacted and a year later the Constitution of 1777 became the fundamental law of Georgia.

The Constitution of 1777 established a government for the state that paralleled the colonial system. The colonial form of government included a Royal Governor, a King's Council (upper house) and a Commons House of Assembly. The new government established a House of Assembly which would pick a Governor and a 12-member Executive Council from its own ranks. The Constitution of 1789 established a General Assembly that was comprised of two houses. Thus the groundwork was laid for the modern legislative system.

Georgia has had ten constitutions since its founding: 1777, 1789, 1798, 1861, 1865, 1868, 1877, 1945, 1976, and 1982. Today, the General Assembly is divided into the Senate (56 members serving two-year terms) and the House of Representatives (180 members serving two-year terms.) The General Assembly convenes once a year for forty days.

Adapting to new circumstances is a way of life for Georgians. So too for its Capitol. The first Georgia

Capitol was in Milledgeville, a town carved out of land acquired from the native Creeks. It was completed in 1807. Twenty years later, the Capitol was transformed from columns and pediments into a Gothic castle -- the first use of Gothic architecture in Capitol construction. In 1832, at the height of the nullification controversy between South Carolina and President Andrew Jackson, Georgia offered her Gothic castle as a meeting place for southern states. Some thirty years later in this Capitol, Georgians voted to leave the United States.

PREVIOUS PAGE: *Miss Freedom* is the name of the statue that tops the Capitol. She raises her torch in memory of the state's war dead. The gold on Georgia's dome comes from its own mines. Eighty-five ounces of gold mined in Dahlonega, GA coat the dome. Gold was first applied in the late 1950's.

TOP: Georgia's leaders during the critical years of the War Between the States were Robert Toombs (left) and Alexander Hamilton Stephens. Both men fought against the secession of Georgia from the Union, but when their state voted to leave they went on to assume roles in the Confederate States' government: Toombs, formerly a U.S. Senator, would become Secretary of State; Stephens was Vice President.

During the War Between the States Atlanta emerged as a major financial center. At the end of the war, a movement was begun to move the capital city there. Ground was broken for the new Capitol in 1884 and the building was dedicated in 1889. Architects Willoughby J. Edbrooke and Franklin P. Burnham designed a classical structure with a rising dome, symbolizing the rebirth of the state. Inside, the duo provided for a cross-designed layout, but the chambers would be located in the front (House of Representatives) and back (Senate).

Throughout the Capitol, portraits and busts of famous Georgians and Americans abound. A bust of Margaret Mitchell, author of *Gone With The Wind*, is displayed.

James Oglethorpe is honored with both a bust and portrait. Towards the end of his career, Oglethorpe was offered command of the British forces in America in 1775 to put down the rebellion. He declined the appointment because the British government refused to give him powers of concession and conciliation. His compassionate nature by now, it seems, was legendary.

TOP: State seal sculpture on the tympanum (the triangular walled surface inside the pediment).

ABOVE: A perspective of the Capitol front from across the street.

RIGHT: *Miss Freedom*, which has topped the Capitol since its opening in 1889. Below her and inside is the Rotunda, which extends from the second floor through the upper stories to a height of 237 feet and 4 inches.

ABOVE: Georgia House of Representatives Chamber.

RIGHT: The Rostrum of the House of Representatives is where
the Speaker of the House presides.

ABOVE: Grand stairway leads to the second floor and the chambers of the House and Senate. A bust of James Oglethorpe sits on the landing.

RIGHT: A perspective of the Georgia Capitol. The statue of Joseph Emerson Brown and his wife, Elizabeth Grisham Brown, honors the former governor who served 1857-1865.

The "Georgia Hall of Fame" (not shown) is a collection of marble busts honoring famous Georgians, including the signers of the Declaration of Independence and U.S. Constitution, the early state governors, and others. Portraits of former governors are featured near the Lt. Governor's office. One man whose portrait is included was not a governor. He was the only Georgian to receive the Nobel Peace Prize. His name: Martin Luther King, Jr.

Official Name: . . . . State of Delaware

Motto: . . . . Liberty and Independence

Citizen: . . . . Delawarean

Capital City: . . . . Dover, DE

Established:. 1776

Joined Union: 1787

Anthem: . . . . "Our Delaware"

Name: . . Named after Sir Thomas West, Lord De La Warr -- the first colonial governor of Virginia

Nickname: . . . . The First State; The Peach State

License Plate Slogan:. . . . . The First State

Total Area: . . . . 2,396 sq mi (49)

The State of
Delaware

Liberty and Independence

Uniquely, Delaware gained its freedom from both Pennsylvania and Great Britain in 1776 when it formed its own state government. "The Three Lower Counties," as it was known, had an assembly but submitted to the Pennsylvania Governor since 1703. With the onset of the Revolution, Delawareans promptly formed a constitution that provided for their own governor. Now Delaware was an independent state. And its leaders moved quickly to insure that their newfound sovereignty was protected.

DELAWARE

In instructions to its delegates to the Continental Congress, the Assembly ordered: "First, that you concur with the other Delegates in Congress, in forming such farther compacts between the United Colonies, concluding such treaties with foreign Kingdoms and states, and in adopting such other measures as shall be judged necessary for promoting the liberty, safety, and interests of America, reserving to the people of this Colony, the sole and exclusive right of regulating the internal government and police of the same."

The Assembly also ordered its delegates "... on every necessary occasion, you are firmly to urge the right of this government to an equal voice in Congress with any other province or government on this Continent, as the inhabitants thereof have their ALL at stake as well as others."

Thomas West, Lord de la Warr, was the first governor of Virginia, arriving at Jamestown in 1610. His voyage into Delaware Bay a year later resulted in that bay, river and state assuming his name. Yet it was the Dutch, then the Swedes, who made the first settlements in Delaware. When England gained New Netherlands from the Dutch, Delaware passed to English control.

The Duke of York gave William Penn "New-Castle, Kent and Sussex, upon Delaware" in 1682. Penn simply referred to Delaware as "the Territories." He issued a Charter of Delaware in 1701 and two years later the people were permitted an assembly, but Delaware remained under Pennsylvania's control until 1776.

Considering its history, Delaware is not easily defined. It was a slave state that voluntarily remained in the Union. It supplied troops to both the northern and southern armies in the War Between the States. Though the second smallest of the United States, Delaware is first in chartering corporations. In fact, nearly 200,000 corporations are incorporated in Delaware, including half of the Fortune 500.

The reason: pro-business incorporation laws. As one of its reserved rights, each state separately

TOP: Delaware's Legislative Hall. *Left*, a Senator's chair.

PREVIOUS PAGES: A view from the second floor looking down to the foyer of Legislative Hall; a perspective of the State House.

regulates the chartering of corporations and business activities in its domain. Yet states are required by the U.S. Constitution to respect the corporations chartered in other states. Thus Delaware, with more lenient laws, has been able to attract companies into its jurisdiction and wield its influence nationally.

Those laws are made by a bicameral legislature: a House of Representatives and Senate, sixty-two members between them. This body sat for 141 years in Delaware's original State House, a small brick building on the east side of The Green, an expansive park surrounded by official government buildings from 1792 to 1933.

The new Legislative Hall on The Green is of the Georgian Revival style, a colonial structure made of handmade brick and 18th-century-style interiors. It is reminiscent of the old Pennsylvania State House (Independence Hall) in Philadelphia. Designed by architect E. William Martin of Wilmington, it was part of the Capitol Square Complex initiative that involved the acquisition of surrounding property. This initiative was made by the State Buildings and Grounds Commission, created by Governor C. Douglass Buck in 1931.

In 1965, the General Assembly authorized an effort to give each legislator an office in Legislative Hall. In 1970, north and south additions designed by George Fletcher Bennett of Dover were completed. In 1994, additional wings were added to provide hearing and caucus rooms under the direction of the Architects Studio, Inc. In 1997 interior renovations on the 1933 building and 1965 additions were completed.

TOP RIGHT: Legislative Hall's steeple and flag rise above the trees.

BOTTOM RIGHT: The central green buffers Legislative Hall from other governmental departments. Known as "The Green," this expansive park has lain at the center of state government since 1792.

TOP: Delaware House of Representatives Chamber.

OPPOSITE: Delaware Senate Chamber.

TOP LEFT: Main stairway to the second floor and the chamber galleries.

TOP RIGHT: House of Representatives Chamber.

BOTTOM LEFT: Pull-down stairs lead to attic.

BOTTOM RIGHT: The state seal appears in the foyer ceiling.

OPPOSITE: The very front of Legislative Hall features a Liberty Bell, a replica Delaware and her sister states received following World War II.

"The government of the counties of New Castle,
Kent, and Sussex, upon Delaware, shall hereafter
in all public and other writings be called
The Delaware State ... a free and independent State."

-- Delaware Constitution, 1776

TENNESSEE 1785

KENTUCKY 1792

OHIO 1799

MISSISSIPPI 1800

INDIANA 1805

ILLINOIS 1812

ALABAMA 1818

MAINE 1819

MICHIGAN 1824

WISCONSIN 1836

MINNESOTA 1849

Charter
States

"Be it enacted by the General Assembly, that it shall and may be lawful for the delegates of this State ... by proper deeds ... to convey ... over unto the United States in Congress assembled, for the benefit of the said states, all right, title and claim, as well of soil as jurisdiction, which this Commonwealth hath to the territory or tract of country within the limits of the Virginia charter ... upon condition that the territory so ceded, shall be laid out and formed into states ... and that the states so formed, shall be distinct republican states, and admitted members of the federal union; having the same rights of sovereignty, freedom and independence, as the other states."

-- From the deed issued by the Commonwealth of Virginia to the United States dated October 20, 1783. In accepting the deed March 1, 1784, Congress declared it "shall stand as fundamental constitutions between the thirteen original States ..."

1785

Official Name: . . . . State of Tennessee

Motto: . No official motto; state seal says "Agriculture and Commerce"

Citizen: . . . . Tennessean

Capital City: . . . . Nashville, TN

Established:. 1785

Joined Union: 1796

Left Union: 1861

Readmitted:. 1866

Anthem: "My Homeland, Tennessee"; "When It's Iris Time In Tennessee"; "My Tennessee"; "The Tennessee Waltz"; "Rocky Top"

Name: . . The Cherokee *tanasi*, given to villages on the Little Tennessee River, is where the name originates

Nickname: . . . . Volunteer State

License Plate Slogan:. . . . . Sounds Good To Me (top); Volunteer State (bottom)

Total Area: . . . . 42,146 sq mi (36)

The State of

Tennessee

Agriculture and Commerce

The first written constitution drawn up by men of American birth was the Watauga Association, made by settlers on the Watauga River in 1772. These people, hailing from Virginia, Pennsylvania, and North Carolina, established an executive council and legislature. Eventually it would become part of the State of Franklin, which in turn would become Tennessee. The story begins in 1768 with the opening of the lands west of the Cumberland Mountains following the Treaty of Fort Stanwix. Leaders of the Regulator Movement, a defeated band of North Carolina rebels who opposed royal authority, came to the banks of the Watauga River and, together with other settlers, established the Watauga Association. Led by James Robertson (founder of Nashville) and John Sevier, the people created an independent commonwealth.

TENNESSEE

Four years later, this independent territory was annexed by North Carolina and renamed Washington District.

Sevier represented the district in the North Carolina Legislature, taking time out to join local militias to beat the British at the Battle of Kings Mountain in 1780. That victory greatly aided American efforts in the south which had been hobbled by Continental Army defeats. At the end of the Revolutionary War, North Carolina ceded the Washington District to the United States. This caused an uproar, for the people there had not been consulted.

So they revolted and established the State of Franklin, proposing to "form themselves into a free, sovereign, and independent body politic or state by the name of the Commonwealth of Franklin." A constitution was drafted and the first legislature of the state met in 1785, though ultimately that constitution was rejected and North Carolina's adopted.

In the meantime, though, North Carolina repealed her cession of land to the United States and attempted to assert authority over Franklin. For a time, the inhabitants suffered under two competing governments, opting in many instances to ignore both, particularly when the matter involved taxes. John Sevier, now Franklin's Governor, was charged with treason against North Carolina and was arrested. He escaped and assumed the position of Brigadier General of the Militia.

Faced with these circumstances, North Carolina again ceded the territory to the United States on condition that slavery be permitted. The U.S. Congress agreed and in 1790 established the "Territory south of the River Ohio." Six years later, the State of Tennessee was admitted into the Union.

Now that they had secured their status as an independent state, Tennesseans set to work on a new government. A constitution was ratified in 1796

after attempts to outlaw slavery failed. Sevier became Governor and served from 1796 to 1809.

As for a Capitol, the state did without one for fifty years. The General Assembly met instead in the old Nashville Inn and other places both in and near Nashville. That changed in 1843 when Nashville was made the permanent capital city and plans were drawn up for a new Capitol. The cornerstone was laid July 4, 1845 and ten years later the final stone laid, yet the Tennessee Capitol was not completed until 1859. It was designed by William Strickland, a noted classic revivalist architect who also designed the Philadelphia Stock Exchange and restored the steeple on Independence Hall. Strickland died in 1854, but not before viewing the House Chamber near completion. He was buried in the building above the cornerstone in a tomb of his own design.

Tennessee's Capitol sits on visible bedrock; its exterior and interior are made of native stone. The exterior is made of Bigby limestone taken from a nearby quarry. Stone masons managed teams of slaves and prisoners who excavated and transported the blocks to the work site. The interior marble was taken from Rogersville and Knoxville. In 1953 renovations were made, including the use of Indiana limestone to repair the exterior.

ABOVE: A side perspective of the Capitol.

PREVIOUS PAGES: Pieces of the original 1850 columns, which were replaced for wear in 1955, are shown. *Right*, the Capitol looking up from the street.

TOP & BOTTOM LEFT: The Jackson Garden includes Polk's Tomb where President James K. Polk and wife Sarah are buried. Strickland designed the tomb and placed it at the Polks' residence. It was moved upon Sarah's death. Other famous Tennesseans in the Gardens are there in statue only: Sergeant York, the heavily decorated hero of World War I (at the top of the stairs) and Andrew Johnson, President Lincoln's successor (not shown).

BOTTOM RIGHT: A scene in the foyer depicts the competition between frontiersmen and natives over control of the land.

PREVIOUS PAGE: The great lantern mounted on the roof's ridge is modeled after the Choragic Monument of Lysicrates. Strickland's Philadelphia Stock Exchange has a similar lantern.

OPPOSITE: The Tennessee Capitol was the first to fall to the northern armies in the War Between the States. In 1862 U.S. Military Governor Andrew Johnson, who had been the state's senator to the U.S. Congress, used it as the seat of the occupation. Not until the 1870's was landscaping completed. Capping those efforts was Clark Mills' equestrian statue of Andrew Jackson, set into place and dedicated May 20, 1880.

TOP: Looking up into the Capitol's grand vault, made by the joining of four massive arches of native marble. The chandelier hangs in the center, a reproduction of the gas model installed in 1850.

OPPOSITE: The House Chamber is monumental in proportion and is the largest room in the building. Flanked by two galleries -- either of which seem as large as the Senate Chamber -- the House Chamber is finished in limestone.

FOLLOWING PAGES: The Senate Chamber (left) is not opposite the House as in other Capitols, but occupies a room to the side of the hallway (right) leading from the House.

TOP: The Capitol is built upon bedrock, as this view from the side shows. Inside, the lawmaking power is vested in a representative system in which Tennesseans are the bedrock. The General Assembly is made up of the Senate and House of Representatives. Members of either house must be a citizen of Tennessee for at least three years, as well as live in the county represented at least one year before election. The House is comprised of 99 members, elected to two-year terms, and representing about 50,000 citizens each. The Senate has 33 members elected to four-year terms, half of whom are elected in two-year intervals. They represent about 150,000 citizens each.

OPPOSITE TOP: The Capitol overlooks Bicentennial State Park, an extensive tribute to Tennessee's history. The park was dedicated on the state's 200th anniversary as one of the United States.

OPPOSITE BOTTOM: A view of the Capitol from the road below encircling its base (left) and from the roof of the Hermitage Hotel (right).

"Be it enacted by the general assembly of the State of North Carolina ... conveying to the United States of America all right, title, and claim which this State has to the sovereignty and territory of the lands situated within the chartered limits of this State west of a line beginning on the extreme height of the Stone Mountain ... that the territory so ceded shall be laid out and formed into a State or States ... the inhabitants of which shall enjoy all the privileges, benefits, and advantages set forth in the ordinance of the late Congress for the government of the western territory (Northwest Ordinance) ... Now therefore know ye that we convey, assign, transfer, and set over unto the United States of America, for the benefit of the said States ... all right title and claim ..."

-- From the North Carolina Deed of Cession of Tennessee, 1790

Official Name: . . . . Commonwealth of Kentucky
Motto: . . . . United We Stand, Divided We Fall
Citizen: . . . . Kentuckian
Capital City: . . . . Frankfort, KY
Established: 1792
Joined Union: 1792

Anthem: . . . . "My Old Kentucky Home"
Name: . . . Kentucky means "plain" and comes from the Wyandot people
Nickname: . . . . Blue Grass State; Tobacco State
License Plate Slogan: . . . . Blue Grass State
Total Area: . . . . 40,411 sq mi (37)

PRECEDING LEFT PAGE: Murals in the lunettes on either side of the nave were painted by Gilbert White. The mural over the east wing shows Daniel Boone's first gaze on the "beautiful level of Kentucke [*sic*]" in 1769. The mural to the west shows Boone and Transylvania Company promoter Richard Henderson signing the Treaty of Watauga in 1775. In the deal with the Cherokee, the company purchased much of present-day Kentucky.

PRECEDING RIGHT PAGE: Perspectives of the Capitol's front. The grounds burst with flowers: in the flowerbed nearest the Capitol are two time capsules. One commemorates the 200th anniversary of the Declaration of Independence and will be opened in 2076. The other commemorates the 75th anniversary of the Capitol in 1985, and it will be opened when the building turns 150.

ABOVE: Looking up towards the eye of the dome.

OPPOSITE: Statues of notable Kentuckians stand in the Rotunda. Both Abraham Lincoln (center) and Jefferson Davis (left) are natives, as well as Ephraim McDowell, a pioneering surgeon (right). The Rotunda floor is made of various marbles including Light Italio, blue and pink Tennessee, and Verde Antique. The walls are made of Georgia marble.

ABOVE: A perspective of the Capitol's front.

RIGHT: An exhibit of Kentucky's First Ladies in miniature was presented to the Commonwealth in 1971 and is just off the Rotunda. The collection is a project of the Kentucky Federation of Women's Clubs and is regularly updated.

OPPOSITE: The legislative chambers of the General Assembly with the Senate (above) and the House of Representatives (below).

OPPOSITE: The Capitol dome at night.

PREVIOUS PAGES: Originally called the Court of Appeals, the Kentucky Supreme Court sits in what could be considered one of the most dignified chambers of any court in any state or nation. Walled in Honduran mahogany paneling, the room's ceilings are finished with a Dutch metal leaf lacquered to resemble bronze. *Right*, looking at the Senate Chamber foyer from the Rotunda.

ABOVE: The main corridor of the Capitol is lined with thirty-six huge, one-piece columns made of Vermont granite and is 300 feet in length. The columns were lifted into place by human muscle; the only engine-powered machinery used in the Capitol's construction was a steam-driven concrete mixer.

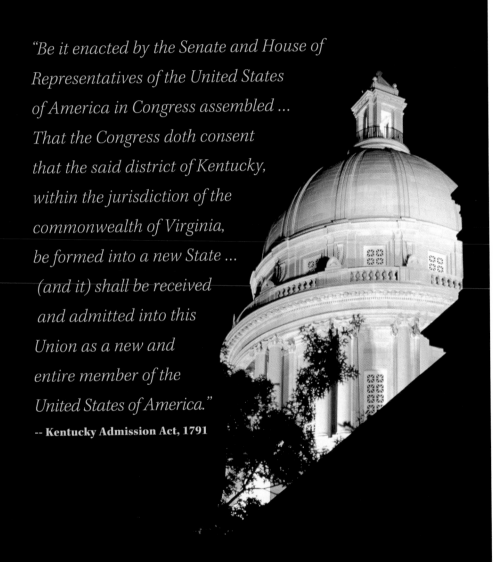

"Be it enacted by the Senate and House of Representatives of the United States of America in Congress assembled ... That the Congress doth consent that the said district of Kentucky, within the jurisdiction of the commonwealth of Virginia, be formed into a new State ... (and it) shall be received and admitted into this Union as a new and entire member of the United States of America."

-- Kentucky Admission Act, 1791

1799

Official Name:...................... State of Ohio
Motto:.......... With God, All Things Are Possible
Citizen: .... Ohioan
Capital City:...................... Columbus, OH
Established:............................... 1799
Joined Union: 1803

Anthem: .... "Beautiful, Ohio"
Name: ... Iroquois name for "beautiful river" is *ohio*
Nickname:...... Buckeye State; Mother of Modern Presidents
License Plate Slogan:........ Birthplace of Aviation
Total Area: .... 44,828 sq mi (34)

The State of
Ohio

With God, All Things Are Possible

America's first "wild west" was east of the Mississippi, in the territories which bordered the middle and lower Original States. The contest for these lands provoked an epic struggle among the natives, Americans, French, and English. Scenes of great courage, tragedy, disaster, and victory were played out on several stages, none more than Ohio. Its geographic position made this inevitable. Immigration from Pennsylvania and the states of the northeast and from Virginia and Kentucky swelled its population. The immigrants were of two kinds: natives who sold or were forced out of their lands in the Original States, and Americans looking to settle the newly opened region.

OHIO

The Virginia-based Ohio Company was established in 1750. On July 3, four years later, a Virginian Lt. Colonel was forced to surrender Fort Necessity to French forces, giving France control of the Ohio Valley. The Lt. Colonel's name: George Washington. Now the French and Indian Wars were underway. These ended in 1763 with the British winning all lands east of the Mississippi River.

The Delawares, one of the great native peoples of the east, would meet their end in Ohio. Also known as the Lenni-Lenape or Lenape people, they lived in the valley of the Delaware River. This area encompassed much of New Jersey and Delaware, eastern Pennsylvania, and southeastern New York. In 1682, the Delawares signed the famous peace treaty with William Penn which lasted for 50 years. Gradually they moved inland, sold their lands as they went

and eventually ended up in the Ohio Valley. Here the Delawares fragmented. Some took the side of the French and lost. Others fought in Pontiac's Rebellion. U.S. General "Mad Anthony" Wayne defeated the Delawares at Maumee Rapids in 1794.

Still others were Christianized and attempted to live a life of peace. One group of these Delawares, on

OPPOSITE: The Ohio Capitol.

PREVIOUS PAGES: Vestibule leading to the Rotunda. *Right*, the Atrium was completed in 1993. It is a self-supporting structure, connecting the State House and Senate Building.

BELOW: State flags line the Capitol's back entrance. Ohio's flag is the only one of the United States that is a pennant. The white and red circle represents the "O" in Ohio; the stars indicate Ohio was the 17th state to join the Union.

a mission to gather their harvest, was captured by a Pennsylvania force headed by Capt. David Williamson. The Pennsylvanians were searching for the natives responsible for recent attacks in the Pittsburgh area and charged these innocent Delawares with the crime. A quick trial sentenced 62 adults and 34 children to death, and they were slaughtered. Surviving elements of the Christianized Delawares fled to Canada and settled on the Thames River.

The remainder scattered across the Mississippi River and eventually were settled with the Cherokees in present-day Oklahoma by the U.S.

Government. Shawnee Chief Tecumseh's failure in 1811 to retake lands lost by treaty effectively ended native involvement in Ohio and neighboring regions. Over the next two decades, their remaining lands were either sold or ceded. Thus the native tribes were taken out of the equation.

New York and Massachusetts surrendered any claims to Ohio to the United States in the 1780's. Connecticut did the same, but retained the Connecticut Western Reserve (which encompasses the present-day cities of Akron, Cleveland, Sandusky, and Youngstown). Virginia, which had the strongest claim, deeded her lands to the United States,

reserving the Virginia Military District (located between the Scioto and Little Miami Rivers). In both instances these lands were in turn sold to the respective state's citizens and jurisdiction eventually passed to Ohio.

By 1799 Ohio established its territorial legislature and in 1803 became an American State. Almost immediately thereafter, a Capitol was contemplated. From 1803 to 1816 the state's capital city changed three times before settling in Columbus. The southwest corner of the current Capitol grounds was where a brick building was built to serve as Ohio's State House from 1812-1852. It was destroyed by fire.

Ohio's State House was designed in the early 1800's and built between 1839 and 1861. It was opened to legislators and the public in 1857, though not yet finished. It is considered a masterpiece of Greek Revival architecture. The building is not the work of a single architect, but of several during the nearly quarter century it took to build it.

The Rotunda features an interior dome, even though the outside is drum-shaped. In the dome is a 29-foot skylight where, in the very center, is a painted Seal of Ohio, a reproduction of the one that was in use in 1861. Ohio school children funded the installation of a skylight around the seal in a penny-collection campaign run by Bob Evans Farms. The Rotunda's floor is made of 5,000 pieces of hand-cut marble from around the world, arranged to tell the story of the United States up to 1860, when it was laid.

The lawmaking authority of the state is lodged in a General Assembly made up of a Senate and a House of Representatives. The Senate's 33 members represent an average 330,000 people.

Its chamber is wired so Senators can plug in laptops and work online. The columns are of Pennsylvania marble, topped with Corinthian capitals. Originally the home of the Ohio Supreme Court that opened in 1901, the Senate Chamber underwent a major restoration that was completed in 1993.

According to state authorities, the House Chamber was designed by architect Nathan B. Kelly. So remarkable were his side galleries in appearance that the building commissioners demanded evidence that the balconies would support large

crowds. Kelly hung 4,000 pounds of iron from the balcony brackets to satisfy the commissioners.

One of the best known people to speak in the House Chamber was Abraham Lincoln, who addressed a Joint Session of the Ohio Legislature. Little did he know at the time that Ohio technically was not part of the American Union of States. Why? Because in 1803 the U.S. Congress failed to vote on the legislation formally admitting the Buckeyes into the United States for reasons unknown. Not until 1953 was such an act passed by Congress.

OPPOSITE: The state seal and motto lie in stone at the entrance to the Ohio State House.

ABOVE: The House of Representatives Chamber as seen from the gallery.

ABOVE: The Senate Chamber.

OPPOSITE: The House of Representatives rostrum and podium. *Below*, at the entrance to the House.

FOLLOWING PAGES: The Senate Chamber framed by pillars; *Right*, looking down into the Rotunda from the Senate's side of the building.

Ohioans met in convention in 1803 in Chillicothe to draft and ratify their constitution. It was not submitted to the vote of the people. "We, the people of the eastern division of the territory of (the) United States northwest of the river Ohio," the preamble begins, "having the right of admission into the General Government as a member of the Union, consistent with the Constitution of the United States, the ordinance of Congress of one thousand seven hundred and eighty-seven, and the law of Congress ... do mutually agree with each other to form ourselves into a free and independent State by the name of the State of Ohio."

OPPOSITE BOTTOM: Inside the Senate Building, which is connected to the State House.

ABOVE: The Peace Statue was erected by the Women's Relief Corps in 1923 to honor Ohioans who served in the American Civil War and the women of the state during this period.

OPPOSITE TOP: *Perry's Victory* by William Powell of Commodore Perry's victory on Lake Erie in 1813. "We have met the enemy and they are ours," he wrote after the surrender of the British. Perry's success secured United States control of Lake Erie in the War of 1812. Perry's ship *Lawrence* was destroyed during the engagement. This scene depicts his transfer to the *Niagara*.

Official Name:................State of Mississippi
Motto:..........................Virtute et Armis
Citizen: ....Mississippian
Capital City: ....Jackson, MS
Established:................................1800
Joined Union: 1817
Left Union: 1861

Readmitted: 1870
Anthem: ...."Go, Mississippi"
Name:.....The Chippewa term for the Mississippi
River, meaning "very large river"
Nickname:............Magnolia State; Eagle State
License Plate Slogan:........................N/A
Total Area: ....48,286 sq mi (32)

The State of
Mississippi

Virtute et Armis | By Valor and Arms

S o obliterated was Mississippi's capital city that Union soldiers called it "Chimneyville" for the smouldering remains it had become. Jackson, Mississippi suffered at the end of the War Between the States like other southern capitals would -- at the hands of victorious army men, some bent on spoils (the ancient custom of stripping a conquered city of its movable property). It would be forty years before the city and state had reason to celebrate.

MISSISSIPPI

The occasion which brought the citizens together in a spirit of hope and a display of Mississippi pride was the dedication of their new Capitol and the setting of the cornerstone. Thousands of state citizens poured into Jackson to witness the event and festivities which surrounded it.

The ceremonies began after an official parade that featured contingents of the United Daughters of the Confederacy, Masons from various southern states, and every sort of politician and dignitary including the Governor and members of the legislature.

The excitement was justified. Though still suffering from the effects of the great war, Mississippi came into some money in the form of back taxes paid by the Illinois Central Railroad -- enough to pay the $1,093,641 it would cost to build a new Capitol.

Even so, economies were built into the structure, though not readily apparent to the eye. Columns and walls that could be touched by visitors were made of real marble; those that were inaccessible, like the columns high up in the Rotunda, were made of scagliola (plaster with marble dust).

Built from 1901 to 1903, the Capitol sits on the site of the old state penitentiary. The architect,

Theodore Link of St. Louis, MO, patterned the structure in the Beaux Arts style. The German-born Link was required by the building commission to change one feature of his Capitol. Instead of a 300-foot bell tower he had envisioned on one end of the structure, the commission demanded a dome like the one submitted by George Mann (who designed the Arkansas Capitol).

Link obliged, topping the Mann-designed dome with a gold eagle made of solid copper. It measures 8 feet high by 15 feet wide and is coated with gold leaf. Inside, the Rotunda walls are made of Italian white marble; the base consists of New York jet-black marble. The eight large scagliola columns rise to support four scenes in the dome: two showing encounters with the natives, one portraying Spanish exploration, and one showing a Confederate General.

Both the Senate Chamber and House of Representatives Chamber are made of art marble with a base of Belgium black marble. A dome in the center of each adds to the grandeur of the chambers. The Senate dome is Bohemian stained glass.

Members of both legislative bodies serve four-year terms. The Senate has 52 members, the House 122. Mississippi's legislative history began in 1798 when the Mississippi Territory was established.

Following the cession of key western lands by Georgia, the present-sized state was admitted into the United States in 1817.

PREVIOUS PAGES & ABOVE: The Mississippi Capitol. According to the state's tour brochure, the tympanum features an all-powerful Mississippi in the center, attended by the elements of her domain. Above her head and atop the dome is an eight-foot-tall gold eagle. *Right*, the Capitol is shown from the lower bank and at the base of the steps.

ABOVE: Looking up towards the eye of the Rotunda.

OPPOSITE: A perspective of the Capitol from the street.

PREVIOUS PAGE: Monument to *The Women of the Confederacy*, erected by the United Daughters of the Confederacy.

TOP LEFT: The House of Representatives.

TOP RIGHT: Grand stairway in the center of the building.

MIDDLE LEFT: State seal in the House of Representatives.

LOWER LEFT: A floral display in the Rotunda.

ABOVE & OPPOSITE: Perspectives of the House of Representatives dome.

FOLLOWING PAGES: Mississippi Senate Chamber; looking up at the Capitol's pediment.

"That the general, great, and essential principles of liberty and free government may be recognized and established, we declare ... That all freemen, when they form a social compact, are equal in rights; and that no man or set of men are entitled to exclusive, separate public emoluments or privileges, from the community, but in consideration of public services."

-- Constitution of Mississippi, 1817

1805

Official Name: . . . . State of Indiana
Motto: . . . . The Crossroads of America
Citizen: . . . . Hoosier
Capital City: . . . . Indianapolis, IN
Established: 1805
Joined Union: 1816
Anthem: . . "On the Banks of the Wabash, Far Away"

Name: . . . . The U.S. Congress created the name,
meaning "Land of the Indians," when it established
the Indiana Territory in 1800
Nickname: . . . . The Hoosier State
License Plate Slogan: . . . . Crossroads of America
Total Area: . . . . 36,420 sq mi (38)

The State of
Indiana

The Crossroads of America

INDIANA

The "Land of Indians" did not have many when the first Europeans visited what is now Indiana. But by the time the French secured control of the region and fortified Vincennes in 1732, the Miami, Wabash, Ottawa, and Delaware native populations were growing. When the British assumed sovereignty over the region in 1763 after defeating the French, the tribes were still able to mount a challenge. What became known as "Pontiac's Conspiracy," named for the Ottawa chief, resulted in native uprisings in the region and along the western borders of Pennsylvania, Maryland, and Virginia.

Pontiac's Rebellion ended in 1765 when he signed a treaty with the British, and nine years later the English united the lands of Indiana with Quebec.

Indiana was liberated from British control in 1779 when Virginia Militia General George Rogers Clark seized Vincennes in a daring mid-winter attack.

ABOVE: The House Chamber as seen from the gallery.

OPPOSITE: The Indiana Capitol.

PREVIOUS PAGES: The Rotunda. Eight Carrara marble statues stand in the Rotunda, declaring the hallmarks of civilization. They represent Law, Oratory, Agriculture, Commerce, Justice, Liberty, History, and Art. *Right*, the Capitol amidst urban environs.

Braving exposure and fatigue, Clark and his men won Indiana for Virginia, and in this way title passed to the Old Dominion.

In 1784 Virginia deeded over the territory to the United States. But the native tribes were not interested in such legal formalities. Shawnee Chief Tecumseh argued that as the region's lands were the common property of all natives, no one group could cede or sell any particular piece. From 1788 to 1795 war raged, settled by a treaty signed in Greenville, Ohio, after U.S. General "Mad Anthony" Wayne's victory in the Battle of Fallen Timbers. In this treaty the tribes were forced to surrender fifty million acres. In turn, the U.S. Congress established the Indiana Territory in 1800.

It comprised present-day Indiana, Illinois, Wisconsin and parts of Michigan and Minnesota.

Chief Tecumseh made one last attempt to control the surrounding territories as well as lands stretching down to Georgia. His plan was to confederate all native tribes in these areas and retake the lands lost in the 1795 treaty. While in the south organizing the league, his brother Prophet attempted to test the Greenville treaty by establishing a settlement on Tippecanoe Creek. Forces led by Virginia-born William Henry Harrison, then Governor of Indiana, attacked the settlement in what is today Battle Ground, IN. Though the fighting ended in a draw, the spirit of Tecumseh's movement was broken and many of the natives migrated to Canada.

In 1872 the last Miami people in Indiana dissolved their tribal bonds, ending Native American involvement as organized bodies in the "Land of Indians."

Vincennes was the capital of the Indiana Territory until 1813 when it was moved to Corydon. In 1825 Indianapolis became the permanent capital. Indianapolis (meaning, "center of the land of Indians") is appropriately in the geographic center of the state. Designed by Alexander Ralston, an assistant to Pierre L'Enfant who laid out Washington, DC, the city's layout is similar to the nation's capital.

An enlarged legislature forced the state to construct a new Capitol to replace the one built in 1832, and the cornerstone was laid September 12, 1880. Architect Edwin May submitted a plan and called it Lucidus Ordo (Latin for "a clear arrangement"). Designed in the classic Corinthian style, the interior was in the modern Renaissance style.

May died in 1880 and Adolph Scherrer, his assistant and draftsman, replaced him. The original contractors, Kanmacher and Denig of Chicago, were replaced by another Chicago firm, Gobel and

Cummings, which finished the work. The exterior was finished July 3, 1886 and the General Assembly held its first session January 6, 1887. The total cost was $1,980,969.18.

The building is made of limestone, marble, brick, and mortar. Indiana materials include blue limestone used for the footings and oolitic limestone for the outer walls. The interior is finished in oak, walnut, white oak, and maple from Indiana's forests.

Inside the building the people's representatives make the laws and regulations of the state. "The Indiana Constitution vests the legislative power in the Senate and House of Representatives and grants each house 'all powers necessary for a branch of the legislative department of a free and independent state,'" states the government's publication *Your Indiana General Assembly*. "Unlike the Congress which has only those powers granted it by the United States Constitution, the General Assembly possesses all legislative powers not denied it or granted to other agencies by the Constitutions of the United States and of Indiana."

The Senate has 50 members who serve four-year terms; the House has 100 members who serve two-year terms. In even-numbered years, the Indiana General Assembly meets for thirty session days; in odd-numbered years, it meets for sixty-one session days.

PREVIOUS PAGE: A gold eagle tops a side of the Capitol. The figures represent early Hoosiers.

ABOVE: A grand colonnade connects legislative chambers and meeting rooms.

ABOVE: Looking into the eye of the Rotunda. Alcoves in the Rotunda (not shown) hold busts of famous Hoosiers and Americans, including George Washington and Abraham Lincoln; Henry F. Schricker (1883-1966), beloved Indiana Governor and the first elected to two terms, 1941-1953; Richard Owen (1810-1890), who helped survey the Northwest Territory and served as Commandant of Camp Morton, a northern prison camp during the Civil War. He had his bust paid for by Confederate prisoners grateful for his kindness; Sherman A. Minton (1890-1965), the only Hoosier to serve on the U.S. Supreme Court, 1949-1956; and others.

"That the general, great, and essential principles of liberty and free government may be recognized and unalterably established, we declare: that all men are born equally free and independent, and have certain natural, inherent, and unalienable rights; among which are, the enjoying and defending life and liberty, and of acquiring, possessing, and protecting property, and pursuing and obtaining happiness and safety ...That the people have a right to bear arms for the defence of themselves and the State ..." -- *Indiana Constitution, 1816*

ABOVE: The Senate Chamber. The most significant change in the original building came with the redesign of the legislative chambers. Offices for House and Senate members were built within the original chambers, shrinking them dramatically in size. This work was completed in the 1950's.

TOP: Indiana Supreme Court Chamber.

RIGHT: A view of the colonnade from the ground floor.

OPPOSITE: The front of the Capitol has a statue of Oliver P. Morton (1823-1877), Indiana's Governor during the Civil War. Initially popular when war broke out, Morton was able to raise 200,000 troops for the northern effort. Yet, as the war dragged on, Morton and Lincoln increasingly faced opposition. Anti-draft riots were frequent in the southern portions of the state. By 1863 the Governor and Legislature were unable to work together, and constitutional government ceased to exist in the State of Indiana as funds went unappropriated. Drawing on his own personal credit, Governor Morton financed state and military operations from 1863-1864 and saw the war through.

OPPOSITE: The Soldiers & Sailors Monument is located in the center of the city, two blocks from the Capitol. It is made of Indiana limestone.

ABOVE: The House Chamber's chandelier contains 100 lights, one for each delegate of the House. According to state tour information, it illuminates a mural entitled *The Spirit of Indiana* by Eugene Savage. The woman in the center represents Indiana statehood, wearing an empire gown. Virginia-native William

Henry Harrison is with her, and behind them is a sycamore tree, the Wabash and Erie Canal, and the Wabash River Valley. Ceres, the Goddess of Agriculture, is to the right and surrounded by industrialization and ships carrying Indiana's products to the rest of the world. The figure Education is throwing valuable possessions into a fire, from which the rising fumes form Pegasus and Apollo. This history of Indiana is shown in cloud formations of pioneers, settlers, soldiers, and development.

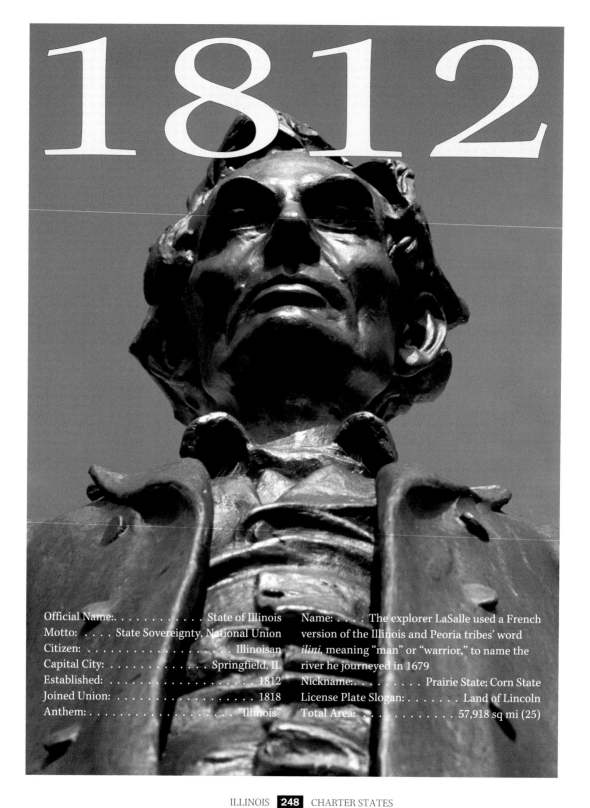

1812

Official Name:. . . . . State of Illinois
Motto: . . . . State Sovereignty, National Union
Citizen: . . . . Illinoisan
Capital City: . . . . Springfield, IL
Established: 1812
Joined Union: 1818
Anthem:. . . . . "Illinois"

Name: . . . The explorer LaSalle used a French
version of the Illinois and Peoria tribes' word
ilini, meaning "man" or "warrior," to name the
river he journeyed in 1679
Nickname:. . . . . Prairie State; Corn State
License Plate Slogan: . . . . Land of Lincoln
Total Area: . . . . 57,918 sq mi (25)

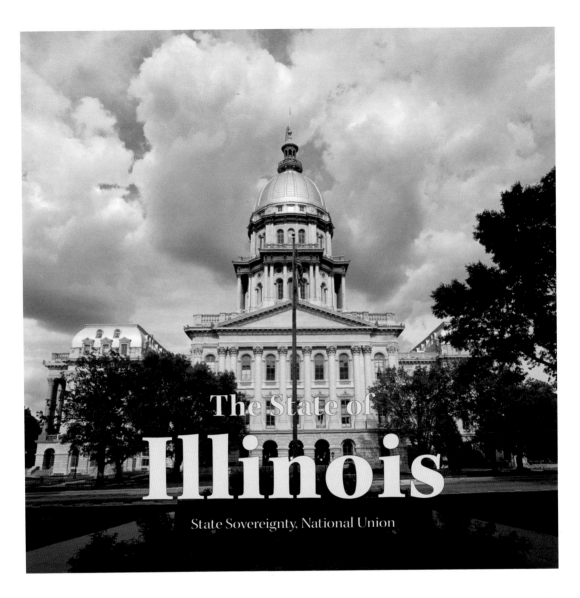

The State of Illinois

State Sovereignty, National Union

G reat men and great ideas cut across the State of Illinois like its three main rivers -- the Rock, Illinois, and Kaskaskia. And like those rivers, they become part of something larger than themselves -- the water into the Mississippi, the state into the union. Father Marquette, a Jesuit missionary, was planning a mission with the Illinois natives when they spoke of a great southern-flowing river. Intrigued, he accepted an appointment from the governor of New France (Quebec) to find it and, with French explorer Louis Jolliet, began an incredible adventure. They set off across Lake Michigan to Green Bay, followed the Fox and portaged across to the Wisconsin, traveled down the Mississippi to the Arkansas River and back home via the Illinois. Thus the Frenchmen proved what heretofore had only been rumored:

ILLINOIS

the Atlantic Ocean and Gulf of Mexico were connected by a tremendous American river highway!

While working on plans for his Illinois mission, Marquette became ill and died. His Jesuit brothers, though, did succeed in establishing one at Kaskaskia in 1700, and there the history of the state begins. Under British control in 1778, the area by now had become a thriving agricultural and trading center. But the American Revolution was underway and change was coming.

A Virginia military detachment under the command of General George Rogers Clark seized Kaskaskia and the neighboring settlements. Clark demanded -- and was given -- pledges of allegiance to the Commonwealth of Virginia by the Catholic inhabitants. Because of his acceptance of their religion and property, the Frenchmen accepted the change. It didn't hurt that France was now an important American ally in the struggle for independence.

TOP & PREVIOUS PAGE LEFT: Bronze statue of Abraham Lincoln graces the front of the Illinois Capitol.

PREVIOUS PAGE RIGHT: A rear perspective of the Capitol.

OPPOSITE: The Capitol viewed from Capitol Avenue.

The Virginia General Assembly then erected the county of Illinois within its borders. It encompassed a district that includes much of the present-day state. Illinois would be part of Virginia through the 1780's, when that commonwealth ceded it to the United States. The Northwest Ordinance of 1787, passed by the Congress of the Articles of Confederation, placed Illinois in the Northwest Territory and governed its creation as a state. By 1812, four years after being split off from the Indiana Territory, Illinois seated the state's first House of Representatives.

As the U.S. Congress prepared the enabling act for Illinois statehood, the matter of its northern border became a major issue. If the Northwest Ordinance were followed, Illinois's boundary would not include direct access to Lake Michigan. Without such access, it was feared, the state would rely on economic development with her southern sisters and not the northern states. So to afford "additional security for the perpetuity of the Union," Congress declared in the enabling act, Illinois would include the lands that today encompass the greater part of its northern frontier, including Chicago, and critical access to Lake Michigan.

State Sovereignty, National Union. With those words as its official motto, the state's constitutional convention, meeting in Kaskaskia in 1818, accepted the congressional terms and established its constitution. Illinois, a product of the Northwest Ordinance which termed the new states "republics," was now in the American Union of States.

State Sovereignty, National Union. From Illinois would come the man who would define the limits of the former, and the authority of the latter.

His name was Abraham Lincoln. Born in the same year the Illinois Territory was established, Lincoln was a Kentuckian who ended up in Illinois at the age of 21. There he held a number of jobs, from postmaster to surveyor. He began his political career in the state legislature, where he served from 1834-1841. His career ended as President of the United States in 1865 with an assassin's bullet.

In his first inaugural address, with the country on the verge of armed conflict, Lincoln quoted the platform of his party, which he termed a law: "Resolved, That the maintenance inviolate of the rights of the States, and especially the right of each State to order and control its domestic institutions according to its own judgement exclusively, is essential to that balance of power on which the perfection and endurance of our political fabric depend ..."

Lincoln went on, noting that the President "derives all his authority from the people, and they have conferred none upon him to fix terms for the separation of the States ... his duty is to administer the present Government as it came to his hands and to transmit it unimpaired by him to his successor."

"I hold that in contemplation of universal law and of the Constitution, the Union of these States is perpetual," said Lincoln, the first President born from outside the Original States. For the next four years he conducted a war to defend that principle.

This idea -- that national union takes precedence over state sovereignty -- led the Illinois Secretary of State to push for a law after the Civil War that would reverse the wording of the motto to "National Union, State Sovereignty." But the State Senate would have nothing of it, passing a bill in 1867 that restored the motto to the original.

It remains to this day on the state's flag and seal, but the place where it was created has since been destroyed. Much of Kaskaskia, the first capital, was destroyed by the shifting course of the Mississippi.

Shortly after forming their state, Illinois legislators selected Vandalia as the new capital city and state business was conducted there when, in 1837, "the Long Nine" -- the name given to nine key legislators because their combined height was fifty-four feet -- successfully moved the capital to Springfield. One of the taller members of the "Long Nine" was a fellow named Abe Lincoln.

It was in the original Springfield State Capitol that Lincoln first enunciated his views. "A house divided against itself cannot stand," he thundered in a speech set in the Hall of Representatives. The year was 1858 and he was debating Stephen Douglas in the electoral contest for federal senator. (At the time the state legislature appointed senators.) Lincoln lost to Douglas, but made such an impression that he was catapulted into the presidential race two years later.

The present Capitol is Illinois' sixth, and the second to be located in Springfield. Ground was broken in 1868 and completed in 1888 at a total cost of $4,315,591. The Illinois Legislature first met in the Capitol in 1877. The original Capitol in Springfield was completed in 1839 and only used for 36 years.

Chicago nearly became the fourth capital city of Illinois, had not the Great Chicago Fire occurred. The General Assembly had authorized the convening of its Fall 1871 session in the Windy City, but tragedy struck October 8 and cancelled the plans. Springfield remained the capital city thereafter.

The Illinois Capitol was designed by John C. Cochrane, a Chicago architect, who formed a partnership with Alfred H. Piquenard for the Capitol's construction. To expedite the movement of building materials, a railroad line from the Toledo, Wabash and Western was constructed around the Capitol.

When Piquenard died in 1876, the project was delayed and then halted for a lack of funds. Seven years later a new architect and funding were secured. W.W. Boylington (designer of Chicago's Water Tower building) was hired to complete the Capitol and, in 1888, he did so. The original cornerstone had been lost for seventy years, buried in the final constructions. It was discovered in 1944.

Designed in the shape of a Latin Cross, the dome rises 361 feet from the ground. The outer walls are limestone from Joliet and Lemont. Pillars on the north and east porticos are granite. The grand staircase, second floor columns, and floors are made of domestic and imported marbles.

Not far away from the dome's soaring heights is Springfield's Oak Ridge Cemetery, final resting place of Illinois' favorite son. Mary Todd Lincoln insisted her husband be buried there, and not Washington, DC. She said Springfield, Illinois was his home. Though forever more, because of him, that home and state would be an inseparable part of a larger community.

TOP AND OPPOSITE: The Capitol Rotunda features the bronze statue *Illinois Welcoming The World* in the center with the history of the state told in an encircling bronze relief above.

OPPOSITE: Stephen Douglas, who defeated Lincoln in the Illinois Senate race in 1858, advocated "popular sovereignty" -- the idea that new territories should decide for themselves whether to allow slavery, and not Congress. In 1860 he ran on the Democratic ticket for President, but the southern politicians refused to support him. When South Carolina fired upon Fort Sumter a year later, Douglas gave Lincoln his full support. In an eloquent address defending the Union in 1861, not far from where his statue stands today, Douglas contracted typhoid fever and later died. The Douglas statue stands directly in front of the Capitol but behind the monument to Lincoln.

TOP LEFT: The old Capitol in Springfield served the people for just 36 years. It was completed in 1839 and is the site of the famous Lincoln-Douglas debates. Lincoln served as a state legislator in this building.

TOP RIGHT: The Illinois Governor's office in the Capitol.

BOTTOM LEFT: Looking up into the eye of the Rotunda.

BOTTOM RIGHT: A ceiling motif.

NOT PICTURED: The Illinois General Assembly chambers were under major reconstruction during the creation of this book and could not be photographed. The General Assembly has two bodies, the Senate and the House of Representatives. Senators serve either four- or two-year terms under a staggered electoral system; the Senate has 59 members. The House has 118 members, each serving two-year terms.

OPPOSITE: Virginia General George Rogers Clark meets with Illinois natives in 1778 to sign a treaty in this famous *Treaty with the Indians* painting by Gustave A. Fuchs. The Virginian was given a pledge of allegiance and support to his commonwealth in the American Revolution; Illinois was later made a county of Virginia. Fuchs was commissioned to do the work in 1886 specifically for the Illinois Capitol for $2,000.

"I consider your further success as depending upon the goodwill and friendship of the Frenchmen and Indians who inhabit your part of the Commonwealth," Virginia Governor Patrick Henry wrote to Clark in 1778 with the establishment of the new county. "Let them see and feel the advantages of being fellow citizens and freemen."

Years later the State of Illinois was born. "The people of the Illinois Territory, having the right of admission into the General Government as a member of the Union," the preamble to the Illinois Constitution of 1818 begins, "... in order to establish justice, promote the welfare, and secure the blessings of liberty to themselves and their posterity ... do mutually agree with each other to form themselves into a free and independent State, by the name of the State of Illinois."

ABOVE: A portrait of George Washington by the Finnish artist George Sigurd Wettenhovi-Aspa was donated in 1973 by the Meyer family of Champaign, IL. It was executed in the 1890's.

Official Name: .... State of Alabama
Motto: .... Audemus Jura Nostra Defendere
Citizen: .... Alabamian
Capital City: .... Montgomery, AL
Established: 1818
Joined Union: 1819
Left Union: 1861

Readmitted: 1868
Anthem: .... "Alabama"
Name: ... Alabama comes from the Choctaw words
Alba and *Amo* meaning "plant gatherer"
Nickname: .... Heart of Dixie
License Plate Slogan: .... Heart of Dixie
Total Area: .... 52, 237 sq mi (30)

The State of
Alabama

Audemus Jura Nostra Defendere | We Dare Defend Our Rights

ALABAMA

S ome of the most dramatic events in American history have occurred in and around Alabama and its Capitol. The first battle between Native Americans and invading Europeans also happened to be the bloodiest such contest waged on the continent. It happened in the Battle of Mauvilla (1540) in which Chief Tuscaloosa, the Alibamu Chief, was defeated by Hernando de Soto's Spanish forces. The Spaniards slaughtered thousands of Tuscaloosa's warriors and people and began the European takeover of the Americas. The historic battle happened in Alabama.

After each of the southern states met in convention and voted to leave the United States, they bonded together to form the Confederate States of America. On February 4, 1861, delegations from the first six states to join met in convention to draft a new constitution and establish a government. Jefferson Davis was sworn in as President and the meeting place was named the Provisional Capitol of the Confederacy.

It all happened in the Alabama Capitol.

In 1965, a century after the rise and fall of the Confederacy, a civil rights leader organized a protest march from Selma, Alabama to Montgomery. The issue: denying people their right to vote because of the color of their skin. He was already successful in having federal authorities end segregation in the city's bus system and pass the Civil Rights Act of 1964.

OPPOSITE: Nations of which Alabama has been a part, represented by their great seals and displayed in the Rotunda (clockwise from top left): Spain, 1540-1560 and 1780-1813; France, 1699-1762; England, 1762-1769; and the Confederate States of America, 1861-1865.

ABOVE: A setting sun's rays drape the Alabama Capitol.

PREVIOUS PAGES: Perspectives of the Capitol; *Left*, Alabama War Memorial at night.

HOSTILE MEETING OF DE SOTO, SPANISH EXPLORER
AND TUSCALOOSA, INDIAN CHIEFTAIN - 1540.

earlier having met in Huntsville under the leadership of Governor William Wyatt Bibb.

The first state capital was Cahaba, some ten miles from Selma, selected when Alabama achieved statehood. State authorities later moved the capital to Tuscaloosa in 1826 before settling in Montgomery, which became Alabama's capital city in 1846.

The first Capitol building there was designed by Stephen Button, a Philadelphia architect. Completed in 1847 in the Greek Revival style, it caught fire in 1849 and was destroyed. On the old foundation a new Capitol was completed in 1851 in a similar revival style. It is essentially the same building that stands today.

Like the State of Alabama itself, the Capitol has undergone numerous changes. A rear wing was completed in 1885 and the two side wings between 1906 and 1912. The neoclassical rear extension was finished in the early 1990's.

Upon entering, the visitor is taken with the pair of three-story spiral stairways in the foyer. Horace King, a noted engineer and bridge builder who was a freed slave, built the staircases and did other work in the Capitol. After the Civil War he was one of the first African-Americans to serve in the Alabama Legislature.

The Rotunda features eight large murals under the dome. Created by Mobile designer Roderick MacKenzie and completed in 1930, the murals depict key moments in Alabama history. To the Rotunda's right is the old House Chamber, to the left the old Senate Chamber. These chambers, along with the old Supreme Court Chamber, Library, and Governor's Suite are faithfully restored.

The real business of the state occurs on Union Street, across from the Capitol. Since the mid-1980's the Alabama Legislature and other state authorities have worked in the modern statehouse. Members of the Senate and House of Representatives both serve four-year terms. The Senate has 35 members, the House 105.

The peaceful protestors were attacked by police on their march. But Martin Luther King finally did reach his goal: the Alabama Capitol steps.

Alabama was claimed and desired by many. The French established the first permanent settlement in Alabama called Fort Conde, the forerunner of Mobile. The English included portions of it in the Carolina charter (1663) and the Oglethorpe Grant (1732). The Spanish retained control of that portion of Alabama in what was then West Florida until 1812.

By 1817 Alabama, which had been a part of Mississippi Territory, was ready to assert control over its present domain. Alabama Territory was created with the admission of Mississippi into the Union, and the first legislature met at the Douglass Hotel in Saint Stephens, the territorial capital.

In 1819 the State of Alabama became one of the United States, the state's constitutional convention

ABOVE: *Hostile Meeting of DeSoto, Spanish Explorer, And Tuscaloosa, Indian Chieftain - 1540,* one of the eight murals in the Rotunda that detail the history of Alabama.

OPPOSITE: Looking into the eye of the Rotunda.

ROTUNDA MURALS: The eight large murals under the dome were created by Roderick MacKenzie and completed in 1930.

TOP LEFT: *Surrender of William Weatherford, Hostile Creek Leader, To General Andrew Jackson, 1814.*

TOP RIGHT: *Governor William Wyatt Bibb And Committee Drafting The First State Constitution At Huntsville, 1819.*

BOTTOM LEFT: *Secession And The Confederacy, Inauguration Of President Jefferson Davis, 1861.*

BOTTOM RIGHT: *Prosperity Follows Development Of Resources, Agriculture, Commerce, And Industry, 1874-1930.*

MURALS NOT SHOWN: *French Establishing First White Colony In Alabama Under Iberville And Bienville, Mobile, 1702-1711; Pioneer Home-Seekers Led Into Alabama Wilderness By Sam Dale, 1772-1841; Wealth And Leisure Produce The Golden Period Of Antebellum Life In Alabama, 1840-1860.*

OPPOSITE TOP: Looking up into one of the twin staircases in the foyer.

OPPOSITE BOTTOM: The old House chamber was vacated for modern chambers in the Alabama Statehouse. The plaque in the center reads: "In this Hall the ordinance of Secession which withdrew Alabama from the Union of Sovereign States was passed Jan. 11, 1861."

ABOVE: A pair of three-story spiral stairways built in 1851 by Horace King, a freed slave, is the focus of the foyer. King later became one of the first African-Americans to walk through the entrance doors as a legislator.

OPPOSITE: The modern Alabama Statehouse was completed in the mid-1980's and includes the Senate Chamber (top) and the House of Representatives (bottom).

Official Name: . . . . State of Maine

Motto: . . . . Dirigo

Citizen: . . . . Mainer

Capital City: . . . . Augusta, ME

Established: 1819

Joined Union: 1820

Anthem: . . . . "State of Maine Song"

Name: . . . . . Named after Maine, France, or possibly named after the explorers' term for the mainland

Nickname: . . . . Pine Tree State; Old Dirigo State

License Plate Slogan: . . . . Vacationland

Total Area: . . . . 33,741 sq mi (39)

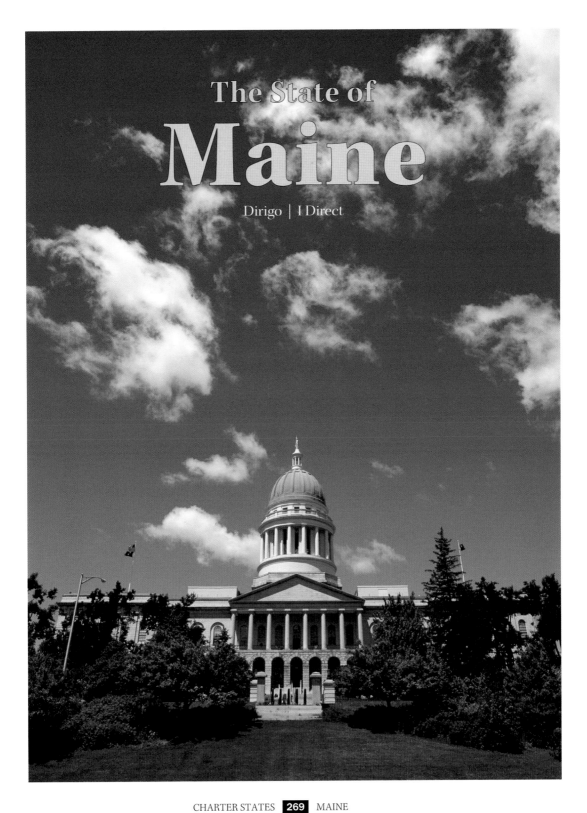

The State of
Maine

Dirigo | I Direct

MAINE

When one thinks of the first settlements in America, immediately Jamestown, Virginia and Plymouth, Massachusetts come to mind. But before colonists even left England for these locations, Europeans were living in Maine.

The first white settlers to the area are believed to have been Norsemen under Thorwald in the 11th century, though not until 1524 was the land's discovery well documented. In that year Verrazzano discovered the Gulf of Maine and named the territory New France. Ninety years later (and six years before the *Mayflower*), explorer John Smith gave the discovered land the name "New England."

Saint Croix Island, located in the Saint Croix River which separates Maine from New Brunswick, Canada, was the site of the first European settlement in North America. In 1604 Pierre Dugua Sieur de Mons, along with Samuel Champlain and 77 colonists, established a settlement on the island. During the project Champlain sailed up the Penobscot and Kennebec and discovered Mount Desert Island, the location of Bar Harbor. The effort was short-lived and the colonists abandoned the island in 1605.

English colonization of North America had its start in 1606 when James I issued to the Virginia Company a charter that created two subsidiaries, the Plymouth and London Companies. The London Company established a settlement on the James River in Virginia in 1607 -- the first permanent English settlement in the New World. In the same year the Plymouth Company planted a colony on the mouth of the Kennebec River in Maine. Whereas

OPPOSITE: The Capitol's columned foyer.

PREVIOUS PAGES: The Maine Capitol as seen from the lower park; *Left*, the view from the second-floor balcony.

ABOVE: Dome of today following a remodeling of Charles Bulfinch's original in 1910.

Virginia settlers were able to tough out a difficult winter in the south, the inhabitants in the north were not and they abandoned the project.

Another attempt at settling Maine was ended by Virginia military action in 1613. Sir Samuel Argall was ordered by Virginia authorities to break up the French colony and Jesuit mission. He was successful, imprisoning the inhabitants and carrying them to England. For his successes, he was made Virginia's Deputy Governor.

In 1622 the Province of Maine was born after the Council of New England (successor to the Plymouth Company) issued patents to Sir Ferdinando Gorges and John Mason. The first permanent settlement, Pemaquid, commenced in 1625. A charter naming the province was issued in 1637, and the first incorporated town in America -- Georgiana -- was founded on the present site of York.

Developments in Maine caught the eye of Massachusetts, which reinterpreted its charter to include almost all of its northern neighbor. By 1677 Massachusetts won the allegiance of Maine's towns and provided for their representation in the General Court. And it purchased the Gorges family's claims. In 1691 Massachusetts' new charter effectively consolidated Maine into its borders.

On the eve of the American Revolution, six months after the engagements at Lexington and Concord, Maine's future capital (Portland) was attacked and burned by the British. It was during the War for Independence that Mainers discussed their own independence. In 1783, the year Great Britain acknowledged Massachusetts as "free, sovereign and independent," a separatist movement began to grow. Meanwhile "The District of Maine" became the new title of the former province.

A convention elected from the counties of York, Cumberland, and Lincoln in 1786 investigated forming a separate government, but the 37 persons there decided not to send a petition of grievances to the Massachusetts legislature. And in the ensuing years, though the Commonwealth of Massachusetts resisted a secession of its northern frontier, it did allow the people of Maine to decide the issue for themselves. In 1792, the Commonwealth authorized another vote on separation. The vote was to stay with Massachusetts, 2,525 to 2,074.

Again, in 1797 and in 1806, Massachusetts permitted a vote on separation and still the Mainers preferred to remain part of the Commonwealth. But then came the War of 1812 against Great Britain. As a frontier district Maine, surrounded by the Canadian provinces of Quebec and New Brunswick, suffered during the war. The British captured and held Bangor, Belfast, Eastport, and eastern Maine. Dissatisfied with the protection provided by the state, Mainers seemed ready for separation.

Massachusetts authorized the Brunswick Convention in 1816, but required that the citizenry first be asked, "Is it expedient that the District of Maine shall be separated from Massachusetts, and become an independent state?" The Commonwealth mandated a 5-4 margin in the affirmative before a convention could be called. By a vote of 11,969 in favor of separation and 10,347 opposed, the Mainers answered, "Yes!" But the work of the resulting convention was nullified by a Massachusetts General Court committee for not meeting the requirements.

Now separation seemed inevitable. Another vote was authorized by the Commonwealth in 1819 and the results were striking: 17,091 in favor of separation, 7,132 against it. A constitutional convention thus met in Portland, October 11, 1819 to form a new state. As to whether it was to be called a commonwealth or a state, the State of Maine was selected. The final constitution was submitted to

popular vote and 90% of the voters approved it.

"We, the people of Maine," the Constitution reads, "in order to establish justice, ensure tranquillity, provide for our mutual defence, promote our common welfare, and secure to ourselves and our posterity the blessings of liberty, acknowledging with grateful hearts the goodness of the Sovereign Ruler in affording us an opportunity, so favorable to the design; and, imploring his aid and direction in its accomplishment, do agree to form ourselves into a free and independent State..."

After two hundred years of dependency on other powers, Maine was now free. She had successfully separated from Massachusetts and petitioned for entry into the Union. Conveniently, she was admitted with Missouri as part of the compromise that gave the South a "slave state" in the U.S. Senate and the North a "free state." Mainers now settled down to order their affairs and at the top of the list was creating a Capitol worthy of the province that became a state. With a tilt of their hat to Mother Massachusetts, officials decided they wanted a copy of the Commonwealth's State House that had been, for many years, their own.

So who better to design and build it than the man who created the masterpiece in Boston? Charles Bulfinch was beginning his work at the U.S. Capitol, finishing what others had started, when he got the call. His creation in Augusta was the Boston State House without the large dome. Rather, "a copy of the Temple of Vesta at Rome," he wrote to state authorities, would mean "a covered cupola of 12' diameter & a walk within the surrounding colonnade."

Completed in 1832, the creation would serve as the Capitol and home of the Maine Legislature until 1910. It was around this time that Mr. Bulfinch's dome was deemed out of proportion with the rest of the growing building and work was undertaken to make it larger and more vertical. The result remains to this day. The dome rises 185 feet above the first floor and is wrapped in copper.

The original Capitol building, paid for with the sale of state lands, cost $145,000.

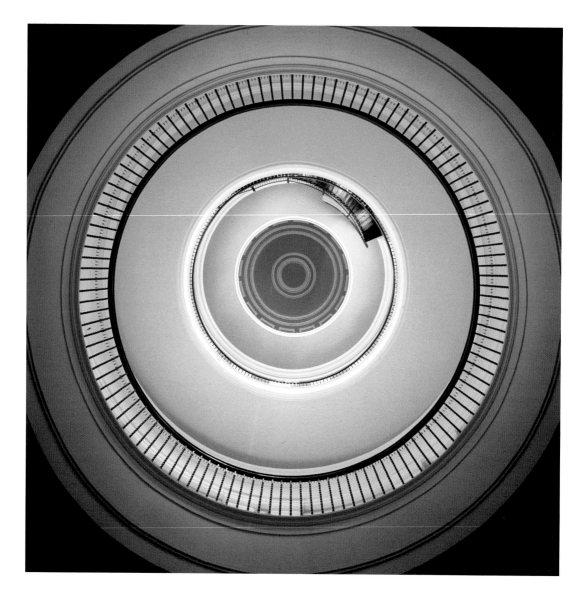

ABOVE: The first place the sun rises in the United States is Mt. Katahdin, northern end of the Appalachian Trail in Maine. That early sun evenly illuminates the Capitol's Rotunda. Its unique position in North America makes Maine the only state to border just one other state (New Hampshire) and two Canadian provinces (New Brunswick and Quebec).

OPPOSITE TOP LEFT: Another view of the Rotunda.

OPPOSITE RIGHT: A side perspective of the Capitol.

OPPOSITE LOWER LEFT: House of Representatives Chamber.

ABOVE: Maine Senate Chamber. Maine's Senate in 1999 had sixteen women senators, ranking it second in this regard among the American States. The first two female senators were elected in 1927, and up until 1976, women legislators were assigned such tasks as selling tickets to the spring dance and picking colors for license plates. Today women serve as Majority Leader and Committee Chair. The Maine Senate is the first of any state in which women hold the top three leadership positions.

OPPOSITE: Maine's House Chamber. The Maine Legislature has two bodies: the Senate and House of Representatives. The Senate has 35 members serving two-year terms; the House has 151 members serving two-year terms.

FOLLOWING PAGE LEFT: Maine Senate Chamber.

FOLLOWING PAGE RIGHT: In 1910 extended wings on the north and south ends were added to the Capitol, giving the Senate new chambers. Minerva, the Roman goddess of wisdom, tops the Capitol. Some twelve feet in height, she holds a pine bough in the form of a torch in an outstretched hand; the other holds a pine cone. The statue was designed by W. Clark Noble.

Official Name: .... State of Michigan
Motto: .... Si Quaeris Peninsulam Amoenam
Circumspice
Citizen: .... Michiganian
Capital City: .... Lansing, MI
Established: 1824
Joined Union: 1837
Anthem: .... "My Michigan"

Name: The Chippewa term for "clearing" is *majigan* and refers to an area on the lower peninsula that was settled. Another interpretation says Michigan is derived from the native word *Michigama* meaning "large lake"
Nickname: ...... Lady of the Lake; Wolverine State
License Plate Slogan: .... Great Lake Splendor
Total Area: .... 96,705 sq mi (11)

OPPOSITE TOP: Looking up at the oculus, or eye of the dome, some 160 feet from the floor. It is painted as a star-filled sky.

OPPOSITE BOTTOM: State seal plate in the sidewalk bordering the front grounds.

ABOVE: A perspective of the Capitol from the street. According to the official Capitol tour booklet, the relief on the pediment features, in the center, Michigan dressed as a Native American. She holds in her hands a book and a globe, representing progress and the future. The weapons of the past lay at her feet, discarded. Agriculture sits, surrounded by plow, horn of plenty, sheaf of wheat, and laurel wreath. Shipping, Commerce, Lumbering, and Mining are represented. "This allegorical composition reflects Michigan's pride in its accomplishments and faith in progress and the future," states the tour booklet.

1836

Official Name: .... State of Wisconsin
Motto: .... Forward
Citizen: .... Wisconsinite
Capital City: .... Madison, WI
Established: 1836
Joined Union: 1848

Anthem: .... "Oh, Wisconsin"
Name: From the Chippewa, Wisconsin means "grassy place" for the lands around the Wisconsin River
Nickname: .... Badger State
License Plate Slogan: .... America's Dairyland
Total Area: .... 65,499 sq mi (22)

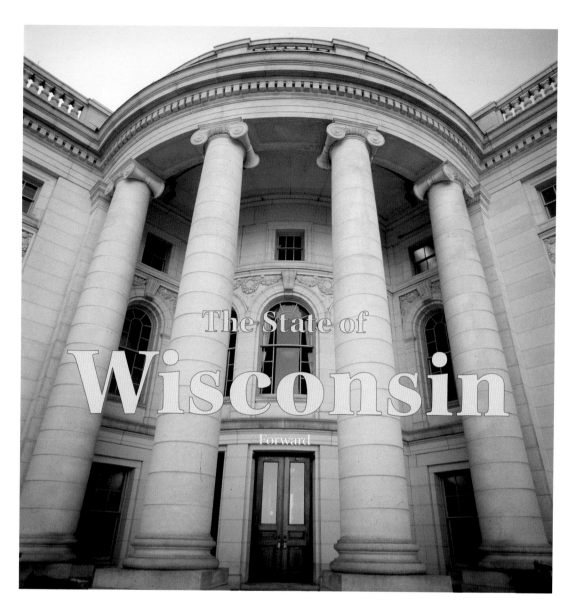

The State of

Wisconsin

Forward

Wisconsin was part of the Indiana Territory (1800-1809), then the Illinois Territory (1809-1818), then the Michigan Territory (1818-1836). When it was formed into the Wisconsin Territory in 1836, it encompassed all of present-day Wisconsin, Iowa, Minnesota, and portions of the Dakotas. Not until 1848, with the parting of Minnesota, did Wisconsin assume its present dimensions. But people had been living in Wisconsin for centuries. When the first French explorers landed on the shores of Green Bay in 1634, well-established Native Americans were found prospering in the region. Winnebago, Dakota, and Menominee natives lived in lodges of bark.

WISCONSIN

Wisconsin over what were, essentially, French trading posts. Scotch fur traders gradually gained prominence after France made peace in 1763; by the time the War of 1812 began, the North West Company gained power as the Scotch, English, French, and the American Astor combined their activities.

In 1816 the U.S. Congress prohibited British citizens from trading in the United States, effectively giving the market to Astor's American Fur Company -- payback for a critical loan Astor arranged for the U.S. Treasury in 1813.

By the end of the century, tribes fleeing warring Iroquois and encroaching Americans also moved there and included the Chippewa, Sauk, Fox, Ottawa, Kickapoo, Huron, Miami, Illinois, and Potawatomi. All of the people in the region, natives and Europeans alike, were involved in some way in the region's biggest business.

And that was fur. The fur trade was a driving force behind European exploration of North America in general, and Wisconsin in particular. In fact, the largest business enterprise in the United States in the first half of the 19th century was the American Fur Company, founded by John Jacob Astor in 1808.

Fur was the primary medium of exchange on the frontier, and the trading posts which it helped found led to the creation of major cities like Detroit, St. Louis, and Chicago.

By their victory over the British in the Revolutionary War did the Americans gain jurisdiction in

By the 1820's Wisconsin was poised for growth. Newly discovered lead mines in the southwest region of the land drew heavy immigration. Illinois miners returned home in the winter; miners from the eastern states took shelter in hovels dug into the hillside. Witnesses likened the miners to the area's burrowing badgers; thus the state's nickname was born.

The first Wisconsin Territorial Legislature to meet did so in Old Belmont (now Leslie) in 1836 and later Burlington (today in Iowa) and selected Madison as the permanent capital. A constitutional convention was authorized by the U.S. Congress and a charter drafted by Wisconsinites in 1848. It provided for rights for married women, an elected judiciary, a prohibition on banks, and other measures. The citizens voted it down; when a new constitution was presented minus the controversial pieces (the ban on banks was in effect until 1852), the citizens approved it. On May 29, 1848 Wisconsin became one of the United States.

Its initially liberal constitution gave a hint of things to come. For from its government would be issued the most progressive legislation ever enacted

ABOVE: *Justice*, one of four murals in the Rotunda.

OPPOSITE: The Capitol under construction.

PREVIOUS PAGES: Wisconsin Capitol at dusk; *Right*, a close-up of the entrance portico.

in the world. And a dose or two of political revolution.

It was Wisconsinites who met in Ripon to protest slavery in U.S. territories in 1854. They proposed to start a new political organization called the Republican Party. The seeds planted here and elsewhere would lead to the election of Abraham Lincoln to the presidency six years later.

It was Wisconsinites who enacted the first laws to regulate utility rates, and the first to implement direct primary elections of candidates. They were the first to create state unemployment benefits, the first to have a kindergarten, the first to have a marked-trunk highway system, and the first to impose a state income tax.

Wisconsin's original constitution, made and approved in 1848, remains in effect (though it has been amended nearly 100 times). That charter empowers the legislature to make laws. It consists of a Senate of thirty-three members, elected to four-year terms, and an Assembly of ninety-nine members, elected to two-year terms.

Lawmakers meet in one of the most admired capitols in North America. It is the state's third. The first (1838-1863) was replaced by the second (1864-1904), which was later destroyed in a fire. In 1906 work commenced on the third Capitol, designed by George B. Post & Sons of New York. It was completed eleven years later at a cost of $7.25 million. By legislative act the Capitol was made to follow a Greek cross plan, as the previous building did. It is in the Italian Renaissance style.

Forty-three varieties of stone were utilized in the making of the Capitol. The exterior is Bethel White granite from Vermont. The Rotunda features marble from France, Italy, Greece and Algeria as well as Minnesota limestone, Norwegian syenite and red granite from Waupaca, Wisconsin.

According to state literature, *Wisconsin* is the name of the statue that tops the Capitol's dome, measuring 15 feet, 2 inches in height. Sculpted by Daniel Chester French of New York and representing the state motto "Forward," she wears a helmet with a badger (state symbol) on top. In her hand is a globe with an eagle. The dome *Wisconsin* stands on is the only one made of granite in the United States; it also has the distinction of being one of the largest by volume in the world.

Wisconsin's progressivity is evident not only in its laws, but in its practical use of the Capitol as well. For instance, a copy of the state constitution is displayed in the Capitol to keep it before the people. And Wisconsin was the first state or nation in the world to install electronic voting machines in its Assembly Chamber, speeding the legislative process.

Forward, indeed!

ABOVE: Looking across the Rotunda.

OPPOSITE: The Capitol was made to follow a Greek cross plan in the Italian Renaissance style. Forty-three varieties of stone were utilized to make the Capitol; the exterior is Bethel White granite from Vermont.

FOLLOWING PAGES: Wisconsin Capitol Rotunda. According to the tour booklet, *Resources of Wisconsin* is in the eye of the Rotunda. This painting is the work of Edwin Blashfield, a leading American muralist. Blashfield's work is also seen in the capitols of South Dakota and Iowa. In the center of *Resources* is a woman with a red headdress representing Wisconsin. She holds wheat in her hands in recognition of agriculture's importance to the state. Numerous other figures hold other products from Wisconsin, including tobacco, fish, fruit, and lead. From the ground floor, the painting rises 200 feet. It is 34 feet in diameter and is framed by a balcony.

ABOVE: A perspective of the Rotunda.

OPPOSITE: The Assembly Chamber features New York and Italian marbles. The mural *Wisconsin* depicts the state's past, present, and future. It was created by Edwin Blashfield, who also painted the *Resources of Wisconsin* in the eye of the Rotunda. According to state tour information: "The woman seated on the rock is *Wisconsin*; she is surrounded by three women representing the bodies of water surrounding Wisconsin: the Mississippi River, Lake Superior, and Lake Michigan. The woman in the green robe symbolizes the present. The group of people in the foreground are farmers, loggers, and miners as they appeared in the early 1900's when this painting was completed. In the far left corner you see *Conservation* pointing to the tree, asking *Future* to preserve Wisconsin's natural resources. On the rock by the soldier with the United States flag you see our state animal, the badger."

OPPOSITE: One of four vaulted corridors.

ABOVE: The Senate Chamber features Italian and French marbles, walnut furniture, and a Kenyon Cox mural entitled *The Marriage of the Atlantic and the Pacific*. It commemorates the opening of the Panama Canal.

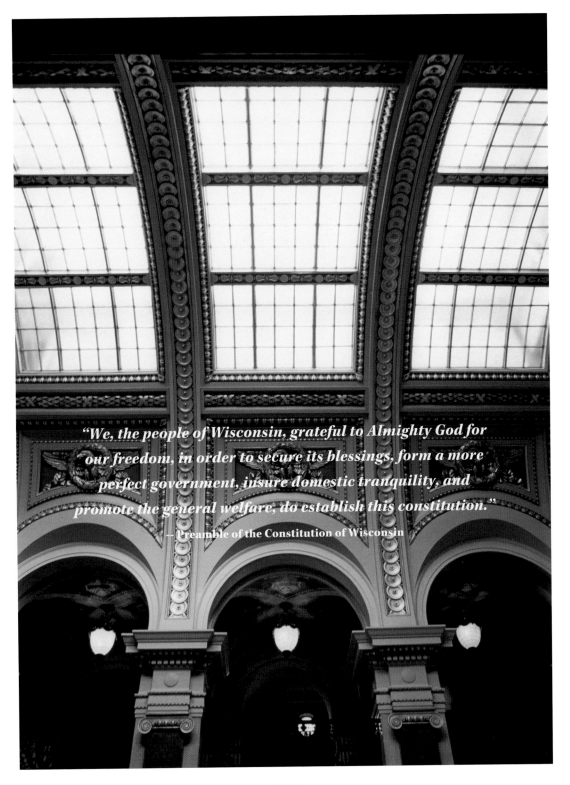

"We, the people of Wisconsin, grateful to Almighty God for our freedom, in order to secure its blessings, form a more perfect government, insure domestic tranquility, and promote the general welfare, do establish this constitution."

-- Preamble of the Constitution of Wisconsin

Official Name: .... State of Minnesota	Anthem: .... "Hail! Minnesota"
Motto: .... L'Etoile du Nord	Name: From the Dakota word *mnishota*, given to the
Citizen: .... Minnesotan	Minnesota River meaning "cloudy" or "milky water"
Capital City: .... St. Paul, MN	Nickname: .... North Star State
Established: 1849	License Plate Slogan: .... Land of 10,000 Lakes
Joined Union: 1858	Total Area: .... 86,943 sq mi (12)

The State of
Minnesota

L'Etoile du Nord | The Star of the North

Minnesota Governor Alexander Ramsey was on an official visit to Washington, DC when word of South Carolina's attack on Fort Sumter reached the city in 1861. Immediately Governor Ramsey offered 1,000 Minnesota troops to President Lincoln. He accepted, giving the second youngest state in the Union then the honor of providing the first soldiers to defend it. Ultimately over 22,000 Minnesotans saw action in Union armies. But it came at a stiff price on the homefront. With its best young men away fighting the southern states, Minnesota was defenseless against a Sioux attack in 1862 that left upwards of 900 state citizens dead.

MINNESOTA

The Sioux (also known as Dakota) natives were the primary occupants of the lands west of the Mississippi River. Before European encroachment, the Sioux populations reached as far east as Virginia and the Carolinas. So large was the Siouan family of native inhabitants that it included the Iowa, Missouri, Omaha, Kansa, Catawba, Crow, and Winnebago peoples. The Sioux or Dakota natives occupied portions of Wisconsin, the Dakotas, and the lands where the Mississippi River originates, Minnesota.

Though visited by French explorers in 1655, it was Daniel Greysolon, sieur du Lhut (Duluth) who claimed it for France in 1679. Not until 1849, though, would the requisite 5,000 people live here to justify the establishment of the Minnesota Territory by the U.S. Congress. These people primarily lived east of the Mississippi, in lands governed by the Northwest Ordinance that were gained in the American Revolution.

PREVIOUS PAGES: The Capitol's East Stair Hall; *Right*, front perspective of the Minnesota Capitol.

ABOVE: Balcony ornament with the state motto.

OPPOSITE: Looking towards the Senate from the Rotunda.

Claims to the lands west of the Mississippi were purchased from France in the Louisiana Purchase. It was here that the Sioux dominated. The Treaty of 1851 between the United States and the Sioux realized the cession of key lands to the U.S. -- over 28,000,000 acres were surrendered in southwestern Minnesota, and the Sioux kept a small reservation along the Minnesota River. Meanwhile the Ojibwa or Chippewa, the Sioux's enemy in the north, relinquished the present northern half of the state and its timber treasures to the United States. These treaties led to an immigration boom that brought Minnesota's population to over 150,000 in 1857, the year it drafted its constitution.

Given these circumstances a band of Sioux, led by Little Crow, felt cheated. When Minnesota became a state in 1858, the Sioux's small reservation was cut in half and government officials attempted to turn the Sioux into farmers. This they resented. In 1862, when the state failed to make timely payments in accordance with the treaties, Little Crow went on the warpath.

No one was safe. Their militia now fighting for the Union, the people of the Minnesota Valley could do little as the warring Sioux destroyed frontier towns. The massacre which followed ranks as one of the bloodiest on the continent, and not until 1867 would the unrest be quelled and some Sioux removed to South Dakota.

Leading the charge against the natives was General Henry Hastings Sibley, the state's first governor. Sibley had been an agent for John Jacob Astor's American Fur Company and was a central figure in the establishment of the territory. Before commanding Minnesota forces, he helped draft the state's constitution. Sibley defeated Little Crow at Wood Lake and pushed the remaining Sioux into North Dakota.

With the natives subdued, the state could now tend to its domestic concerns at the Capitol in St. Paul, a city owing its provenance to the establishment of a church. In 1805 Zebulon Pike and a small group of U.S. soldiers purchased White Rock from the natives for 60 gallons of whiskey, assorted trinkets, and $2,000 in cash from the U.S. Congress. In 1819 the U.S. Army established Fort Snelling, the

first permanent American settlement in Minnesota. Later Father Gaultier built the church of St. Paul in the little community and, as the area is at the head of the navigable Mississippi River, it became known as St. Paul's Landing and eventually just St. Paul.

The lands to the west of St. Paul were first visited by Franciscan friar Louis Hennepin in 1680, whereupon he named the Falls of St. Anthony. Those falls today are in the center of Minneapolis, Minnesota's largest city and St. Paul's twin.

Today the twin cities account for more than half of the state's citizens.

Minnesota's political identity was born in the convention at Stillwater in 1848 where a petition for territorial status was drafted. Sibley presented it to Congress in 1849 and the Territory of Minnesota was created.

The first meetings of the Minnesota Legislature were held in a St. Paul hotel made of logs while preparations were made for the first Capitol building. It opened in 1854. A constitutional convention met in July, 1857 and drafted what remains the first and only constitution of the State of Minnesota. This compact was submitted to popular vote in the

fall of that year and received near-unanimous approval. Congress admitted the state May 11, 1858.

A fire broke out during a session of the Legislature in 1881, destroying the building. A second Capitol was immediately built, but within ten years plans for the present structure were being drawn. In 1893 a building was authorized and a competition begun which drew forty entries. The winner: noted architect Cass Gilbert (1859-1934), who also designed the Arkansas State Capitol, West Virginia State Capitol, Woolworth Building in New York, and the U.S. Supreme Court in Washington, DC.

Ground was broken on the project May 6, 1896. The building was opened to the public January 2, 1905, and the next day Minnesota's 34th Legislature convened. The total cost of the construction project was $4.5 million.

And who was the man who laid the cornerstone of the new (and present) Minnesota Capitol in 1898?

He was none other than the state's first territorial governor and its second state governor. It was Alexander Ramsey, the man who some 35 years earlier was the first to pledge state troops to President Lincoln.

OPPOSITE: Looking into the Rotunda.

ABOVE: A large, single star representing the North Star State lies in the center of the Rotunda floor. Looking up one sees four large murals which tell the allegorical story, *The Civilization of the Northwest*. They rise over cases of flags that were carried by Minnesota soldiers in the Civil War and Spanish-American War.

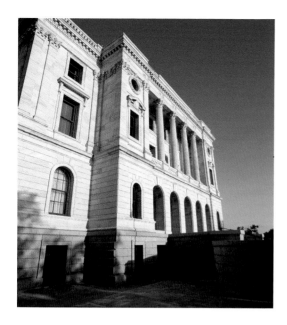

TOP: Side perspective of the Capitol.

BOTTOM: The four names on the House Chamber's ceiling -- La Salle, Hennepin, Perrot, and Duluth -- are the French explorers who journeyed through Minnesota.

OPPOSITE: House of Representatives Chamber. This legislative body is authorized by the Minnesota Constitution of 1857, which begins: "We, the people of the State of Minnesota, grateful to God for our civil and religious liberty, and desiring to perpetuate its blessings, and secure the same to ourselves and our posterity, do ordain and establish this constitution."

ABOVE: According to the tour information, the sculpture *Minnesota, the Spirit of Government* in the front of the House of Representatives was built with Depression-era State Emergency Relief Act funds by the father-son duo, Carlo and Amerigo Brioschi. The pair had moved to St. Paul from Italy. The sculpture features Minnesota as a Goddess on a pedestal that bears the state seal. Below this are the words, "The Trail of the Pioneer Bore the Footprints of Liberty." Flanking Minnesota are Native Americans to her right and explorers and trappers to her left. It was installed in 1938.

ABOVE: The Senate Chamber. The Minnesota Legislature is authorized to meet in regular session each biennium for a maximum of 120 legislative days. The Minnesota Senate is comprised of sixty-seven senators serving four-year terms. The House of Representatives has 134 members serving two-year terms.

OPPOSITE: *The Progress of the State*, a golden sculpture that sits at the base of the dome and at the top of the triumph arches, is referred to as the "Quadriga" (Roman word for a two-wheeled chariot). According to Minnesota Historical Society literature: "Two women, symbolizing Agriculture and Industry, lead the horses that represent the forces of nature (Earth, Wind, Fire and Water)." The outside dome is made of white Georgia marble, one of the world's largest self-supporting marble domes (the others include St. Peter's in Vatican City, the Taj Mahal in India, and the Rhode Island Capitol).

VERMONT 1777

TEXAS 1836

HAWAI'I 1840

Nation States

"We the Representatives of the freemen of Vermont ... ordain, declare, and establish, the ... declaration of rights, and frame of government, to be the Constitution of this Commonwealth ..."

-- From the Constitution of Vermont, proclaimed July 8, 1777.

"... the people of Texas do now constitute a free, sovereign, and independent republic, and are fully invested with all the rights and attributes which properly belong to independent nations."

-- From the Texas Declaration of Independence, issued March 2, 1836.

"God hath made of one blood all nations of men to dwell on the earth in unity and blessedness. God has also bestowed certain rights alike on all men and all chiefs, and all people of all lands ... (including) life, limb, liberty, freedom from oppression."

-- From Hawai'i's first Declaration of Rights, issued June 7, 1839.

Official Name:.................State of Vermont	Anthem:.........................."Hail! Vermont!"
Motto:......................Freedom and Unity	Name:.. From the French *verd mont* ("green moun-
Citizen:.............................Vermonter	tain," in 17th-century spelling)
Capital City: ....Montpelier, VT	Nickname: ....Green Mountain State
Established: 1777	License Plate Slogan:........Green Mountain State
Joined Union: 1791	Total Area: ....9,615 sq mi (43)

The State of
Vermont

Freedom and Unity

VERMONT

"I AM AS RESOLUTELY DETERMINED to defend the independence of Vermont as Congress are [*sic*] that of the United States and rather than fail will retire with hardy Green Mountain Boys into the desolate caverns of the mountains and wage war with human Nature at Large." Thus wrote Ethan Allen, the father of Vermont independence, in 1781, and no doubt his enemies in New York knew he meant every word.

The reason for the bold talk was simple: self-preservation. Settled by citizens from the other New England States after land grants were issued by the Governor of New Hampshire in the mid-1700's, Vermonters saw their claims repudiated by New York officials who did not honor the New Hampshire grants. New York won on appeal to the British King in 1764 in the dispute, claiming the land of the Green Mountain -- some of the oldest mountain ranges in North America, running the length of the state.

But Ethan Allen and the Vermonters would have nothing of it, forming themselves into the Green Mountain Boys to repel attempts by New York to assert control in 1770. With Remember Baker and Colonel Seth Warner ably managing military operations throughout the American Revolution, Allen was able to fight both the military and political cause of Vermont. On May 10, 1775, more than a year before the Declaration of Independence, Allen and the Green Mountain Boys, working with forces under

PLEASE KEEP OFF

the command of Benedict Arnold, captured Fort Ticonderoga. In 1777, the Republic of Vermont declared its independence. New York indicted the leaders for treason and offered a bounty on Allen's head. The little republic established a government instead. "Whereas, all government ought to be instituted and supported for the security and protection of the community as such and to enable the individuals who compose it, to enjoy their natural rights ..." the preamble to Vermont's Constitution of 1777 declares.

The document detailed the realities of the day: Britain's authority had been cast off by the new American Commonwealths, which Vermonters now declared their land to be.

The Vermont Constitution lists the abuses of New York authorities, who were bent on forcing the little republic to submit to New York sovereignty. "Therefore, it is absolutely necessary for the welfare and safety of the inhabitants of this State, that it should be, henceforth, a free and independent State ..." the preamble continues.

For the next fourteen years, Vermont diligently maintained her independence. And for legal protection in this society, the people looked to the Declaration of Rights included in the 1777 constitution. This little republic has the distinction of being the first in America to abolish slavery. "That all men are born equally free and independent," the Declaration of Rights reads, "and have certain natural and inherent rights, amongst which are the enjoying and defending of life and liberty; acquiring, possessing, and protecting property, and pursuing and obtaining happiness and safety. Therefore no male person ... (nor female) ... ought to be holden by law, to serve any person, as a servant, slave or apprentice ..."

During the Revolution, Green Mountain Boys aided the American cause, though their allegiance was to Vermont. Warner served with New Hampshire's Stark to stop Burgoyne. Though he hinted Vermont would join with Canada (and thus the British) after the Revolution, Allen and the Vermonters saw their future in union with the other American States. New York relinquished all claims to the Green Mountain lands in 1790, and Vermont joined her former adversary as one of the United States.

Today a statue of Ethan Allen greets those entering the State House of Vermont, as does his famous quote about defending Vermont's independence. According to the tour brochure, the present Capitol is the third in the state's history. Built in 1859 on the same site as the previous one following the

damaging fire of 1857, it cost $150,000 to build and two and a half years to complete. Concomitant with its completion, Vermont was invaded by Confederate soldiers at St. Albans during the Civil War. The raiders were quickly repelled back into Canada.

The front portico is the only remaining part of the earlier State House of the 1830's, though the original foundation remains and the new building was created within the ruins of the old. The lobby floor was made with black tiles from the Isle Motte on Lake Champlain and white tiles from Danby, VT. The black tiles hold an ancient relic: fossils are embedded in the stone.

A new gold dome was placed above the previous Grecian temple facade and atop it a statue called *Agriculture*. It is the second version, having replaced the original in 1938. Acclaimed sculptor Larkin Mead, the Vermont native, made the original which was found to be rotting. In the effort to replace *Agriculture*, eighty-six-year-old Sergeant-at-Arms Dwight Dwinell carved a new statue with the aid of his janitorial staff. *Agriculture* is 14-feet tall.

The bust of Abraham Lincoln at the end of the Hall of Inscriptions is the only remaining work by Larkin Mead in the Vermont Capitol. The bust was created as part of the effort to make the bronze statue for Lincoln's tomb in Springfield, IL. Other significant state possessions include the Constitution Chair, carved from the timbers of "Old Ironsides," *the U.S.S. Constitution*. It has served as the Vermont Governor's chair since it was presented to the state in 1858. And Vermont's Hall of Flags on the second floor holds some of the 72 flags carried by Vermont soldiers in the Civil War, many of which have elaborate designs painted on silk.

The capital, Montpelier, is the smallest in America and home to the General Assembly. It consists of 30 Senators and 150 Representatives.

PREVIOUS PAGES: Perspectives of the Vermont State House, a Grecian temple on a hill in Montpelier.

OPPOSITE: A statue of Ethan Allen greets visitors.

ABOVE: In the front looking at *Agriculture* on the dome's top.

ABOVE & OPPOSITE: The Vermont House of Representatives and its entrance. The House Chamber features an original Cornelius and Baker bronze and gilt gas chandelier. On the chandelier's underside are eight individual Vermont coat-of-arms. When fire ravaged the House Chamber, an alert person grabbed the 1836 copy of Gilbert Stuart's portrait of Washington. It hangs today exactly where it always has: above the Speaker's rostrum.

TOP: The Senate Chamber. Renovations for the chamber were to begin shortly after this picture was taken.

OPPOSITE: *Agriculture* tops the Capitol dome. It is the second version, having replaced the original in 1938. Acclaimed sculptor Larkin Mead, the Vermont native, made the original which was found to be rotting. This new statue was carved from the original. It stands 14 feet tall.

TOP LEFT: Vermont high-school students in a mock meeting of the House of Representatives. Students participate in the program annually to practice the art of self-government.

ABOVE & OPPOSITE: A perspective of the Senate Chamber from the Senate President's chair. The elliptically-shaped Senate Chamber seats 30 members. At the front is the rostrum and in it is an elaborate carving of Vermont's coat-of-arms. Above it are lights that symbolize the muses of Inspiration and Meditation, according to tour literature.

LEFT: Entrance foyer of the Governor's office. Adjoining this office is the Cedar Creek Reception Room which features *The Battle of Cedar Creek* painting. Completed in 1874, it measures 20'x10' and hangs amid elaborate wall stencils, brass chandeliers and stained glass skylights. Painted by Julian Scott, a Medal of Honor recipient for his own valor in the Civil War, it depicts a battle in Virginia's Shenendoah Valley in 1864 with the Old Vermont Brigade leading a rally that would end a Union retreat.

OPPOSITE BOTTOM: The Hall of Inscriptions features quotes from Vermonters throughout the centuries including this comment from U.S. Ambassador George Harvey in 1921.

THE RECORD OF VERMONT as a resolute champion of individual freedom, as a true interpreter of our fundamental law, as a defender of religious faith, as an unselfish but independent and uncompromising commonwealth of liberty-loving patriots, is not only unsurpassed, but unmatched by any other state in the Union.

—GEORGE HARVEY, 1921
United States Ambassador to Great Britain

"VERMONTERS FOR 200 YEARS have handed down certain attitudes of mind from generation to generation. Some folks call us old-fashioned and backward-looking for adhering to the ideals and principles characteristic of the people who settled our State. We value our heritage of ideals."

-- George D. Aiken, 1938

Sixty-seventh Governor of the State of Vermont
Recorded in the Hall of Inscriptions

ABOVE: A meeting and reading room in the State House.

OPPOSITE: Admiral George Dewey, commander of the American fleet responsible for taking Manila Bay, Philippines in the Spanish-American War (1898), was born across the street from the State House. To the building on which steps he played as a boy, the Admiral donated two Spanish naval guns that were captured in that battle which now flank the building's front. Admiral Dewey's portrait hangs inside.

1836

Official Name: .... State of Texas
Motto: .... Friendship
Citizen: .... Texan
Capital City: .... Austin, TX
Established: 1836
Joined Union: 1845
Left Union: 1861
Readmitted: 1870

Anthem: .... "Texas, Our Texas"
Name: ...... *Teysha* (Caddo indian meaning, "hello friend") and *tejas* ("friendship," a Spanish term for the people from Louisiana to Oklahoma) are believed to be the foundation of Texas
Nickname: .... Lone Star State
License Plate Slogan: .... Lone Star State
Total Area: .... 267,277 sq mi (2)

The State of
Texas

Friendship

TEXAS

Everything is bigger in Texas. Literally. The drive across the state is some 1,000 miles. The geography, ranging from desert to plain to forest to mountains and valleys, is perhaps the most varied of any state or province in North America. Encompassing 267,277 square miles, it is the largest of the 48 contiguous American States and is larger than France, Spain, Great Britain, and Germany. So like its geography is its history: a grand story fit for a nation, which for about ten years Texas was.

To know Texas one must understand something about Mexico, the country it was constitutionally attached to until the Texas Revolution of 1835-36.

The native culture of greater Mexico blossomed into advanced civilizations like the Mayan and Aztec centuries before confrontation with the first Europeans (Cordoba in 1517 and later Cortez). By 1535 greater Mexico was conquered and established as New Spain. Unlike the American States, the native peoples were incorporated into the society and not placed on reservations.

A strong central government was at the heart of New Spain, and power was lodged with a viceroy who acted for the Spanish king. For nearly two hundred years New Spain was thus managed. When France invaded Spain the people of Mexico revolted and declared independence in 1821. A federal union was established in Mexico in 1824 with sovereign states like the American system.

Texas and neighboring Coahuila united to form one of these Mexican states, and issued a constitution declaring it to be "free and independent of the other Mexican United States and of every other power and dominion whatever."

The new state asserted, "the sovereignty of the state resides originally and essentially in the general mass of the individuals who compose it." The Confederation of Mexican Republics approved this constitution, and thus Texans owed allegiance to two sovereignties like their eastern cousins in the U.S.: the federal and their state.

This was short-lived. In 1833 the Texans petitioned for separation from Coahuila to form their own state. It was denied, but it did not matter: in 1835 the federal government was overthrown in Mexico City by the military and replaced with a strong central government. The constitutions of the member states were destroyed; the states were converted into mere departments of the nation. Texans now had a choice: submit to the central authority or fight for the right of self-government.

The Texans fought.

Like the Original States and their American Revolution, Texas struggled in her own war of independence and won. And like the originals, Texas declared independence and constituted a republic complete with a congress and a president.

This republic was culturally diverse, encompassing native Mexicans, immigrants from the

OPPOSITE: The foyer of the Capitol annex.

PREVIOUS PAGES: The mural depicting Texas Independence is in the Library & Archives building on the grounds. *Right*, the Cowboy statue dominates this perspective of the Texas Capitol.

ABOVE: Visitors are greeted in the South Foyer by the original life-sized marble statues of Stephen F. Austin and Sam Houston (far right) created by Elisabet Ney. Unveiled in 1903, copies were made and donated to the U.S. Capitol's Statuary Hall.

American States, French influences from the neighboring Louisiana Purchase, African-Americans, and the original colonizers who were Mexican citizens. A leader of these revolutionaries, the man called "The Father of Texas," was Stephen F. Austin.

Austin inherited a grant of land in Mexico from his father, who had secured it from Spain, and 300 colonists settled along the banks of the Colorado River in 1822. When Mexico achieved independence from Spain in 1823, Austin sought and received reconfirmation of the land grant. Settlement began in earnest, drawing large numbers of Americans from the neighboring states east and north.

It was Austin who went to Mexico City on the directive from the Texas Convention in 1833 to seek separate statehood for Texas within Mexico. After the authorities turned him down, Austin wrote and instructed the Convention to proceed anyway. For this he was imprisoned. When Mexico's federal government was overthrown and all state constitutions abolished, he returned to Texas and later led efforts to get international support for the Texas independence movement.

"... (The) political connection with the Mexican nation has forever ended, and that the people of Texas do now constitute a free, sovereign, and independent republic, and are fully invested with all the rights and attributes which properly belong to independent nations," states the Texas Declaration of Independence, issued March 2, 1836.

Ominously it included these words: "we fearlessly and confidently commit the issue to the decision of the supreme arbiter of the destinies of nations." Texans knew they had a fight on their hands. They had to beat none other than Mexico's revolutionary hero, Santa Anna, and his much larger armies.

The Alamo was the name of the Spanish mission-church-turned-fort in San Antonio in which Texans fought off Santa Anna. All of the Texans in the mission church -- 188 fighters led by Col. William B. Travis and including legends Davy Crockett and Jim Bowie -- staved off a force of 4,000 Mexicans before perishing.

Only six Texans survived to surrender, including Crockett. But after promising they were safe, Santa Anna ordered all six executed.

Three weeks later on March 27, 1836, James Walker Fannin and his small Texan force were captured in Goliad and slaughtered. On Santa Anna's orders, 330 out of 445 rebels were executed with the commander Fannin the last to take a bullet.

Thirty days after declaring independence, Texas appeared doomed.

Winning these battles, Santa Anna overconfidently pursued the Texas Army and its commander, Sam Houston. The two met on April 21, 1836 in the Battle of San Jacinto along the banks of the river by that name. With the Mexicans in hot pursuit, Houston suddenly stopped at the river and turned his forces to fight.

"Remember the Alamo! Remember Goliad!" was the Texans' cry as they charged the enemy.

The results were staggering: a large portion of the Mexican army was either killed or captured. Santa Anna was now a prisoner of the Texans.

And Texas was free!

"We, the people of Texas," began the new constitution, adopted in 1836 and bearing close

ABOVE: Front perspective of the Texas Capitol. Note the national seals under the flags, representing the various nations Texas has been associated with.

OPPOSITE: The Capitol from the entrance gate. Steps away is the oldest surviving state office structure, the Texas General Land Office Building, completed in 1856-57. It housed the official maps and records of Texas' extensive public lands which the state retained control of after it was annexed to the United States. Today the building serves as the Capitol Visitors Center.

resemblance to the U.S. Constitution. The Texans, many of whom were born in one of the states or territories eastward, knew well the song of freedom and independence.

Houston's stunning success led to his election in 1836 as President of Texas, defeating Stephen Austin, who became Secretary of State. Both born in 1793, Texas' founding fathers would part company with the death of Austin in December. Meanwhile, Houston had a republic to run.

Born a Virginian, Houston was adopted by the Cherokee and grew up in Tennessee. In 1827 he was elected governor of that state. When his new bride suddenly left him, Houston retired from politics and moved to what is now Oklahoma to live with the Cherokee people and marry. Shortly thereafter he returned to politics, serving in the convention that declared Texas' independence. He was later named Commander-in-Chief of the Republic's troops.

Under strong leadership, Texas declared her independence and maintained it for nearly a decade,

ABOVE RIGHT: The eye of the Rotunda.

ABOVE LEFT: The painting *Surrender of Santa Anna* graces the foyer wall.

OPPOSITE: The outside wall of the Library & Archives Building showcases a portion of the Republic of Texas Declaration of Independence, 1836.

with a constitutionally established system of government. Texas treated with the United States, Great Britain, and France as a nation. Even Mexico finally recognized Texas' sovereignty, but then only if the new republic remained independent of the United States.

What was it like to live in the Republic of Texas? Much like life in any state or nation. Texas established her boundaries and cut the territory up into counties. Militia secured her borders. A judicial system was extended over the land. A customs service was created and duties collected; post offices and post roads connected the republic; and a land office granted property for development.

It was well known that Texans preferred joining the United States, having voted for annexation in the election following independence. But northern representatives and senators in the U.S. Congress opposed it because Texas permitted slavery. By 1845 Great Britain and France engineered a Mexican offer to recognize Texas' independence, provided Texas remain separate from the U.S.

U.S. negotiations on a Treaty of Annexation commenced with the Texas Republic and a treaty was finally submitted to the U.S. Senate in 1844. That body rejected it 35 to 16. A year later it was submitted not as a treaty, which requires the Senate to approve it with a two-thirds majority, but rather as a joint resolution of the Congress, which only needs a

THE PEOPLE OF TEXAS DO NOW CONSTITUTE A FREE SOVEREIGN AND INDEPENDENT REPUBLIC, AND -- WE FEARLESSLY AND CONFIDENTLY COMMIT THE ISSUE TO THE DECISION OF THE SUPREME ARBITER OF THE DESTINIES OF NATIONS.

DECLARATION OF INDEPENDENCE, REPUBLIC OF TEXAS, 1836

simple majority. This squeaked through (120-98 in the House, 27-25 in the Senate).

Now it was the Texans' turn.

Meeting in convention, they had to decide whether to sign the Mexican treaty and stay independent or approve the terms laid out in the U.S. Congress' resolution and join the Union of American States. The terms of the annexation were unique: Texas retained the right, at its discretion alone, to divide itself into as many as five separate states of the United States. It also retained ownership of its vast and valuable public lands (as well as its debt).

The Texans made their decision: the Lone Star Republic was to become the Lone Star State.

"As soon as the act to admit Texas as a State shall be passed the union of the two republics will be consummated by their own voluntary consent," said U.S. President James Polk, in his State of the Union address in 1845. "Toward Texas I do not doubt ... she will never have cause to regret that she has united her 'lone star' to our glorious constellation."

The capital city, named in Stephen Austin's honor, was laid out in 1839 by the Republic of Texas, three years after it achieved independence. The Texas Congress met in a one-story, wooden Capitol in Austin until a new structure was completed in 1853 -- the first Texas statehouse.

"Capitol Square" was designated in 1839 by the republic's surveyors; this new statehouse would be the first to occupy the four-block perimeter. It was made of limestone and its three stories measured 140' x 90'. That building burned in 1881, though efforts had been underway before the accident to replace it with a grander structure.

Elijah E. Meyers of Detroit won the competition to design the new Capitol. To pay for the project the state offered contractors three million acres of prime Texas Panhandle land.

Meyers, who had served as the architect of the Michigan Capitol a decade earlier, chose the Renaissance Revival style. For two years there was a debate over what exterior stone was best for the job. The owners of Granite Mountain donated to the state the distinctive Sunset Red granite seen today, provided the authorities do the quarrying. The labor of a thousand convicts was used to quarry the stone.

Groundbreaking was held on February 1, 1882 and the 12,000-pound cornerstone was laid March 2, 1885. By the middle of 1887 the walls were erected and in 1888 the zinc *Goddess of Liberty* statue was placed atop the dome. In all, the massive structure took seven years to build and measured 566' x 288'.

Dedicated in May 1888, the Capitol of Texas had 392 rooms, 924 windows, and 404 doors. It stands 310 feet in height, making it seven feet taller than the Capitol of the United States.

Everything is bigger in Texas.

ABOVE & OPPOSITE: Looking up into the Rotunda.

FOLLOWING PAGES: The Republic of Texas Great Seal was retained when Texas became a state and is placed directly beneath the dome on the first floor. Laid in the terrazzo floors, the seal is surrounded by smaller seals, one for each of the six countries whose flags have flown over Texas. These include Spain, France, Mexico, England, Confederate States of America, and the United States of America. Portraits of the Presidents of the Republic and Governors of the State encompass the Rotunda's four public levels.

DIED
FOR STATE RIGHTS
GUARANTEED UNDER THE CONSTITUTION.
THE PEOPLE OF THE SOUTH, ANIMATED BY THE SPIRIT OF 1776, TO PRESERVE THEIR RIGHTS,
WITHDREW FROM THE FEDERAL COMPACT IN 1861.   THE NORTH RESORTED TO COERCION.
THE SOUTH, AGAINST OVERWHELMING NUMBERS AND RESOURCES,
FOUGHT UNTIL EXHAUSTED.
DURING THE WAR, THERE WERE TWENTY TWO HUNDRED AND FIFTY SEVEN ENGAGEMENTS;
IN EIGHTEEN HUNDRED AND EIGHTY TWO OF THESE, AT LEAST ONE REGIMENT TOOK PART.
NUMBER OF MEN ENLISTED:
CONFEDERATE ARMIES, 600,000;   FEDERAL ARMIES, 2,859,132.
LOSSES FROM ALL CAUSES:
CONFEDERATE, 437,000;   FEDERAL, 485,216.

OPPOSITE & TOP: Confederate Soldiers Monument.

ABOVE: A cannon used in the Texas Revolution and Civil War.

RIGHT: Terry's Texas Rangers Monument and plaque close-up.

ABOVE: The Senate Chamber features a collection of Texas historical paintings, one of the oldest being that of Stephen F. Austin which hangs behind the Lieutenant Governor's desk. Two paintings of critical battles in Texas' fight for independence are also featured: *Dawn at the Alamo* and the *Battle of San Jacinto*, both by one of Texas' first artists, Henry Arthur McArdle. The chamber's walnut desks are the original ones purchased from the A.H. Andrews Company of Chicago. The Texas Senate has 31 members, each serving a four-year term.

RIGHT: Governor's Public Reception Room where important pieces of legislation are signed into law.

OPPOSITE: The House Chamber has been restored to its 1910 appearance. It is the largest room in the Capitol "epitomizing the grand scale and tour de force that is Texas," according to official literature. It holds 150 representatives. Behind the Speaker's desk are the remains of the original Battle of San Jacinto flag. The Texas Legislature meets every odd year for one 60-day session.

PREVIOUS PAGES: "God And Texas, Victory Or Death," reads the plaque on the Heroes of the Alamo Monument in front of the Capitol. It looks through to the Terry's Texas Rangers Monument. *Right*, a perspective of the Capitol offers a glimpse of the *Goddess of Liberty* holding one star atop the Capitol. In the mid-1980's a new statue replaced the deteriorating original as part of an overhaul of the exterior dome.

ABOVE: A courtyard in the Capitol Extension. To preserve the view of the Capitol on the north side but add needed office space, a Preservation Master Plan was created in 1989 that placed a building extension underground. Some 40,000 truckloads of dirt and stone were removed. It was completed in 1993.

OPPOSITE: Outside the gates of the Capitol. Texas' sovereign authority is established in the state's constitution of 1876 in these words: "'Texas is a free and independent State, subject only to the Constitution of the United States; and the maintenance of our free institutions and the perpetuity of the Union depend on the preservation of the right of local self-government unimpaired to all the States ... No power of suspending laws in this State shall be exercised except by the legislature.'"

"*WHEREAS, General Antonio Lopez de Santa Anna and other Military Chieftains have, by force of arms, overthrown the Federal Institutions of Mexico, and dissolved the Social Compact which existed between Texas and the other Members of the Mexican Confederacy -- Now, the good People of Texas, availing themselves of their natural rights,*

SOLEMNLY DECLARE --

"... That Texas is no longer, morally or civilly, bound by the compact of Union; ... That they hold it to be their right ... to withdraw from the Union, to establish an independent Government, or to adopt such measures as they may deem best calculated to protect their rights and liberties ... These DECLARATIONS we solemnly avow to the world and call GOD to witness their truth and sincerity ..."

-- Texas Declaration of Independence, 1836

Official Name: .... State of Hawai'i
Motto: .... Ua Mau ke Ea o ka Aina i ka Pono
Citizen: .... Hawaiian
Capital City: .... Honolulu, HI
Established:............................... 1840
Joined Union: 1959
Anthem: .... "Hawai'i Ponoi" (Our Hawai'i)

Name:......... Legend holds that Hawai'i Loa was discoverer of the islands in ancient times; linguistic analysis finds *Hawa* means "homeland" and *ii* means "small"
Nickname: .... Aloha State
License Plate Slogan:................ Aloha State
Total Area: .... 6,459 sq mi (47)

The State of
Hawai'i

Ua Mau ke Ea o ka Aina i ka Pono |
The Life of the Land is Perpetuated in Righteousness

HAWAI'I

The Pacific Ocean is the largest body of water in the world, occupying one-third of the globe's surface. The navigator Magellan named the ocean "peaceful" because of the moderate winds he experienced on a journey. But it was not appropriately titled. Violent storms and geological activities make the Pacific Ocean as volatile as her sister, the Atlantic. In this vastness, in the North Pacific and not quite halfway between Asia and the Americas, volcanoes on the ocean floor exploded and gushed forth the earth's molten interior. The explosions and outpourings grew higher and higher, rising in the water until there was water no more. Only air, sky, sun, moon.

In time all kinds of life would find their way to this dry oasis traveling on the desert sea. Polynesian peoples are believed to have reached the islands some two thousand years ago from other isles thousands of miles away. Soon a distinctive culture took root. The people called the islands "Hawai'i," from *Hawaiki*, the ancient name of the Polynesians' homeland in the west.

Rich soils and plentiful water combined with a tropical climate to produce a vibrant agriculture. From the sea, fish. On the shores, coconuts. In the valleys, taro, a native vegetive root. The lower slopes grew sweet potatoes and bananas. The mountains, wood. And everywhere flowers, powerful expressions

of affection in the culture. Such was the agricultural society that grew up on these Pacific isles.

The men were unsurpassed in sailing, swimming, and fishing. Great warriors, they excelled in the skills of war but had organized inter-island athletic competitions. Champions from each island would compete in surfing, boxing, bowling, wrestling, and more. In the evenings music and dance filled the night.

The culture was advanced, in a natural way. The Hawaiian calendar had 12 lunar months and a leap year. The language has only 12 letters, and up until the 19th century, it was spoken only and not written. Great stores of knowledge from many

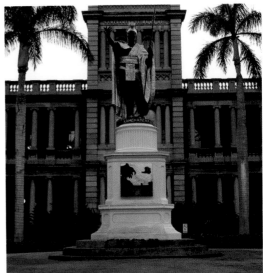

disciplines were passed orally from generation to generation by professionals trained for the job.

Four kingdoms existed in Hawai'i until the leader of one of them conquered the other three. This first successful union of the various Hawaiian Islands took place in 1790 when Kamehameha I, the father of a united Hawai'i, conquered all of the isles except Kauai and Niihau, which he later gained by cession in 1810. Kamehameha would lead this new consolidated kingdom through various trials and tribulations, thwarting Russian designs on the isles in 1816 and stopping Spanish piracy in 1818.

His most striking features were wisdom and compassion. Under his rule a fair government was organized, oppression of the people ended, and crime reduced. He began to break the power of priests and sorcerers, intertwined in a political-religious system best described as a polytheistic theocracy.

PREVIOUS PAGES: A perspective of the Capitol at dusk. *Left,* the giant medallion on the front and back of the Capitol is the state seal. It incorporates elements of the original royal crest.

OPPOSITE: The royal Hawaiian flag was retained as the state flag and flies with the U.S. flag in front of the Capitol.

ABOVE: A perspective of the Capitol. *Right,* King Kamehameha stands in front of the Royal Palace. This statue is a copy of the original, which was lost at sea and then recovered and set near his birthplace on the Big Island. It was made by Thomas Gould.

Kamehameha began a dynasty that lasted until 1872, including a nine-year rule by his widow Kaahumanu and four successive kings thereafter. The great reforms he undertook were broadened in successive generations. Kamehameha II abolished taboos (kapus), a system of prohibiting certain actions under penalty of supernatural forces. These social rules weighed heavily on the isles' women.

Kamehameha III crafted Hawai'i's first Declaration of Rights on June 7, 1839, its Edict of Toleration June 17, 1839, and its first constitution October 8, 1840. "God hath made of one blood all nations of men to dwell on the earth in unity and blessedness," the Declaration of Rights begins. "God has also bestowed certain rights alike on all men and all chiefs, and all people of all lands." Those rights include "life, limb, liberty, freedom from oppression."

The Hawai'i Constitution established the legal footing of the kingdom. A representative body chosen by the people was chartered, as was a House of Nobles, a Supreme Court, a Premier, and Governors for the various islands. The king's rights and powers were detailed, including administration of the land which "to him belonged all the land from one end of the Islands to the other, though it was not his own personal property, it belonged to the chiefs and people in common."

In 1842 the United States recognized the independence of Hawai'i, President Tyler noting that the

ʻLEI HOʻE LILIʻU LANI Eʻ   LILIʻUOK[...]

Kealakekua Bay must have reconsidered, for Cook was killed in a dispute over a missing boat.

Future immigrants would be more successful, notably Protestant missionaries from the New England States who arrived in 1820. Under the auspices of the American Board of Commissioners of Foreign Missions, more than a dozen companies of these missionaries journeyed to Hawaiʻi in the ensuing 35 years, 150 people in all. Among their ranks were ministers, doctors, teachers, printers, farmers, and businessmen. Led by Hiram Bingham, the Americans infiltrated key aspects of the Hawaiian society, with the blessing of the king and wide acceptance of the people. Hawaiians took well to these eastern influences. Missionaries and Hawaiians worked to establish a written language and translated the Bible and the dictionary to boot. A vibrant printing program ensued; two native-language newspapers were in circulation in 1834.

And in areas of government the missionaries helped establish democratic principles and served in key positions and promoted "reforms." One of these "reforms" would be the beginning of the end for the kingdom. "The Great Mahele of 1848" legally changed the Hawaiian tradition of land ownership. Now land could be held privately. For a people whose culture was based on community control of limited resources, individual ownership of the land was not well comprehended.

But the Americans and Europeans knew the principles of private property and soon most of the ancient lands of the Hawaiians became theirs. Essentially the Great Mahele privatized the royal authority over the island's property, and the foreigners bought it up cheap.

"They came here to do good, and stayed and did very well." This is how the Hawaiians have characterized the success of the missionaries.

Now the valleys and hillsides that grew taro, sweet potatoes, yams and bananas for the locals were converted to grow sugarcane for export for peoples thousands of miles away. The Hawaiian Islands yield some of the heaviest (and thus most valuable) sugarcane in the world.

With sugar unavailable from Louisiana during the War Between the States, the northern states began importing from Hawaiʻi and the boom was

islands are "the stopping place for almost all vessels passing from continent to continent across the Pacific Ocean. It cannot but be in conformity with the interest and wishes of the Government and the people of the United States that this community, thus existing in the midst of a vast expanse of ocean, should be respected and all its rights strictly and conscientiously regarded ..." Tyler told Congress.

Daniel Webster, then Secretary of State, formalized the recognition of independence in 1843.

English navigator Captain James Cook is credited as the first European to land on the islands, though the Spanish are believed to have visited earlier. Capt. Cook named them the Sandwich Islands after the Earl of Sandwich. Landing in 1778 on Kauai, the Hawaiians believed he was the god Lono. When he returned a year later, the Hawaiians near underway. When the United States permitted Hawaiian sugar to be imported duty-free by the Reciprocity Treaty of 1876, the kingdom was transformed into a giant producer nearly overnight. Production exploded from 13,000 tons in 1876 to 229,414 tons in 1898. By 1932, Hawaiian sugar production topped one million tons.

To work the cane fields, vast numbers of laborers were imported -- first Chinese "coolies" in 1852 and later tens of thousands from Puerto Rico, the Philippines, Japan, Portugal, and elsewhere. Immigration laws were relaxed around the same time private property was instituted, and the effects were devastating to the native islanders.

Several hundred thousand people are estimated to have occupied the islands in the 1700's. In 1832 the census showed 130,313 Hawaiians and a handful of foreigners. By 1900, the number of Hawaiians and part-Hawaiians was down to 37,656. The foreigners, most being workers in the fields, now numbered 116,345.

The interaction with the Americans and Europeans devastated the population in seen and unseen ways. As a central trading port the island was constantly being invaded by alien flora and fauna, not to mention human disease, transmitted by foreign ship crews intermingling with the local populations. Diseases foreign to their long-isolated environment destroyed much of the population.

In 1890 Hawaiian sugar plummeted in value as the U.S. set tariffs to aid Cuban farms and subsidize domestic production. To maintain the value of their investments, the businessmen realized, Hawai'i would have to become part of the United States. Only one obstacle blocked the sure prosperity of the planters and merchants: the constitutional government and Queen Liliuokalani. The last Hawaiian monarch, a talented poet and composer, ascended to the throne on the death of her brother, Kalakaua, in January, 1891.

Immediately Liliuokalani worked to re-establish royal authority and native rights lost when the elected Kalakaua had been forced to sign the "Bayonet Constitution" four years earlier. The newly formed "Hawai'i League" of influential businessmen, led by missionary Lorrin Thurston, pushed through this sham constitution.

OPPOSITE: A statue of Queen Liliuokalani stands between the Iolani Palace and the new Capitol. After being overthrown she lived at the governor's residence until her death in 1917.

ABOVE: Perspectives of Hawai'i's Capitol. Note the pool in the top photo and palm tree columns in the bottom, symbolizing the islands' rise above the Pacific as an oceanic state.

On January 16, 1893 between 4:00-5:00 p.m., the marines landed without resistance, no locals knowing what was afoot. One-hundred-sixty troops with two pieces of artillery set themselves up within 76 yards of the Iolani Palace. The next day, an American stood on the palace steps and announced the provisional government would manage Hawai'i until "terms of union with the United States had been negotiated and agreed upon."

Initially the whole affair went unnoticed by the people, Hawaiians and the non-native public alike. But Queen Liliuokalani knew the time had come. When Minister Stevens immediately recognized the illegal government on behalf of the United States, the Queen had little choice but to issue a surrender statement "to avoid any collision of armed forces, and perhaps loss of life."

It begins: "I, Liliuokalani, by the grace of God and under the constitution of the Hawaiian kingdom Queen, do hereby solemnly protest against any and all acts done against myself and the constitutional government ..."

On January 17 the conspirators proclaimed the new Provisional Government of Hawai'i and a number of them headed to Washington to conclude a treaty of annexation. In a dispatch to Washington February 1, 1893, Minister Stevens wrote: "The Hawaiian pear is now fully ripe, and this is the golden hour for the United States to pluck it." On February 14, Thurston, W.R. Castle, W.C. Wilder, C.L. Carter, and Joseph Marsden signed a treaty with the U.S. annexing the isles.

President Benjamin Harrison forwarded the treaty to the U.S. Senate, citing the "reactionary and revolutionary policy on the part of Queen Liliuokalani" who had made the monarchy "effete." "The influence and interest of the United States in the islands must be increased and not diminished," he declared. With only 30 days left in his term, Harrison urged fast action on the treaty. He didn't get it.

President Cleveland took office shortly after and withdrew the treaty from the Senate pending an investigation. Its findings led him to declare the treaty a fraud, saying both the Senate and President were misled to believe no U.S. force was used to overthrow the constitutional government of Hawai'i. "It is hardly necessary for me to state that the

Officially known as the "Constitution of 1887," it legalized the plutocracy. Liliuokalani devoted her reign to reversing its most negative aspects, notably the disenfranchisement of most of the Hawaiian natives. Governmental power resided in a cabinet of rich businessmen, each required to be a member of the Hawai'i League. Finally in 1893, she presented a new constitution and asked her hostile cabinet to sign it. They stalled and, shortly thereafter, executed the secret plan that would overthrow the government.

We know the details of this plan because U.S. President Grover Cleveland made public a presidential investigation from James Blount of Georgia.

Working closely with John L. Stevens, the U.S. minister to Hawai'i, the plotters implemented the *coup d'etat*. The Hawaiian League was converted into a "Committee of Safety" on January 14 and finalized plans for a provisional government. Meanwhile, the *U.S.S. Boston* lay in Honolulu harbor with marines aboard -- the great irony being that the warship is named after the city where the first missionaries departed years before.

ABOVE: From the floor of the House of Representatives.

OPPOSITE LEFT: The eternal flame honors Hawaiians who served in the armed services of the United States.

OPPOSITE RIGHT: The royal gates open to the new Capitol, which was required to be built in view of Iolani Palace.

questions arising from our relations with Hawai'i have caused serious embarrassment," Cleveland wrote in his State of the Union Address, 1893.

"Mr. Blount submitted to me his report, showing beyond all question that the constitutional Government of Hawai'i had been subverted with the active aid of our representative to that government and through the intimidation caused by the presence of an armed naval force of the United States, which was landed for that purpose at the insistence of our minister," reported the President.

"Upon the facts developed it seemed to me the only honorable course for our Government to pursue was to undo the wrong that had been done by those representing us and to restore as far as practicable the status existing at the time of our forcible intervention," he wrote.

That did not happen. Cleveland asked the queen to grant the conspirators a general amnesty. And he asked Sanford Dole, president of the new government, to restore the queen to her throne. Liliuokalani hesitated initially and Dole, who was born in Hawai'i of missionary parents, refused and helped create the Republic of Hawai'i in 1894.

President Cleveland recognized that government. Meanwhile, an armed revolt by the Hawaiians was put down with the arrest of Liliuokalani, who swore she knew nothing of the plans. No one was killed.

"Oh, honest Americans," the queen pleaded, "as Christians hear me for my downtrodden people! Their form of government is as dear to them as yours is precious to you."

She continued: "The people to whom your fathers told of the living God, and taught to call 'Father,' and whom the sons now seek to despoil and destroy, are crying aloud to Him in their time of trouble; and He will keep His promise, and will listen to the voices of His Hawaiian children lamenting for their homes."

The coup was complete. "My palace is my prison," the queen wrote. In 1896 she was moved to her residence at Washington Place where she remained until her death in 1917. Her passing ended a century of monarchy, which was descended from centuries of kingdoms back to ancient times.

In her book *Hawai'i's Story*, the Queen confessed: "It had not entered into our hearts to believe that these friends and allies from the United States ... would ever go so far as to absolutely overthrow our form of government, seize our nation by the throat, and pass it over to an alien power."

In Washington, meanwhile, the new Republic's men worked the U.S. Congress. Their lobbying, at

the time an unregulated activity, was aided by the Spanish-American War. The strategic importance of Hawai'i was underscored when its port proved to be indispensable to the United States' takeover of the Philippine Islands.

When Cleveland left office, President McKinley submitted the treaty of annexation but it was blocked by opponents. Later, with war just starting against Spain, Congress by joint resolution annexed Hawai'i to the United States in 1898.

The oligarchy was now secure. "The Big Five" companies -- Alexander & Baldwin, Theo H. Davis,

Castle & Cooke, C. Brewer, and Hackfield & Company -- asserted their dominance unhindered. Territorial government was established in 1900.

And with the United States it would remain a territory for sixty years, though its population was sufficient for statehood during annexation. This one-time independent nation was denied statehood 22 times by Congress, beginning with the first application and refusal in 1903.

In 1940, less than a year before Pearl Harbor was attacked, 67% of the inhabitants voted for statehood.

Iolani Palace, where kings and queens had ruled, served as the territorial, and later, the State Capitol. Built in 1883, it followed the design of Thomas J. Baker. For sixty-six years the Republic, Territorial, and State Legislature sat there. The Throne Room, used by the king to entertain ship captains, ambassadors, and businessmen, became the House of Representatives. The Senate was seated in the State Dining Room across from the Throne Room.

The palace stands today as a reminder of the royal past. While it was in service as legislative chambers, between breaks it was returned to the look of the

ABOVE & OPPOSITE: Hawaiʻi's Capitol is rich in symbolism, from the legislative chambers to the central open-air court. One enters the center of the Capitol without going inside, for it is "open to the sun and moon, rises to the sky like the throat of one of the volcanoes that help build this land," according to state literature. The Senate and House chambers are on opposite sides of the court and are entered from it. Each chamber is "cone-shaped, like volcanoes, symbolic of the geological origin of the Hawaiian Islands which rose upward from the sea floor over eons." The world's tallest mountain, measured base to peak, is Hawaiʻi's Mauna Kea. Though only 13,796 feet are visible, Mauna Kea rises 32,000 feet from its base in the Pacific. Mt. Everest rises 29,028 feet. Above Hilo Bay in eastern Hawaiʻi the rainfall is the heaviest anywhere in the world, some 100-250 inches a year.

old Throne Room for Hawaiians and visitors to see, according to state tour literature. The new Capitol was designed by Belt, Lemmon and Lo and John Carl Wernecke and Associates. It was dedicated in 1969. Rich in native symbolism, the Capitol was ordered to be placed within view of Iolani Palace.

On November 23, 1993 President William Clinton signed the "Apology Resolution" passed by the U.S. Congress in which that body directly "apologizes to Native Hawaiians on behalf of the people of the United States for the overthrow of the Kingdom of Hawai'i ... and the deprivation of the rights of Native Hawaiians to self-determination."

OPPOSITE: The royal Hawaiian coat-of-arms on an entrance gate on the Capitol grounds.

ABOVE: Iolani Palace, the original Hawaiian Capitol. In the center of the grounds is the statue of King Kamehameha. This is the only royal palace in the United States.

FOLLOWING PAGES: The House of Representatives. Note the chandelier, which is named "Sun" and is made of gold-plated copper and brass. The Senate's chandelier is named "Moon" and is made of polished aluminum and chambered nautilus shells. Otto Piene designed each. *(The House Chamber was being used to process recent election results when this picture was taken.)* *Right*, entrance to the Governor's office on the top floor.

LOUISIANA 1804

MISSOURI 1812

ARKANSAS 1819

FLORIDA 1826

IOWA 1838

OREGON 1843

WASHINGTON 1854

NEBRASKA 1854

KANSAS 1854

COLORADO 1861

IDAHO 1863

MONTANA 1864

WYOMING 1869

NORTH DAKOTA 1889

SOUTH DAKOTA 1889

OKLAHOMA 1890

ALASKA 1912

Purchased States

"... the First Consul of the French Republic, desiring to give to the United States a strong proof of friendship, doth hereby cede to the said United States, in the name of the French Republic, for ever and in full sovereignty, the said territory ... The inhabitants of the ceded territory shall be incorporated in the Union of the United States, and admitted as soon as possible, according to the principles of the Federal Constitution, to the enjoyment of all the rights, advantages, and immunities, of citizens of the United States ..."

-- From the treaty ceding Louisiana to the United States, made in 1803. The Louisiana Purchase, as the territory became known, encompassed 827,987 square miles from which fifteen states were made or enlarged. Other treaties acquired, through purchase or negotiation, four additional states.

Official Name: . . . . State of Louisiana
Motto: . . . . Union, Justice and Confidence
Citizen: . . . . Louisianian
Capital City: . . . . Baton Rouge, LA
Established: 1804
Joined Union: 1812
Left Union: 1861
Readmitted: 1868

Anthem: . . . . "Give Me Louisiana"
Name: . . . . The mouth of the Mississippi River was
given the name *La Louisianne* by the explorer La
Salle in honor of King Louis XIV of France
Nickname: . . Child of the Mississippi; Bayou State;
Sugar State; Pelican State
License Plate Slogan: . . . . Sportsman's Paradise
Total Area: . . . . 49,651 sq mi (31)

The State of
Louisiana

Union, Justice and Confidence

LOUISIANA

"The Father of Waters" is the nickname of the Mississippi, the greatest river of North America. In fact, if the Missouri and Mississippi Rivers were considered one, it would be the longest river in the world. The Mississippi cuts through the Mississippi Valley, the agricultural and industrial heart of the United States, to reach its destination: New Orleans and the Gulf of Mexico. It is here Louisiana's story begins.

The struggle of European powers for world dominance came to North America in the 1700's. Great Britain's colonies were ganged on the east coast. Spain held colonies in the south, from the Floridas to Mexico. France cultivated the vast areas of the north and mid-west. LaSalle first traversed the Mississippi River in 1682 and named the western lands it cut through "La Louisianne" in honor of King Louis XIV.

Thus in 1718 the Louisiana Province was drawn and later Sieur de Bienville established New Orleans as its capital, extending its reach into the Illinois country. But when Quebec fell to British troops in 1759 and Montreal in 1760, France was forced to surrender her possessions east of the Mississippi to Great Britain; the lands west, together with New Orleans, went to Spain.

Yet the inhabitants remained French-Americans. They kept their language, their culture, and their Roman Catholic religion. And they retained a fierce desire to remain independent. One group of settlers, known as the Acadians, lived in Nova Scotia and New Brunswick, Canada and numbered upwards of 10,000. When their capital Port Royal (where earlier in the century the French launched attacks against New England fishermen) fell to the British in 1755, they were given an ultimatum: swear allegiance to the British crown or leave. Most refused and were deported, some going to Quebec, but the majority found their way to present-day Louisiana.

Like the Acadians (corrupted to *Cajuns*), numerous other French settlers found their way to this haven on the Gulf of Mexico. By 1800 its population was the most diverse in North America. It included Creoles, the descendants of the original French and Spanish settlers, as well as thousands of free African-Americans. Well established on both sides of the lower Mississippi, the total population numbered some 50,000 including the province's slaves who worked in the sugarcane and cotton fields.

The people resisted the Spanish takeover. In 1768 they sent the newly-arrived Governor Ulloa packing and began organizing an independent republic. Spain ordered Alexander O'Reilly, an Irish officer in the Spanish army, to New Orleans with 3,000 soldiers. Instead of immediately using military force, the crafty O'Reilly made nice with the locals. Once he identified the key leaders of the movement, he invited them to a reception whereupon five were executed and the remainder sent to prison in Cuba. Spain was now in control of Louisiana.

And so it would be until 1800 when Napoleon regained the province for France in a secret treaty. The United States had passed its first Tariff Act in 1789, specifying that British and French vessels

LEFT: Part office tower, part ceremonial chamber, the Capitol is the first not to have a dome in the twentieth century.

ABOVE: The entrance frieze, one of the panels wrapping the building's base that details Louisiana's history and unique legal system.

PREVIOUS PAGES: The Capitol viewed from the park and at the steps. The statue at the entrance's left is titled *The Pioneers* by Lorado Taft. "We have lived long, but this is the noblest work of our whole lives ... From this day the United States take their place among the powers of the first rank ..." These words from Robert Livingston, spoken as he signed the Louisiana Purchase, are chiseled in stone at the entrance.

were to be taxed at the same rate. The French, upset that preferential treatment was not granted after helping the Americans beat the British, looked to other options. They saw New Orleans as a tariff-free port. The importance of that city now became manifest.

Preventing the dissolution of the American Republic was the principal motivation for the acquisition of New Orleans. President Jefferson believed that the developing states with Mississippi River access would ultimately be loyal to the authority which regulated shipping from New Orleans. Early on Kentuckians, Tennesseans, and even western Virginians and Pennsylvanians relied on the Mississippi and the New Orleans market for survival.

Initially, Jefferson wanted to buy only the Isle of Orleans (so named because of the lakes, rivers, and swamps that surround it) and West Florida for $2 million. Napoleon offered to sell that and all lands west of the Mississippi. The final price was $15 million, or four cents an acre. The "Louisiana Purchase" thus encompassed the territory between the Mississippi River and the Rocky Mountains, less than 1% of it settled at the time. Congress now divided the territory in two: north of the 32nd parallel became the District of Louisiana (later the Missouri Territory); south became the Territory of Orleans (present-day Louisiana).

This Territory of Orleans was already a distinct society. It wrapped the last 300 miles of the mighty Mississippi and became one with it, creating a unique community around the swampy banks and slow-moving bayous. The people did not take warmly to the United States anymore than they did to Spain. When an effort was made to introduce English-style legal proceedings over their French-based system, agitation for self-government began.

In 1805 a petition to the U.S. Congress demanded that the Territory of Orleans be made an independent state, in accordance with the Louisiana treaty. That request was denied, but Congress did permit the Orleans people to elect their own legislature and stipulated that once the territory's population reached 60,000, it could become a member state.

Debating Louisiana's entry as one of the United States in 1812, U.S. House Minority Leader Josiah Quincy of Massachusetts insisted the Constitution gave no power to acquire new territory. To do so without authorization was grounds for a state to leave the United States, he declared. The House of Representatives was in an uproar, this the first time disunion had been suggested in the chamber. Congressman Poindexter from Mississippi asked for a call to order, saying no one had the right to speak of dissolution of the United States. The Speaker of the House agreed and ruled such talk out of order. Quincy appealed, and in a vote 56-53, the Speaker was overruled.

Quincy said he "uttered the statement ... not for agitation, but as a warning ..." He asserted, and many believed, that the Founding Fathers never envisioned a republic extending beyond the Mississippi and the diminution of the Original States' power.

Despite the protests, the Congress authorized Louisiana to form itself into an independent state. And it approved the state's annexation of Spanish West Florida, which had declared its independence from Spain in 1810 and formed a republic. This would become the eastern portion of Louisiana.

However, Congress required Louisiana to guarantee trial by jury in criminal cases and make English

OPPOSITE: Stately Memorial Hall has in its center a bronze relief of Louisiana and its 64-parish subdivisions.

ABOVE: The statue *The Patriots* depicts a soldier with mourners of a dead combatant. It flanks the entrance's right side. Lorado Taft was commissioned to do this and *The Pioneers*; he was paid $50,000 per statue, according to the tour pamphlet.

the official language. The former requirement was necessary to conform the French-based Napoleonic Code, which the state operated under, to the federal constitution. Louisiana agreed to the conditions but retained her unique Spanish-French legal code because of the nature of the United States Constitution. That document established a republic of sovereign states to make a single nation, each state retaining all powers not delegated to the federal government.

Each of the Original States developed its own body of law separately while a colony and maintained that right with statehood. Not all embraced English common law, yet each was influenced by the notion of

precedent: that what a judge ruled in a previous case should be given weight in the present one. Simply stated, the English law of equity is judge-made law. Roman or civil law, which Louisiana's Code Napoleon operates under, looks not to judicial precedent but to the actual code passed by a legislature.

To this day, technically speaking, there is no single "American Law" nor has there ever been a common law of the United States as a sovereign state. Not even the U.S. Supreme Court is empowered to unify the legal doctrines in the separate states; instead, federal courts are required to use the laws of that state holding jurisdiction when hearing a case.

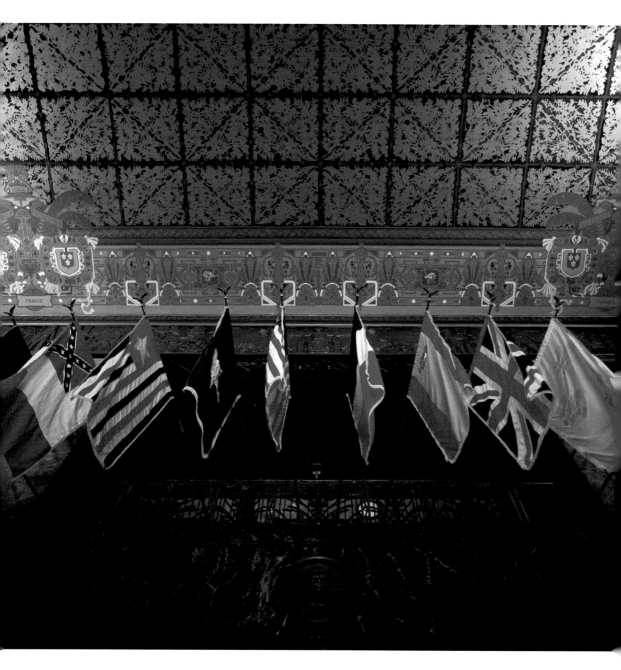

OPPOSITE LEFT: The entrance doors to the Senate Chamber are, like the House, made of bronze. Each door weighs one ton. The Senate doors feature scenes from Louisiana's rich past before it became one of the United States.

OPPOSITE CENTER & RIGHT: Sieur de Bienville, Louisiana's first governor who established New Orleans as its capital; *Right*, the benevolent Governor Allen, who held office during the Civil War.

ABOVE: Flags of the nations that have ruled Louisiana or some portion thereof are displayed in Memorial Hall. They include the flags of Castile and Leon; Bourbon France; Bourbon Spain; England; French tricolor; 15-star U.S. flag; Republic of West Florida's flag; Louisiana national flag; the Confederate States flag; Louisiana state flag; and modern U.S. flag.

Under the French, the people possessed little political power and still less under the Spanish. As a state, Louisiana went about the business of self-government under these influences. Legislative acts were printed in both French and English, a practice that would last until the War Between the States. The state reinstituted the parish system of subdivision used by the Catholic Church there (instead of the civilly-created county found elsewhere). And a strong governor -- a permanent feature of the colonial period -- was constitutionally provided for. Unlike other states, the Governor (with Senate approval) appointed all judges and local officials.

New Orleans remained the capital city until 1849 when the new Louisiana Capitol was completed in Baton Rouge. The building, a gothic castle that would be at home in medieval Europe, made physical the uniqueness of the state. And so would its next, and present, Capitol.

In the midst of the depression in the 1930's, Governor Huey P. Long, who won office on the promise to make each citizen a king, lobbied for new governmental quarters. Once approved, construction was completed in March, 1932, just fourteen months from groundbreaking. The result was a modern, skyscraper-like monument, the tallest in America. Long did not live long to enjoy it; he was assassinated inside the Capitol in 1935.

The Louisiana Capitol is set in a 55-acre park located on the Mississippi River. Sugarcane grows nearby, and the petrochemical industries make their presence known. Standing 450 feet high with 34 floors, the Capitol is faced in Alabama limestone. At the 22nd floor, the square tower becomes an octagon. Four winged figures, representing Law, Science, Philosophy, and Art, guard the corners. At the base begins a grand staircase of 48 steps, one for each of the United States, placed in order of their entry into the union. (Alaska and Hawai'i were added to the top step, which originally only had carved *E Pluribus Unum*.)

The interior was made with marble from Vermont and Italy. Throughout the building the Pelican, Louisiana's symbol, appears. Upon entering the building one steps into Art Deco-styled Memorial Hall where a large bronze-relief map of Louisiana details the state's 64 parishes. To the left of the Hall is the Senate Chamber; to the right is the House Chamber, each Chamber featuring bronze-relief doors.

Designed by Weiss, Dreyfous & Seiferth, the building's style is termed "modern classic." When completed it drew attention because it lacked a dome, the first state capitol not to have one in the twentieth century.

By now, however, this was to be expected: Louisianians always did things a little differently.

ABOVE: The Louisiana House of Representatives Chamber. The Louisiana Legislature is bicameral and all members serve four-year terms. The Senate has 39 members; the House of Representatives has 105 members.

OPPOSITE: The Senate Chamber wall features many kinds of stone; the desks are of walnut and Australian laurel wood. The ceiling is made of Celotex which comes from bagasse, a by-product of sugar production.

TOP LEFT: Memorial Hall looking towards the Senate Chamber.

TOP RIGHT: The doors to the House of Representatives Chamber are made of bronze and depict life after statehood in relief.

ABOVE: A ceiling mural in Memorial Hall recalls Louisiana's membership in the Confederate States of America.

OPPOSITE: Ceiling mural of the United States shield over the U.S. Navy and War Department emblems recalls the U.S. military occupation of Louisiana after the War Between the States.

FOLLOWING PAGES: A ceiling mural of the earliest authority over the lands of Louisiana. *Right*, a front perspective of the Senate Chamber.

"We, the representatives of the people of all that part of the Territory or county ceded under the name of Louisiana ... in order to secure to all the citizens thereof the enjoyment of the rights of life, liberty, and property, do ordain and establish the following constitution ... and do mutually agree with each other to form ourselves into a free and independent State, by the name of the State of Louisiana." -- CONSTITUTION OF LOUISIANA, 1812

Official Name: .... State of Missouri
Motto: .... Salus Populi Suprema Lex Esto
Citizen: .... Missourian
Capital City: .... Jefferson City, MO
Established: 1812
Joined Union: 1821

Anthem: .... "Missouri Waltz"
Name: The name of the Missouri natives, meaning "canoe possessor;" also given to the river they traversed
Nickname: .... Show Me State; Cave State
License Plate Slogan: .... Show Me State
Total Area: .... 69,709 sq mi (21)

The State of

Missouri

Salus Populi Suprema Lex Esto |
The Welfare of the People Shall Be the Supreme Law

Three of the worst earthquakes ever to strike North America hit the heart of the continent in 1811-12. Each is estimated to have been well over 8 on the Richter scale; fortunately few lived near the line of death. But people did live in the territory where the ground split in two. And from this same ground during that same time came the first tremors of a schism that separated and destroyed not rock, but a great family. That spewed not dirt and stones, but blood and bones.

MISSOURI

This is the story of Missouri's beginning.

When President Thomas Jefferson bought the Louisiana Territory from France, St. Louis -- the capital of Upper Louisiana -- was already 39 years old and many communities were established in the interior of the present-day state. Slave labor was employed by the French to extract lead from the region's mines. In 1812 the Territory of Missouri was created and six years later the people petitioned for statehood. But to gain entry into the Union, two bargains were struck and a new border drawn.

When the United States assumed control, slaveholder and non-slaveholder alike lived in Missouri. Large migrations from the Original States and Charter States made for a diverse population. Missourians expected to join the United States without condition, just as Kentucky, Tennessee, Mississippi, and Alabama had years before. But some raised an issue broached in the Continental Congress during the drafting of the Declaration of Independence in 1776: namely, what is slavery's place in a community of liberty-loving states?

Northern congressmen wanted to prohibit the importation of new slaves into Missouri and free children of slaves who turned 25. When these attempts failed, a new idea was put forth: prohibit slavery in all territories north of 36° 30', which was Missouri's

southern border, exempting Missouri of course. This was a continuation of Virginia's chartered southern border that ran across Kentucky's bottom, under the Mississippi, and on past Missouri to present-day Utah.

This was approved, marking the first time United States law divided the republic into two separate spheres. An actual border between two distinct worlds was now legislated. Up until this "Missouri Compromise," each state separately dealt with the injustice of the ancient practice of slavery. Many had outlawed the immoral system. Over a period of several decades numerous Missourians worked diligently on a program of emancipation and education of the state's slaves.

Now, instead of a union of equal states, the republic was to be of different states. An aging Jefferson said the drawing of such a line splitting the republic was like a fire bell in the night.

"I regret that I am now to die in the belief that the useless sacrifice of themselves by the generation of 1776, to acquire self-government and happiness to their country is to be thrown away by the unwise

ABOVE: The state seal is found on the portico's ceiling.

PREVIOUS PAGES & OPPOSITE: Perspectives of the Missouri Capitol. Overlooking the Missouri River, the Capitol measures 437 feet x 300 feet. The dome rises 262 feet from the basement floor. On top is Ceres, goddess of agriculture with one hand holding a sheaf of grain and the other held outstretched, blessing the state.

and unworthy passions of their sons, and that my only consolation is to be that I live not to weep over it," he wrote in a letter.

The Congress required Missourians to revise their constitution, which had ordered the legislature to keep freed slaves out of the state. Missouri had to promise she would never impair the rights of citizens from other states. She did, and the State of Missouri was born. And it thrived, though built over the fault line of state rights. Her diverse economy boomed. Caravans brought thousands of mules

from Santa Fe for the state's extensive mule trade, along with products and other goods. Wildlife was plentiful: some 250,000 buffalo were killed in 1848 alone and 25,000 buffalo tongues were shipped to St. Louis. In 1860 over 5,000 steamboat vessels docked at that city. Now Missouri's population had reached

1,182,000 of which 144,000 were slaves and 29,000 were masters. By the time of the Civil War, the slave population had increased tenfold since 1820; emancipation efforts within the state bore no fruit.

Missouri, the offspring of now-warring parents, was like a child, with the mind of her father and the heart of her mother. And a love for both. The northern states needed a strong national government for the protection of their multi-state economic interests; the southern states needed strong state governments and a compliant federal authority for the maintenance of order in their slave-based agriculture. Missourians embraced both economic systems and wished to be left alone during the messy divorce proceedings.

And then the first shock wave struck. The Missouri Legislature called for a Convention of the People to meet February 28, 1861 and decide whether Missouri should remain one of the United States or become independent as some southern states had done. The people elected delegates, who in turn met in convention with the solemn formality the function demanded. Finally a vote was taken: *Missourians voted to stay in the Union.* The state, the people decided, should remain neutral in the conflict, and a call was made for a Convention of the States to settle all differences peacefully.

When President Lincoln called for troops to keep by force those states in the Union whose people decided differently from Missouri, Governor Claiborne Jackson refused. "Your requisition, in my judgement," he wrote the President, "is illegal, unconstitutional, and revolutionary ..."

The good governor then proceeded to secure the state's armory, but federal troops quickly seized

possession of it. Now Jackson embarked on his own illegal and unconstitutional activities. Acting against the will of the Missouri Convention he was supposed to enforce, he fled Jefferson City and commanded the state militia against invading federal forces.

ABOVE: The Missouri Senate Chamber.

OPPOSITE: Resting on the south bank of the Missouri River (the principal means into the Louisiana Territory) is a monument to the Louisiana Purchase entitled *The Signing of the Treaty*. It was made by Karl Bitter.

Though it wanted to remain neutral in the War Between the States, Missouri was now confronted with its own civil war and two competing state governments. Governor Jackson and elements of the legislature, meeting in Neosho, voted to secede and join the Confederacy. The original People's Convention had already reconvened, fired Jackson, appointed a provisional state government and appealed for aid from the United States. Jackson, Sterling Price and tens of thousands of other Missourians who tied their fate to the southern confederacy ultimately lost with that cause.

Thomas Jefferson, after whom Missouri named its capital city and graced the Capitol entrance with a statue of him titled *Patria*, would have surely wept at the destruction of the United States. But he would have been proud of his children in Missouri. For in the face of an overwhelming struggle outside its borders, the people peacefully met and decided to remain a member of his cherished republic and neutral among the combatants.

And Jefferson would love what the Missourians have done with their Capitol.

"Missouri's State Capitol is a monument to her citizens," declares the pamphlet *Missouri State Capitol* from the Dept. of Natural Resources, noting its dominance of the skyline of Jefferson City. It "is literally a museum of public art, remarkable not only for its quality and abundance, but as a reflection of the themes, events and people of Missouri," the publication continues.

The architectural firm of Tracy and Swartwout of New York was selected from 68 submissions in a national competition. The Capitol was designed in

the Roman Renaissance style. Native limestone from Carthage faces the exterior.

It is the third Capitol in the city: the previous two (the first, 1826-1837; the second, 1840-1911) were destroyed by fire. The Capitol's destruction February 5, 1911 is considered "one of the most spectacular fires in Missouri's history," the tour pamphlet notes. Construction on a new building commenced immediately after the fire with the groundbreaking May 6, 1913 and laying of the cornerstone June 24, 1915. The Capitol was completed in 1918. Dedication was made October 6, 1924.

OPPOSITE & ABOVE: A bronze chandelier hangs from the eye of the dome. British painter Frank Brangwyn shipped the mural panels that dominate the Rotunda from his studios in England. In the center of the dome he painted four figures that represent Agriculture, Commerce, Science and Education. Other murals show the four periods of Missouri's development: the discovery by Pierre Laclede in 1764; the pioneer movements; the settlement age; and the modern age. The natural elements of earth, water, air, and fire are shown in the dome's lower areas.

LORD GOD OF HOSTS BE WITH US YET-LEST WE FORGET

OPPOSITE TOP & MIDDLE: Perspective of the dome and pediment. Missouri is an enthroned woman in the center of the Capitol's pediment, designed along with the other figures by Adolph A. Weinman. Her left arm rests on a shield bearing the state's coat-of-arms. The figure to her right is a boy holding a winged globe which represents the spirit of progress, according to the souvenir guide to the Missouri Capitol.

OPPOSITE BOTTOM: Perspective of the Rotunda.

TOP: Looking up into the eye of the dome.

ABOVE: An inscription on a wall adjacent to the Rotunda.

"We, the people of Missouri ... by our representatives in convention assembled at Saint Louis ... do mutually agree to form and establish a free and independent republic, by the name of the State of Missouri, and for the government thereof do ordain and establish this constitution ..." -- MISSOURI CONSTITUTION, 1820

ABOVE: Using $1 million in revenues from a special Capitol property tax levied on Missourians, the state gathered a team of notable artists to decorate the interior. This team included N.C. Wyeth, James E. Fraser, sculptor Alexander S. Calder, and British painter Frank Brangwyn. Their combined work presents in glass, statues, carvings and murals the story of Missouri, including this stained-glass window in the House Chamber. The House walls detail the elements of a noble society: liberty, equality, law, justice, fraternity, progress, honor, truth, virtue, and charity.

OPPOSITE TOP: *The Glory of Missouri In Peace* is a magnificent stained-glass mosaic with Missouri sitting on a throne, surrounded by Commerce, Mining, and Agriculture on her left and Justice, Art and Science on her right, according to the tour booklet. It dominates the front of the House Chamber. *Missouri At War* (not shown) is the unofficial name of the Charles Hoffbauer painting that depicts Missouri soldiers fighting in France in World War I. Hoffbauer was a noted French artist who was appreciative of the Missourians' assistance in that great struggle. *Social History of Missouri* (not shown) by native Thomas Hart Benton in 1935 is a mural on four walls in the House Lounge depicting life in the state.

OPPOSITE MIDDLE: Perspectives of the House of Representatives Chamber. The House's 163 members serve two-year terms.

OPPOSITE BOTTOM: The Senate Chamber, meeting place of the state's 34 senators. It features a portrait of U.S. General John Joseph Pershing, one of Missouri's famous citizens, and the Commander of the American Forces in World War I.

LEFT: The Thomas Jefferson Statue is placed on the front steps of the Missouri Capitol. His achievements -- third President of the United States, author of the Declaration of Independence, and Father of the Louisiana Purchase -- are carved in marble.

TOP: The state seal in the House of Representatives.

OPPOSITE: A perspective at the base of the Capitol steps.

ABOVE: Ten Commandments marble marker on the Capitol grounds was given to Missouri by the state's Aerie Fraternal Order of Eagles in 1958.

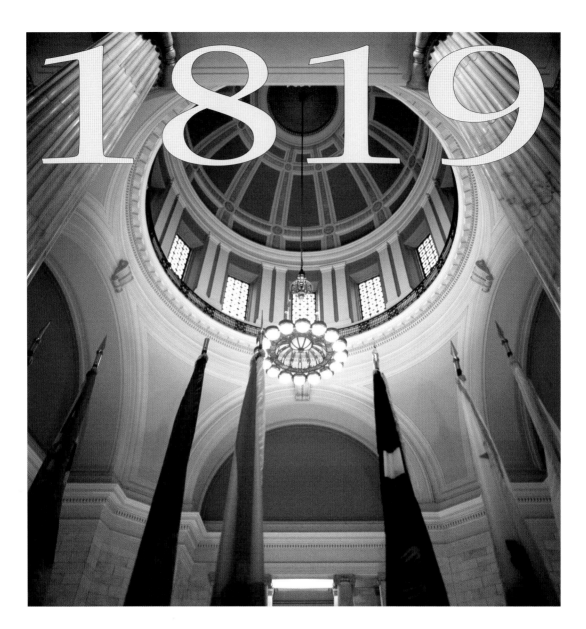

Official Name: . . . . State of Arkansas
Motto: . . . . Regnat Populus
Citizen: . . . . Arkansan
Capital City: . . . . Little Rock, AR
Established: 1819
Joined Union: 1836
Left Union: 1861

Readmitted: 1868
Anthem: . . . . "Arkansas"
Name: . . . From the French pronunciation of "Kansas," the Algonkin name for the Quapaw natives
Nickname: . . . . N/A
License Plate Slogan: . . . . The Natural State
Total Area: . . . . 53, 182 sq mi (28)

The State of
Arkansas

Regnat Populus | The People Rule

ARKANSAS

A duchy is a type of state in which a duke or duchess possesses sovereign power over a territory and people. Such noblemen held the highest position in society and from their ranks monarchs were drawn. Common in Europe, they were much less so in America where a spirit of liberty prevailed, and where finally sovereignty would be understood as emanating not from a royal class of nobles but from each person in a society.

But there were duchies in America, and none more famous than the Duchy of Arkansas.

Present-day Arkansas came into the possession of the United States as part of the Louisiana Purchase in 1803. In 1812 it became a county of the Territory of Missouri, and seven years later it achieved separate territorial status. In 1836 Arkansas became one of the United States.

Palatinate in Germany. Confidence among colonizers and investors alike was high, for Law had the power, so to speak, to turn paper into gold.

Law built France's state bank on a system of paper money, establishing the principle that money's value is not an objective standard measurable in gold or silver, but rather value that is agreed upon by the people using it. So many people benefitted from investing in his projects that a new word had to be created for them. That word was *millionaire*.

More than a century before, all that existed in the region was Arkansas Post, a French settlement founded in 1686. It was here that Scottish financier John Law, in service to the French government, established the Duchy of Arkansas with himself as Duke: In 1719-20 Law brought 1,000 colonists and slaves to Arkansas Post to begin farming the land. The duchy drew slave-holding colonists from the

Unfortunately the good times for Law and many wealthy people in France came to an end when the bubble burst, and with them, the Duchy of Arkansas. The settlers retreated to New Orleans.

Visitors to Arkansas Post and the surrounding lands were taken by the varied plant life and geography. Even to this day vast forests make up more than half of the state, holding no fewer than 130 species of tree. Arkansas is also famous for its springs -- ancient marvels, the most notable in Hot Springs where the water bubbles from the mountain at a temperature of 135 degrees. The springs are created when water seeps into the deep, subterranean depths of the earth to come into contact with

ABOVE: Arkansas State Seal on a wooded dais in the foyer.

OPPOSITE: Front perspective of the Capitol.

PREVIOUS PAGES: Looking up into the Rotunda. *Right*, the Arkansas Diamond Flag (the diamond in the center represents the fact that Arkansas is the only American State with diamond mines) flies at the Capitol.

contact with burning rock. Rain that collects in a great basin between the mountains falls to these depths, is heated to boiling, rises through the rock crevices as steam, and condenses back to water. The result is some of the purest, warmest water on earth that has attracted visitors for centuries.

The hot waters of power and greed burned Law. But what he could not make work, others did -- not as a duchy, but as an American State where the people are sovereign. The first elected legislature of Arkansas met in 1819 in temporary quarters. Soon the

representatives of the people desired a permanent place to conduct business, so Governor John Pope, a noted Kentuckian, spearheaded the drive for a new "Territorial Assembly Building" in 1833.

The design of the first Capitol followed that of an ancient temple. This was to be a temple of sovereignty. Based on a design by Gideon Shryock, it was completed in 1840 and stands to this day, though it was replaced by a new Capitol. Ground was broken on Independence Day, 1899 for the new temple, but it would take sixteen years and two different

architects before the edifice was completed. It was designed by St. Louis architect George R. Mann in the neo-classical style. He was later fired, along with the contractors, amid accusations of bribery.

Though only a few people were actually indicted (Mann was not), Governor George Donaghey opted for a fresh start and hired Cass Gilbert (1859-1934) to finish the job. (Gilbert designed the West Virginia Capitol and Minnesota Capitol). The dome was not completed when Mann was fired. In working with Gilbert, Governor Donaghey suggested the Arkansas Capitol be topped with a dome similar to that of

ABOVE LEFT: The Rotunda in the Arkansas Capitol.

ABOVE RIGHT: Special recognition in the Rotunda is made of Arkansas Governor William Jefferson Clinton, the 42nd President of the United States and native of the state.

OPPOSITE: A barrel vault mural, one of four in the Capitol, was painted by native Paul Heerwagon.

Mississippi. Gilbert obliged, not knowing that Mann had in fact designed the Mississippi dome.

The Capitol cost $2.2 million. It measures 440 feet long by 190 feet wide. The dome top is 213 feet from the ground. The giant front brass doors, six in all, were purchased by Gilbert from Tiffany's in New York for $10,000. They are four inches thick.

He also purchased the twelve-foot chandelier for the Rotunda and smaller ones for the legislative chambers.

The lawmaking powers of the state are vested in the Arkansas General Assembly which has a Senate of thirty-five members, each serving four-year terms; and a House of Representatives of 100 members, each serving two-year terms. One senator represents 65,000 citizens, while one representative answers to 23,000.

The General Assembly first met in the new Capitol in 1911, and has met there every other year to conduct its regular legislative business in accordance with the state constitution.

OPPOSITE & FOLLOWING: The House of Representatives Chamber in the evening, business for the day having just concluded. Arkansas' unique government system breaks the state into 75 counties, each headed by a county judge. This government is established through the state constitution, which was first written in 1836. It declares: "We, the people of the Territory of Arkansas, by our representatives in convention assembled ... having the right of admission into the Union as one of the United States of America ... and by virtue of the treaty of cession, by France to the United States, of the Province of Louisiana ...do mutually agree with each other to form ourselves into a free and independent State ..."

ABOVE: Looking straight into the eye of the dome from which a two-ton chandelier hangs.

ABOVE: Arkansas Senate Chamber.

FOLLOWING PAGES: Looking up to the House Chamber entrance from the Rotunda; *Right*, a front perspective of the Capitol.

1826

Official Name: .... State of Florida
Motto: .... In God We Trust
Citizen: .... Floridian
Capital City: .... Tallahassee, FL
Established: 1826
Joined Union: 1845
Left Union: 1861
Readmitted: 1868

Anthem: .... "Old Folks At Home" ("Swanee River")
Name: ... Ponce de Leon named the land *La Florida* when he landed on Easter Sunday, 1513 in recognition of Pascua Florida, the Spanish holiday "Flowering Easter"
Nickname: .... Sunshine State; The Orange State
License Plate Slogan: .... Sunshine State
Total Area: .... 59,928 sq mi (23)

The State of

Florida

In God We Trust

F lorida is a state outsiders migrate to and, once there, rarely ever leave. It was discovered by those seeking the Fountain of Youth 500 years ago. Today Florida's healthful
climate is enjoyed by older Northerners in search of their second life. Like its population, Florida is old. St. Augustine was founded in 1565, making it the oldest continuous European settlement in the United States -- some 40 years before Jamestown, Virginia was
founded. Florida was much bigger when it was a Spanish province. At the beginning of the
eighteenth century, it stretched from St. Augustine to Baton Rouge and down to the Keys.

FLORIDA

With Columbus' second visit to the Caribbean in 1493 came Ponce de Leon, who became Governor of Puerto Rico. In 1513 he landed near present-day St. Augustine on Easter Sunday and named the land Florida in honor of Pascua Florida. Part of his mission was to find the fabled Fountain of Youth spoken of by the natives. So taken with the Eden-like qualities of the Americas in general, the Spanish believed such a fount possible. He did not find it, but he did claim North America for Spain.

The Spanish Empire, at its height, encompassed vast portions of South and Central America, as well as southern North America. It stretched across the Pacific to the Philippine Islands near China. From the conquered the Spanish conquistadors plundered gold and valuables, placed the treasure on Spanish ships, and sent them home. On this journey the ships passed the strategic peninsula known as Florida.

That gold indirectly helped to develop the American economy. Today's U.S. dollar is descended from the Spanish dollar, pieces of eight and the *peso duro* ("hard dollar"). These coins were widely used in the Original States, before and after the American Revolution, because Great Britain restricted hard currency in her colonies.

With the Spanish settlers came another invaluable commodity: the seeds of various fruits (including oranges) that engendered Florida's great agricultural wealth.

Hostilities between Florida and its neighbors Georgia, South Carolina, and Louisiana were constant in the eighteenth century. By the Treaty of 1763, Spain relinquished Florida to England in return for Cuba. The British divided Florida into two

TOP RIGHT: The Old Capitol, now a museum.

TOP LEFT: The state seal is incorporated in a mural at the new Capitol's lower entrance foyer.

OPPOSITE: A rounded mural details Florida's history at the entrance of the Senate Chamber.

PREVIOUS PAGES: The Old Capitol, as it is known, was built in 1845 in Tallahassee -- the meeting spot in between the capital cities of two distinct provinces, St. Augustine (East Florida) and Pensacola (West Florida). *Right,* in the back of the Old Capitol Florida built its present one, photographed at the entrance looking up the tower. Title to the lands now known as Tallahassee were presented as a gift to Marquis de Lafayette from the U.S. Congress. The 1824 present was for his contributions in the American Revolution. He died before he could retire to Florida.

provinces, East Florida and West Florida. Throughout the American Revolution, the Floridas remained, like Canada, loyal to Britain.

In fact, the Castillo de San Marcos in St. Augustine served as a prison for several of the signers of the Declaration of Independence. When the British lost the war, Spain was given the peninsula once again, but ruling it again proved difficult.

France purchased West Florida in 1795 and a portion passed to the United States with the Louisiana Purchase, though much controversy surrounded exact borders. Some West Floridians remaining under Spain's authority rebelled against Spanish misrule. Backed by the area's notorious "filibusters," or buccaneers, they plundered Spanish ships and possessions.

In 1810 the West Florida Republic was born. Delegates meeting in Baton Rouge drafted a Declaration of Independence and Constitution for the "State of Florida." It was short-lived. The western part of this republic was incorporated into the State of Louisiana in 1812 by the U.S. Congress, and the remaining territory became part of Mississippi and Alabama.

The United States thought little of its southern neighbor. "Adventurers from every country, fugitives from justice, and absconding slaves have found an asylum there," reported President James Monroe to Congress in 1818.

"Several tribes of Indians, strong in the number of their warriors, remarkable for their ferocity, and whose settlements extend to our limits, inhabit those Provinces. These different hordes of people, connected together, disregarding on the one side the authority of Spain, and protected on the other by an imaginary line which separates Florida from the United States ... committed every kind of outrage on our peaceable citizens

which their proximity to us enabled them to perpetrate," continued President Monroe.

He ordered General Andrew Jackson into Florida's present-day Leon County to expel the Seminoles and others who provided safety to (and sometimes married) runaway slaves from Georgia and the Carolinas.

A year after these military incursions into Spanish East Florida, the peninsula was ceded to the U.S. by a weakened Spain. The deal called for $5 million to be paid to American claimants having suits against Spain. No direct payment was made to Spain.

A unified territorial government for Florida was formed in 1822 by Congress, with a governor and a legislative council of 13 citizens -- all appointed by the President. Four years later, Floridians were

given the right to elect their lawmakers, a right denied them for 261 years.

Florida's development to this point was largely focused on the coasts and borders; native populations occupied the central lands and its fertile ground. The Seminole (translated "runaways") descended from the Creek natives of Georgia and Alabama and lived with other Florida native groups who jointly took the name "Seminole." The U.S. offered these people lands in Oklahoma in 1832, and some accepted.

But many other Seminoles refused to leave, including their guiding spirit, Chief Osceola. The son of a Creek woman and European trader, Osceola fled to Florida after the Creek Wars. He fought authorities only after his wife was seized as a fugitive slave. War raged between the Seminoles and federal troops for seven years; it ultimately cost $20 million and the lives of 1,500 American soldiers before the remaining Seminoles fled to the swamps of the Everglades where their descendants live to this day.

OPPOSITE: One of two entrance murals.

ABOVE: The Old Capitol appears anchored to the new one.

It was the longest and costliest native war in the history of the United States.

Osceola was tricked while negotiating under a flag of truce with General Thomas Jesup. He was arrested and sent to Fort Moultrie in South Carolina where he later died. The trickery violated military protocol and outraged Americans, who sympathized with Osceola and admired his bravery. Several towns and counties in Florida today bear his name.

The Seminole now suppressed and the buccaneers outlawed, Florida was admitted into the United States on March 3, 1845. Tallahassee, county seat of Leon County, was made the territorial capital in 1823, replacing St. Augustine for the honor. The Florida Legislature accepted a plan by Col. Robert Butler, the state's surveyor-general, for a Capitol, according to state documents. This was to be built in three parts; the first wing was authorized in 1825. Work languished; in 1839 the state received $20,000 from Congress for government buildings. The old wing and unfinished walls were replaced with a new structure. It was completed the year statehood was proclaimed.

The original building did not follow the temple model of Capitol; the columns were placed on the building's sides and not its ends. There was no dome. It was made of plastered brick. A dome and wings with Beaux-Arts detailing were later added.

The present Capitol, built behind the old one, continues the tradition of uniqueness. A 22-story tower rising 514 feet above sea level divides the legislative branches: the House of Representatives on the north end, the Senate on the south. The finished structure cost $45,000,000.

The designer of this towering symbol of sovereignty is famous for his Kennedy Center in Washington, DC, the General Motors Building in New York, and the U.S. Embassy in India. Edward Durell Stone & Associates teamed with the Jacksonville firm of Reynolds, Smith and Hills in 1969 to design the new complex. It was completed August 19, 1977.

"For those of us who work here are only tenants," Governor Reubin Askew said at the dedication. "We do not own the building. So I think we should dedicate this building to the owners."

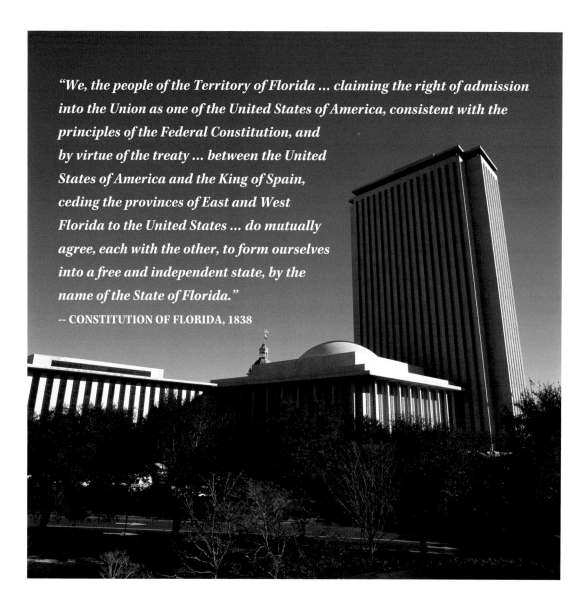

"We, the people of the Territory of Florida ... claiming the right of admission into the Union as one of the United States of America, consistent with the principles of the Federal Constitution, and by virtue of the treaty ... between the United States of America and the King of Spain, ceding the provinces of East and West Florida to the United States ... do mutually agree, each with the other, to form ourselves into a free and independent state, by the name of the State of Florida."

-- CONSTITUTION OF FLORIDA, 1838

OPPOSITE: The Senate on the day of the opening of the Florida Legislature, November 21, 2000.

ABOVE: The Florida Capitol as seen from the balcony of city hall. The difference in size between the old and new capitols is testimony to the tremendous growth in population. Ponce de Leon may never have found the Fountain of Youth here, but 500 years later senior citizens from throughout North America find the Peninsula State's climate to be the next best thing to such a tonic. And the population continues to grow. Tourists from the northeast have been traveling to Florida since the 1850's.

FOLLOWING PAGES: The House of Representatives on its opening November 21, 2000 at the height of the Bush-Gore presidential election controversy. Rumors swirled that the Florida Legislature would exercise its rights delineated in the U.S. Constitution and settle the dispute itself. According to that document, each state's legislature ultimately speaks for the state's body politic in determining how presidential electors are selected. The legislature decided to leave the matter to the courts and not exercise its powers. *Right*, the flags of Florida and the United States join the MIA banner over the Old Capitol.

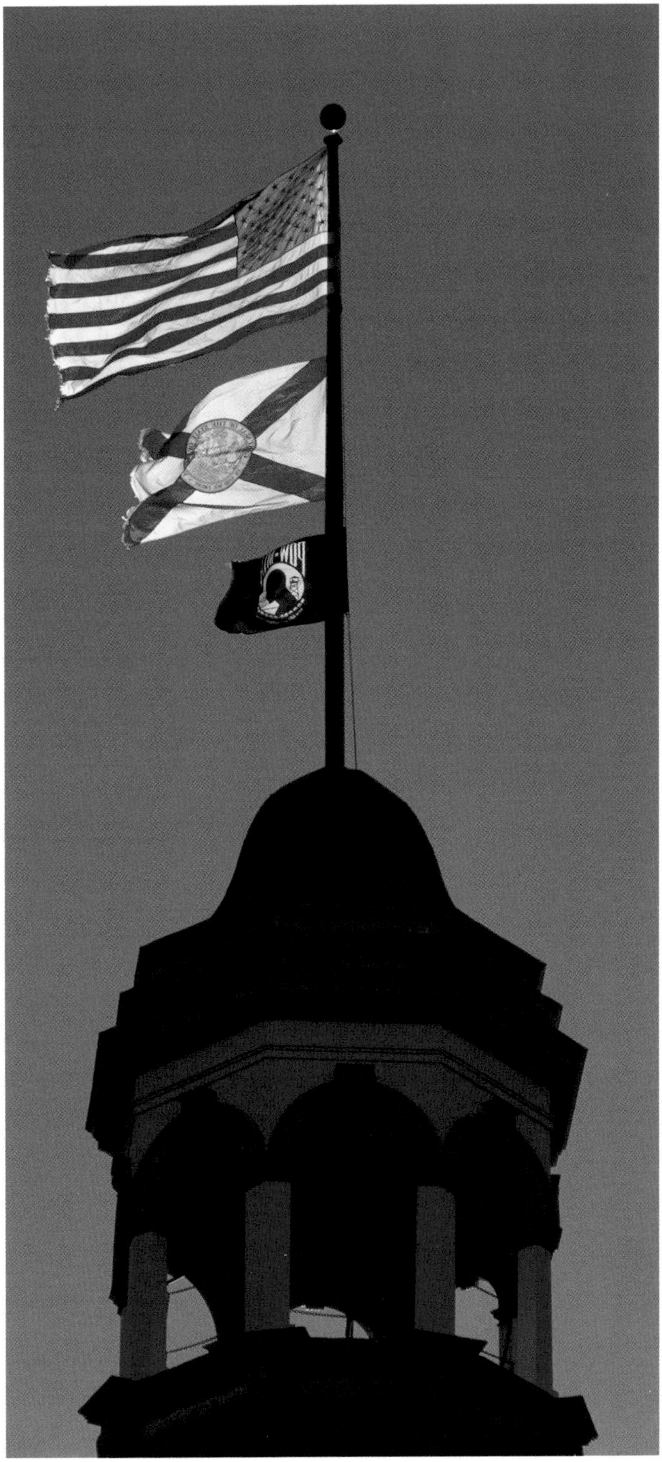

Official Name: . . . . State of Iowa

Motto: . . Our Liberties We Prize, and Our Rights We Will Maintain

Citizen: . . . . Iowan

Capital City: . . . . Des Moines, IA

Established: 1838

Joined Union: 1846

Anthem: . . . . "The Song of Iowa"

Name: . . . . The Iowa natives called themselves *ayuxwa*; this was corrupted by the English to "ioway" and by the French to "ayoua"

Nickname: . . . . Hawkeye State

License Plate Slogan: . . . . N/A

Total Area: . . . . 56,276 sq mi (26)

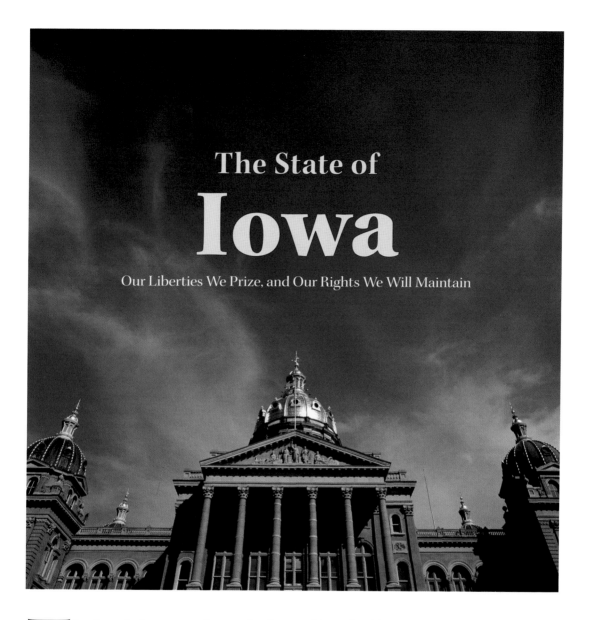

The State of
Iowa

Our Liberties We Prize, and Our Rights We Will Maintain

T he domain known today as the State of Iowa had been under the jurisdiction of France, then Spain, then France again, who sold what was then known as Ioway to the United States as part of the Louisiana Purchase in 1803. Under the control of the U.S. Congress, Iowa was made a part of the Missouri Territory, the Michigan Territory, and the Wisconsin Territory successively. It's no wonder that when Iowans finally turned to the business of governing themselves, the state's borders were in doubt. Soon a boundary dispute erupted with Missouri that brought the two neighbors to the brink of war. It would result in Iowans rejecting statehood to defend their territorial claims.

IOWA

Moines River west to the Missouri River. It encompassed over 2,500 square miles. When a Missouri man cut down valuable bee trees in this disputed region, Iowa authorities ordered him to pay a fine.

In 1839 the Governor of Missouri declared his state sovereign over the area and dispatched a sheriff to collect taxes. The people there, believing themselves Iowans, in turn captured the sheriff.

War was imminent. Missouri ordered up its state militia to report to the border. Iowa, still a territory and without a formal militia, organized its first for the purpose of defending the southern claim.

Each state raised over a thousand troops, and the "Honey War," as it became known, was ready to begin.

Iowa and Missouri were replaying the earlier American border conflicts (Connecticut vs. Pennsylvania, New York vs. Vermont; Michigan vs. Ohio; Florida vs. Georgia). Fortunately nothing happened in this one, and a political solution was sought instead.

The matter with Missouri wasn't the only border conundrum facing the Iowans. Governor Robert Lucas also claimed what today is southeastern Minnesota and declared the Missouri River to be Iowa's

The Grand Divide is a vast stretch of land in which a road known as the "Bee Trace" (now US 63) accommodated natives and later Americans in search of honey -- the only widely available sweetener on the frontier. Honeybees were introduced in North America by Europeans in 1638. So well did the honeybee take to the Grand Divide that wild bee trees were regularly harvested by settlers looking to satisfy their sweet tooth and for candle wax. This part of America truly was a land of milk and honey.

Iowa and Missouri both claimed a portion of the Grand Divide, an 11-mile strip between the Des

PREVIOUS PAGES: A Senate Chamber ceiling mural shows the recording of Iowa's history; *Right*, a perspective of the Capitol.

ABOVE: Looking across the Senate Chamber.

RIGHT: A side perspective of the Iowa Capitol.

OPPOSITE: Statues in the Rotunda by S. Cottin represent History, Science, Law, Fame, Literature, Industry, Peace, Commerce, Agriculture, Victory, Truth, and Progress.

western border. In 1844 the Iowa Constitutional Convention concurred and submitted the proposed boundaries in its petition for statehood to the U.S. Congress, retaining the right to "ratify or reject" any changes Congress made.

The conventioneers knew something about the workings of Washington, DC, for Congress changed the borders, making Iowa a smaller state than what exists today. An act admitting Iowa into the Union was then sent to President John Tyler, which he signed.

But the Iowans rejected the act and turned down the opportunity to join the United States. Further, they re-submitted their original proposal to Congress and garnered support from Illinois Representative Stephen Douglas for their present-day borders. The Iowans and Congress in agreement, the state was admitted by an Act of Admission signed by President Polk in 1846.

Three years later, in 1849, the controversy that engendered the "Honey War" was finally resolved in Iowa's favor by the U.S. Supreme Court.

Though an important part of the frontier diet, honey could not rival a crop that established Iowa's future: corn. So valuable is Iowa's farmland that the state estimates its fertile earth is worth more than all of the gold and silver ever mined in the world. In fact, half of the corn produced in the United States comes from Iowa. An Iowa cornfield can hold fifteen thousand corn stalks to the acre.

During its territorial years, Iowa first made Burlington its capital (1838) and later moved it to Iowa City (1841) where the state was governed for eleven years. In 1857 the capital moved for the final time to Des Moines. In 1868 the Iowa General Assembly authorized construction of a new Capitol to "reflect the strength of Iowans," according to *The Iowa Capitol,* a pamphlet produced by the General Assembly. Ground was broken in 1871, and the building was dedicated in 1884. Two years later the Capitol was completed.

Faced in limestone, granite, and sandstone, the Capitol's coloring and multiple domes make it unique in North America. It was designed by Alfred H. Piquenard, a naturalized citizen born in Paris and graduated from Ecole Centrale with a degree in civil engineering. He formed a partnership with John C. Cochrane of Chicago. The Iowa Capitol is similar to the Illinois Capitol, though Springfield does not have the pleasure of so many domes. Both buildings were constructed at the same time and are connected through Mr. Cochrane, who had employed the designer of the Illinois Capitol.

Iowa oak, walnut, and butternut are used extensively throughout the interior. Native materials were preferred during the construction as a means of lowering costs, but also "to take advantage of the valuable contributions Iowans could make to their Capitol," according to the tour pamphlet.

The dimensions of the building are 363 feet by 246 feet. The main dome is covered in 23-karat gold and rises 275 feet from the ground. Re-gilding in 1965 cost $80,000. The cost to re-gild the dome in 1998 was $400,000.

The Capitol holds the General Assembly which is comprised of the House of Representatives and the Senate. The House has 100 members, each serving a two-year term. The Senate has 50 senators, each serving a four-year term. Legislative sessions are held annually for approximately a hundred days.

"We, the people of the State of Iowa, grateful to the Supreme Being for the blessings hitherto enjoyed, and feeling our dependence on Him for a continuation of those blessings, do ordain and establish a free and independent government ..."

-- CONSTITUTION OF IOWA, 1846

ABOVE: The Iowa Senate Chamber.

OPPOSITE: A side view of one of the domes over the Iowa House of Representatives with the main Capitol dome.

PREVIOUS PAGES: A monument in front of the Capitol depicts the arrival of Americans and their encounter with the natives. *Right*, a front perspective of the Capitol taken from the street.

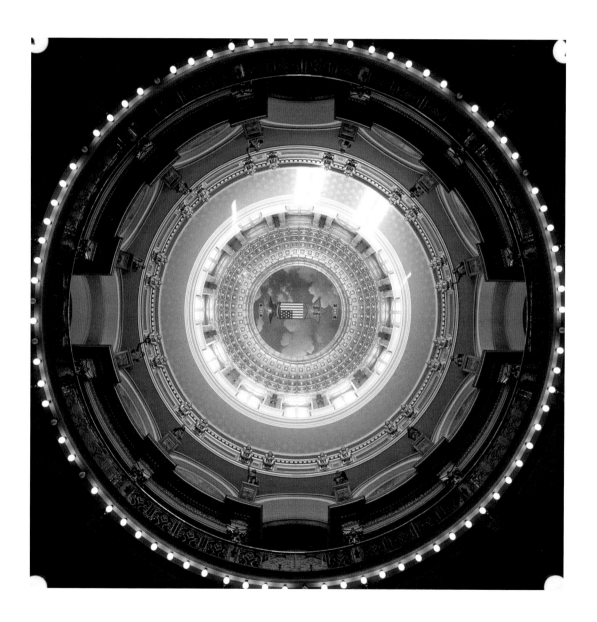

PREVIOUS PAGE LEFT: Entering into the Rotunda one passes a bell that was used aboard the *USS Iowa* battleship. A model of the ship, on loan from the U.S. Navy Department, is nearby.

PREVIOUS PAGE RIGHT: The Iowa House of Representatives. Outside the chamber in the Secretary of State's office is the original Iowa Constitution of 1857 in a special case.

OPPOSITE & ABOVE: The Rotunda features artwork and symbols of the past. Encircling the Rotunda is *The Progress of Civilization*, eight lunettes by Kenyon Cox of New York. They depict Hunting, Herding, Agriculture, the Forge, Commerce, Education, Science, and Art.

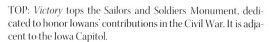

TOP: *Victory* tops the Sailors and Soldiers Monument, dedicated to honor Iowans' contributions in the Civil War. It is adjacent to the Iowa Capitol.

OPPOSITE: The base of the Sailors and Soldiers Monument features the inscription: "Iowa, her affections, like the rivers of her borders, flow to an inseparable union."

TOP RIGHT: The emblem of the Grand Army of the Republic stretches across the dome's eye in recognition of Iowa's contributions in the Civil War.

BOTTOM RIGHT: A hallway ceiling in the Capitol.

IN THE SOULS OF ITS CITIZENS WILL BE
FOUND THE LIKENESS OF THE STATE WHICH
IF THEY BE UNJUST AND TYRANNICAL
THEN WILL IT REFLECT THEIR VICES BUT
IF THEY BE LOVERS OF RIGHTEOUSNESS
CONFIDENT IN THEIR LIBERTIES SO WILL
IT BE CLEAN IN JUSTICE BOLD IN FREEDOM

Official Name: . . . . State of Oregon
Motto: . . . . The Union
Citizen: . . . . Oregonian
Capital City: . . . . Salem, OR
Established: 1843
Joined Union: 1859

Anthem: . . . . "Oregon, My Oregon"
Name:. . Oregon's origin is unknown; it was first used
in 1765 to reference a mythical river in the west
Nickname: . . . . Beaver State
License Plate Slogan: . . . . N/A
Total Area: . . . . 97,132 sq mi (10)

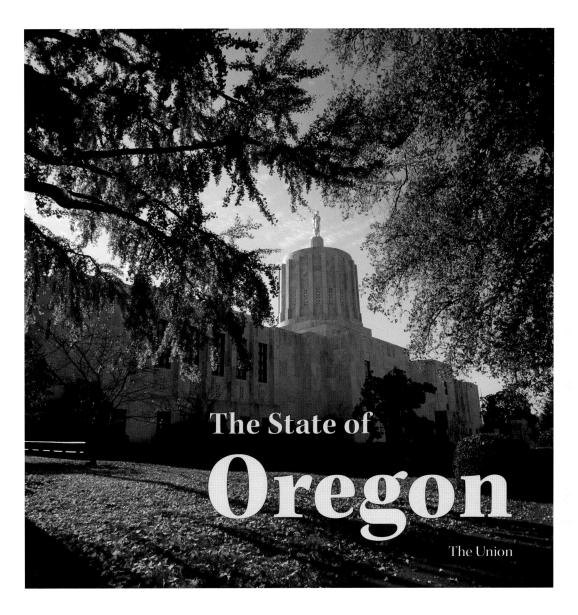

The State of
Oregon

The Union

People who travel great distances by wagon, fend off natives resentful of invasion, and persevere through the harshest weather to reach a destination vivid in mind alone are transformed by the experience. Like the colonists who left England for the shores of Massachusetts and Virginia in pursuit of happiness, the Oregon Country pioneers endured much just for the promise of hard work. And like the first American settlers in the east, they were not only strong in mind and spirit: they knew and asserted the rights of free people. They understood the concept of individual sovereignty and the liberties that spring from it, most notably the right of self-government.

TWARD THE STAR OF EMPIRE TAKES ITS WAY

THE MIND OF MAN
KNOWS NO EMPLOYMENT
MORE WORTHY OF ITS POWERS
THAN THE QUEST OF RIGHTEOUSNESS
IN HUMAN AFFAIRS
NO GOAL OF ITS LABOURS
THAT IS SUPERIOR TO
THE DISCOVERY OF THE GOOD
IN THE GUIDANCE OF LIFE

people. To this flagrant disregard of its authority Congress did nothing but admit Oregon as one of the United States in 1859. Her hearty spirit of independence had earned the privilege.

Salem replaced Oregon City as the capital in 1851, but fire destroyed the newly completed State House December 30, 1855. The legislature would not meet in permanent chambers again until 1876, when the second Capitol was completed. This new building was modeled after the U.S. Capitol, but it too was destroyed by fire on April 25, 1935.

The present Capitol is the third to stand in Oregon. Dedicated October 1, 1938, it is best classified as Modern Greek in style, yet strikingly original. The building is faced with white Danby, Vermont marble, the Rotunda in a Rose Travertine from Montana. Designed by Francis Kelly of the Trowbridge and Livingston firm, New York, its total cost was $2,500,000. Wings were added in 1977 to provide offices and underground parking.

Oregon's citizens have always maintained a feisty independence when it comes to self-government. Women were afforded the vote well before the amendment to the federal constitution. Likewise, Oregonians nominated their federal senators through a direct primary system years before this right was given in other states. Oregon was among the first to pass initiative and referendum laws, giving average citizens the power to put proposed laws to popular vote. And all officials in Oregon are subject to recall.

Of late the state has instituted voting by mail for local, state, and federal elections. Voter turnout using this method has soared, surpassing every state in the Union.

the next year, again without "permission," the state elected two governments: one territorial in accordance with the wishes of Congress, one for the State of Oregon in accordance with the wishes of the

And so it continues to build its reputation as North America's most democratic commonwealth, in a temple designed for that purpose.

OPPOSITE: Atop the tower (dome) is the *Oregon Pioneer* by Ulric Ellerhusen. The statue weighs 8.5 tons and is 23 feet tall. From the ground to the top of his head is 163 feet. Access to the top is possible by climbing 121 steps through the tower to the promenade.

ABOVE: Looking up into the eye of the dome at an angle. Murals around the Rotunda *(not shown)*, painted by Barry Faulkner and Frank H. Schwarz, depict Oregonian history, according to the state tour brochure. They include: Capt. Robert Gray at the Columbia River in 1792; Lewis and Clark in 1805; the first women to cross the continent, welcomed by Dr. John McLoughlin in 1836; and the first wagon train migration in 1843. A bronze Oregon Seal lies on the floor in the center of the Rotunda. It was sculpted by Ulric Ellerhusen. One hundred sixty feet above the seal, the dome rises. In the eye of the Rotunda are thirty-three stars, the very center one larger than the others, symbolizing Oregon and its order in joining the United States.

OPPOSITE: The Oregon House of Representatives is made up of 60 members who meet in an oak-paneled chamber with a large mural at the front. Painted by Barry Faulkner, it shows Oregonians meeting in 1843 to create their provisional government. At the time Oregon was not part of the United States. The carpet pattern features the Douglas Fir, the state's official tree.

The friezes above the galleries in the Senate and House Chambers are inscribed with the names of 158 men and women who contributed to the development of Oregon.

ABOVE: The Oregon Senate Chamber holds 30 members and, like the House, features a large mural in the front. Painted by Frank H. Schwarz, it depicts a Salem street scene when news of Oregon's acceptance into the Union of the United States was announced.

TOP LEFT: Entrance to the Senate Chamber.

TOP RIGHT: Columns saved from the Capitol fire of 1935.

ABOVE: The mural in front of the House Chamber.

OPPOSITE & RIGHT: A perspective of the Capitol during repair of the *Oregon Pioneer*, the statue after work was completed.

"We, the people of the State of Oregon, to the end that justice be established, order maintained, and liberty perpetuated, do ordain this constitution." -- CONSTITUTION OF OREGON, 1857

1854

SENATE CHAMBER

Official Name: .... State of Washington
Motto: .... Alki
Citizen: .... Washingtonian
Capital City: .... Olympia, WA
Established: 1854
Joined Union: 1889
Anthem: .... "Washington My Home"

Name: ..... Named in honor of George Washington, Commander-in-Chief of the Continental Army in the American Revolution and first U.S. President; known as the "Father of His Country"
Nickname: .... Evergreen State; Chinook State
License Plate Slogan: .... Evergreen State
Total Area: .... 70,637 sq mi (19)

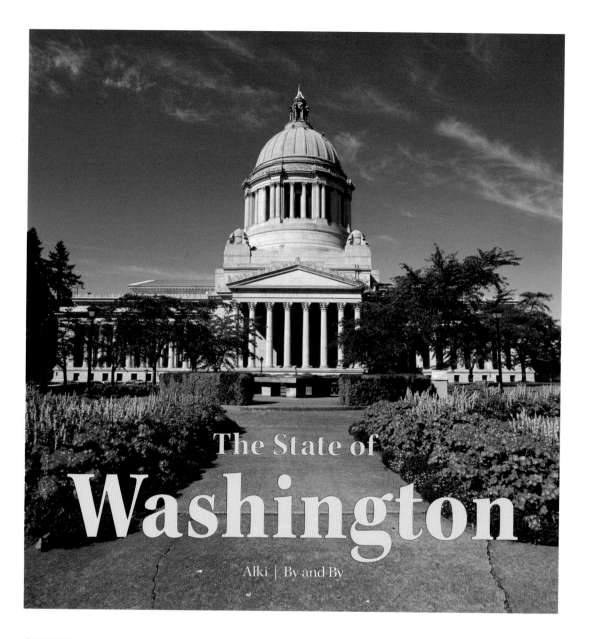

The State of
Washington

Alki | By and By

The United States began as a confederation of thirteen states on the eastern seaboard of the Atlantic Ocean. Their independence from Great Britain was achieved through armed revolution, hard fought on land and sea. One veteran seaman who did his part to help the states win their independence was a Rhode Islander named Robert Gray. With the experience gained in the war and a reputation for courage, he would later live a life of adventure on the high seas. Among his accomplishments, Captain Gray was the first person to sail around the world in a U.S. flagged ship.

WASHINGTON

The year was 1787, and delegations from the newly independent states were secretly meeting in Philadelphia to write a new charter. Thousands of miles away, Capt. Gray was sailing around Cape Horn just off the South American continent, barking orders as commander of the *Columbia* and her sister ship *Washington*.

In 1788, while each state was meeting in convention to debate its accession to the U.S. Constitution, the feisty Rhode Islander was picking up sandalwood in Hawai'i for trade in China.

By the time George Washington was settling in as the first U.S. President, Capt. Gray was returning to Boston Harbor by way of the Cape of Good Hope in 1790. The trip around the world had taken nearly three years, about the same amount of time it took Washington to help begin and lead a new federal government. Both men went about making their unique contribution to the young republic. Washington in his role as President; Capt. Gray as discoverer of Washington which, a century later, became a member of the Virginian's sacred Union.

OPPOSITE LEFT: One of four Tiffany firepots in the Rotunda.

OPPOSITE RIGHT: State Reception Room drapery.

PREVIOUS PAGES: Outside the Washington Senate Chamber; *Right*, a back view of the Legislative Building.

ABOVE: The first flag of the state; *Left*, a view of the Legislative Building from the Temple of Justice.

But just now his Rhode Island still had not joined the United States. Capt. Gray didn't mind; he cared about setting out again as soon as possible to explore that area just before the island (today known as Vancouver Island) where the Kwakiutl and Nootka natives lived. The first trip established trade between them and China, thereby successfully completing Columbus' goal set three hundred years before: establishing trade routes to the Orient.

Capt. Gray left Boston again on the *Columbia* in 1790. In the spring of 1792, after again traveling around South America, he came to the northern continent and discovered that great legendary river widely spoken of, but never found. The Columbia River was now named. And an American claim was laid to the lands, the northern part of which is named for the noble Virginian: Washington State.

Years later, in 1805, Lewis and Clark crossed the continent, traveled down the Columbia, and ended their journey at the mouth of the river, blazing the way for thousands to settle the land.

At this time Washington was part of the Oregon Country, a quasi-independent territory of the Pacific Northwest claimed by both Great Britain and the United States. The Spanish were the first Europeans to land on Washington's soil, arriving near Port Grenville in 1775. English explorer George Vancouver surveyed Puget Sound in 1792, establishing a

northern Idaho and western Montana under its domain. Olympia became the territorial capital.

Washington is the only state or nation in the Western Hemisphere named after a person born in the Americas. Not until 1889, though, would she have enough souls to justify statehood.

Washington's Capitol is a complex of separate buildings arranged as a group around a centerpiece: the Legislative Building. The Temple of Justice (north) is included in the group, as is the Executive Building (west), Insurance Building (east), and Representative/Senator Building (south). The Capitol buildings were built in sandstone mined from quarries near Mt. Ranier. Frederick Law Olmstead, designer of New York's Central Park, laid out the Capitol's grounds, according to tour literature.

It is estimated that 500 craftsmen and artisans from around the world contributed to the effort, the last classically-styled State Capitol built in America. The project was begun in 1923 and completed in 1928. The Capitol's dome rises 287 feet and is one of the tallest masonry domes in the world.

The Washington Legislature is a part-time citizen legislature. Sessions of the Senate and House of Representatives are 60 days during even-numbered years, 105 days during odd. The Senate is comprised of 49 senators, serving four-year terms. The House has 98 members serving two-year terms.

The Rotunda features four large firepots, one in each corner. Created by Tiffany & Co., these firepots replicate Roman signal lights that called the Senate into session 2200 years ago. Behind the firepots are the flags of Washington's counties, 39 in all. Those counties are empowered by a light felt but not seen: the original constitution of 1889, which remains the basic law of the state.

British claim. That same year Capt. Gray made his discovery.

People in the Oregon Country first agitated for self-rule in 1843 and created the Organic Act. This established a provisional government in anticipation of joining the United States *(see Oregon)*. The laws of Iowa were adopted in instances when the government had no law, and a Bill of Rights crafted. A legislature, executive arm, and judiciary were created. Oregon City was made the capital.

The United States gained possession of the Oregon Country in 1846 from the British and two years later established the Oregon Territory. From this, Washington Territory was broken off and established in 1853 by the U.S. Congress, including

PREVIOUS PAGES & ABOVE: After entering the Legislative Building one walks up two flights of steps to reach the chambers. The Rotunda features four large firepots, modeled after ancient Roman signal lights that called the Senate into session. Behind the firepots are the flags of Washington's 39 counties. In the center is the golden Washington Seal.

OPPOSITE: Hanging from the eye of the dome on a 101-foot chain is a 5-ton bronze chandelier, the largest ever created by Tiffany Studios in New York. Statues of Marcus Whitman, a physician who brought settlers to the state, and Mother Joseph, who helped develop hospitals and social service institutions, are steps away from the Rotunda (*not shown*).

OPPOSITE: The *Winged Victory Monument* is a bronze sculpture of *Winged Victory* surrounded by a soldier, sailor, marine, and nurse. Alanzo Victor Lewis of Seattle sculpted the monument, which was dedicated May 30, 1938, to World War I veterans. Three years later the United States entered World War II and the State of Washington was transformed again. Its factories made B-29 bombers; its ports launched warships. And in a secret place known as the Hanford Engineering Works on the Columbia River, nuclear material was created for the first atomic bomb.

ABOVE: The Washington Senate Chamber as seen from the gallery. The front of the room is on the left.

OPPOSITE: The House of Representatives Chamber.

ABOVE: Side view of the House of Representatives Chamber. Behind the curtains a hallway leads to legislative offices.

FOLLOWING PAGES: Workers scale the dome to make repairs; *Right*, another view of the Legislative Building. The Capitol Complex overlooks Capitol Lake and the southern tip of Puget Sound.

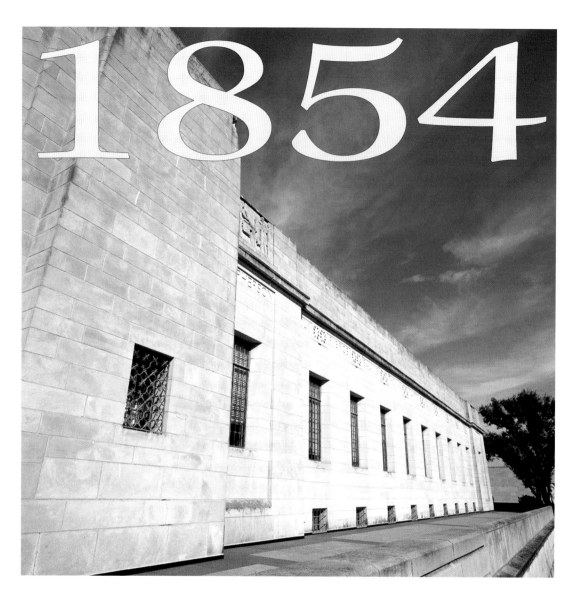

1854

Official Name: .... State of Nebraska
Motto: .... Equality Before The Law
Citizen: .... Nebraskan
Capital City: .... Lincoln, NE
Established: 1854
Joined Union: 1867

Anthem: .... "Beautiful Nebraska"
Name: .. Omaha Indian name for the Platte River is *niboathka*, meaning "broad river"
Nickname: .... Cornhusker State
License Plate Slogan: .... N/A
Total Area: .... 77,358 sq mi (16)

The State of
Nebraska

Equality Before The Law

NEBRASKA

In 1933 the people of Nebraska were in the depths of an economic depression. Prices for farm products, a vital part of the state's economy to this day, were the lowest in state history. A year earlier 600,000 acres were abandoned as scarce rainfall left farmers fearing the return of the "Great American Desert." The effects of these great hardships were felt throughout Nebraska, right up the steps of that just-completed, revolutionary Capitol and into its chambers. For it was here in 1934, under a 400-foot, gold-domed skyscraper tower, that Nebraskans did the unthinkable: *they abolished the House of Representatives and gave its power to the Senate.*

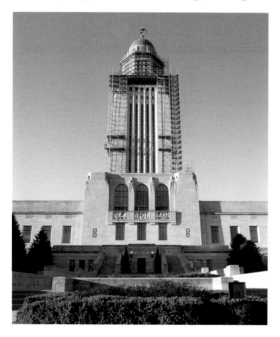

ABOVE: South facade of the Capitol as it undergoes renovation.

OPPOSITE: A setting sun paints the likeness of Hammurabi, one of many ancient leaders of western civilization memorialized on the Capitol. His code protected the helpless and sanctioned "an eye for an eye" retributive justice.

PREVIOUS PAGES: A side perspective of the Capitol's base. Each county's name is included in a frieze that wraps the building. *Right*, the figures representing Wisdom, Justice, Power, and Mercy greet visitors to the Capitol; actual words are not used to identify the building. Above the entrance doors is carved: "The salvation of the state is watchfulness in the citizen."

Since then Nebraskans have entrusted their state sovereignty to a single, powerful legislative body. Forty-nine senators are elected on a non-partisan basis: no party labels are permitted next to candidates' names in the voting booth. It is the only American State to employ unicameralism, but worldwide many national legislatures are of one chamber.

When it became a Territory in 1854, Nebraska encompassed portions of present-day North Dakota, South Dakota, Wyoming, Montana, and Colorado. The Homestead Act of 1862 gave settlers 160 acres of free land provided they settle on it. Thousands poured in -- so many that by 1867 Nebraska was ready to become one of the United States. Its present borders were established with admission that year. But becoming a state wasn't easy for Nebraskans, many of whom were known as "sod busters" because they built their houses from blocks of sod bricks, the prairie practically devoid of trees.

The constitution Nebraskans approved did not extend the right to vote to those of African descent. When Congress required an adjustment of this provision before certifying statehood, President Andrew Johnson vetoed the act. He argued that the U.S. Constitution left with the states the power to determine voter qualifications. Congress overrode the veto and Nebraskans agreed to the change. Three years later, the Fifteenth Amendment became part of the U.S. Constitution, guaranteeing federal and state voting rights for all law-abiding citizens.

The Nebraska Legislature became unicameral in 1934 after the state's citizens approved a constitutional amendment. Bicameralism in the United States developed from the earliest colonial times when there was a legislative body elected by the people, a separate council and governor appointed by the Crown. This council, varying by colony, was part legislative and part executive in its duties. It would become the foundation for the modern Senate.

Some states established bicameral systems with independence; others had unicameral systems. Georgia (1776-1790), Pennsylvania (1776-1789), and Vermont (1777-1836) retained a unicameral legislature.

In the unicameral Continental Congress that directed and won the American Revolution, true legislative power was not its realm -- it being but a congress of deputations from sovereign entities meeting for specific purposes. But it did conduct the war and serve important executive functions on behalf of the states. When the Articles of Confederation went into effect in 1781, the Congress remained as a single body but was still unable to raise its own revenue. The U.S. Constitution created a bicameral Congress, adding a chamber for state representation based on population (House), while maintaining a chamber for the states as states (Senate).

Bicameral systems require a bill to go through the lawmaking process twice through separate, independent bodies of representatives from different jurisdictions -- a critical check on lawmakers designed to ensure only well-considered legislation.

According to Capitol literature, when the voters approved the change in the power to make laws, the senators abandoned their smaller East Chamber in the Capitol and took over the larger House Chamber. Half of the seats were taken out, affording each Senator more room. Today it is known simply as Legislative Chamber. Senators serve four-year terms with half of the body being elected every two years. Sessions are

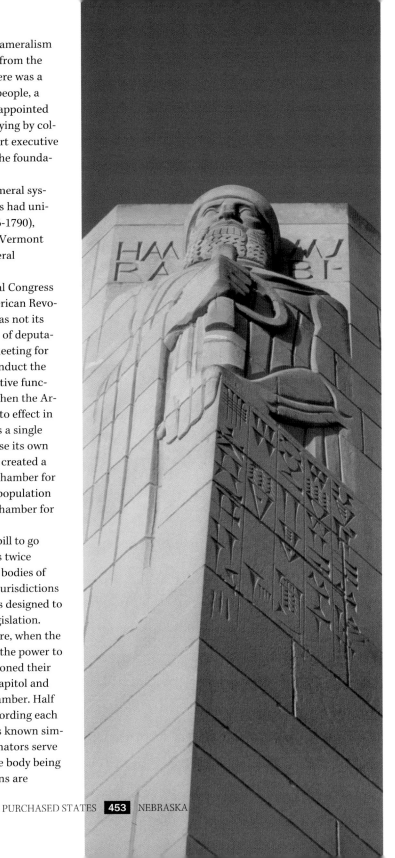

to state documents. It was based on just-evolving "sky-scraper" technology, with a steel frame wrapped in brick and faced with limestone. Despite these modern attributes, Goodhue's building incorporates a variety of architectural elements including Assyrian, Egyptian, Roman, Greek, and Gothic. Ten years and ten million dollars later, the Nebraska Capitol -- known as the "Tower on the Plains" and the first with an office tower -- opened to wide acclaim. Tour literature says the tower resembles the grain elevators found throughout the state.

The base of the Capitol is 436 feet on each side. Impressive stone carvings -- 23 panels in all -- detail the evolution of law in a time line that begins with Moses and ends with Nebraska. The person responsible for the philosophical ideals inscribed within and out of the Capitol was Hartley Burr Alexander, one-time Professor of Philosophy at the University of Nebraska.

limited to 90 days in odd-numbered years, and to 60 days in even-numbered years.

If State Capitols can rightly be called Temples of Sovereignty, then Nebraska's edifice is more like a cathedral. New York architect Bertram Grosvenor Goodhue's design was selected after a national competition, and construction began in 1922, according

OPPOSITE: The likeness of Caesar and Justinian on the Capitol.

ABOVE: *The Spirit of the Law as shown in its History* depicts the development of western civilization in separate relief panels laid out on the four sides of the exterior of the Capitol. Among those panels are *The Signing of the Declaration of Independence* (top), *The Writing of the United States Constitution* (middle), and *The Magna Carta* (bottom).

The person responsible for the carvings was sculptor Lee Lawrie, whose work is also visible on Rockefeller Center. He believed external sculptures should be incorporated into the building itself and not left standing on the Capitol grounds. The result: the birth of modern architectural sculpture. According to state documents, *The Spirit of the Law as shown in its History* stone-carved panels include:

1. Moses Bringing the Law from Sinai (1270 BC): Moses delivers the ten laws written by God to the people of Israel.

2. Deborah Judging Israel (circa 1150 BC): The children of Israel submit to the guidance of Deborah, the sole woman judge of Israel.

3. *The Judgement of Solomon (circa 970 BC):* Solomon knew how to get to the truth of the dispute by suggesting the babe be cut in half, knowing the true mother would save the infant. The people recognized this "wisdom" of God in his judgements.

4. *Solon Gives Athens A New Constitution (circa 570 BC):* Solon reformed the Athenian constitution by creating an assembly for all freemen, an upper assembly for the rich, and the right to jury trial.

5. *The Publishing of the Twelve Tablets in Rome (circa 450 BC):* Early code of Roman law, amended and codified to meet the needs of the society.

6. *The Establishment of the Tribunal of the People (circa 442 BC):* Patrician judge Appius Claudius misuses his power, causing a plebian revolt that earns the lower classes a say on the tribunal.

7. *Plato Writing His Dialogue on the Ideal Republic (circa 380 BC):* "Laws and constitutions spring from the moral dispositions of the members of the state," he wrote.

8. *Orestes Before the Areopagites (performed 458 BC):* The play "Eumenides" by Aeschylus shows how trial by jury came into existence.

9. *The Codification of Roman Law Under Justinian (circa 560):* The revision of all imperial constitutions from the time of Hadrian is publicized in this Code, which is assumed by the people to be the law.

10. *The Codification of Anglo-Saxon Law under Ethelbert (circa 600):* The first written code of law in English is promulgated by King Ethelbert.

11. *The Magna Carta (1210):* This charter limited the powers of the central authority, protected the customs of the English towns, and is a precursor to other English liberties.

12. *Las Casas Pleading the Cause of the Indian (circa 1540):* Father Las Casas worked to establish humanitarian laws and European-style rights for Native Americans.

13. *Signing of the Mayflower Compact (1620):* Before setting foot in a new land, the Pilgrims establish themselves as a body politic and set basic law.

14. *Burke Defending America in Parliament (1775):* Edmund Burke urges reconciliation with the various American colonies and acknowledgement of their liberties.

15. *Declaration of Independence (1776):* Establishes the rights of people to life, liberty, and the

pursuit of happiness; declares each state free and independent.

16. *United States Constitution (1789):* Establishes a government for the United States with specific delegations of power from the individual states and the people; codifies basic liberties of the people in a Bill of Rights modeled after state constitutions.

17. *The Purchase of Louisiana from Napoleon (1803):* The purchase of the Louisiana Territory would double the United States and enable the establishment of the State of Nebraska.

18. *The Kansas-Nebraska Bill (1854):* This Act of Congress established the territories of Kansas and Nebraska and recognized the state's right to prohibit or permit slavery (Nebraska opposed slavery).

19. *The Emancipation Proclamation (1863):* Lincoln declares slaves in seceded states to be free.

20. *Nebraska Enters The Union (1867).*

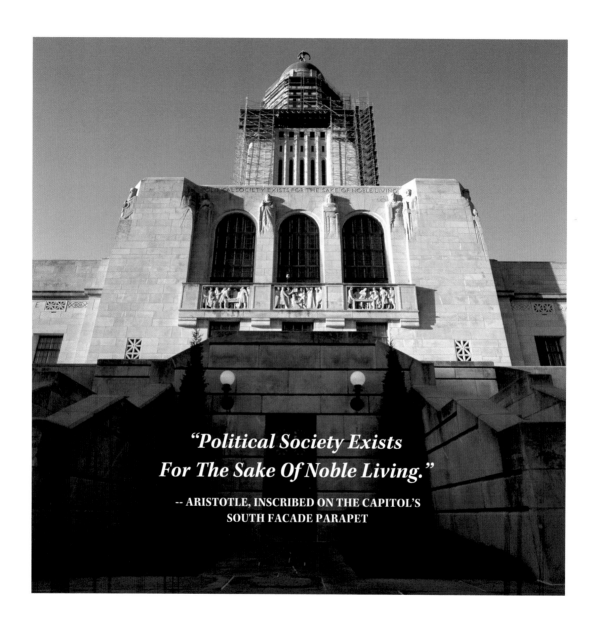

"*Political Society Exists*
For The Sake Of Noble Living."

-- ARISTOTLE, INSCRIBED ON THE CAPITOL'S
SOUTH FACADE PARAPET

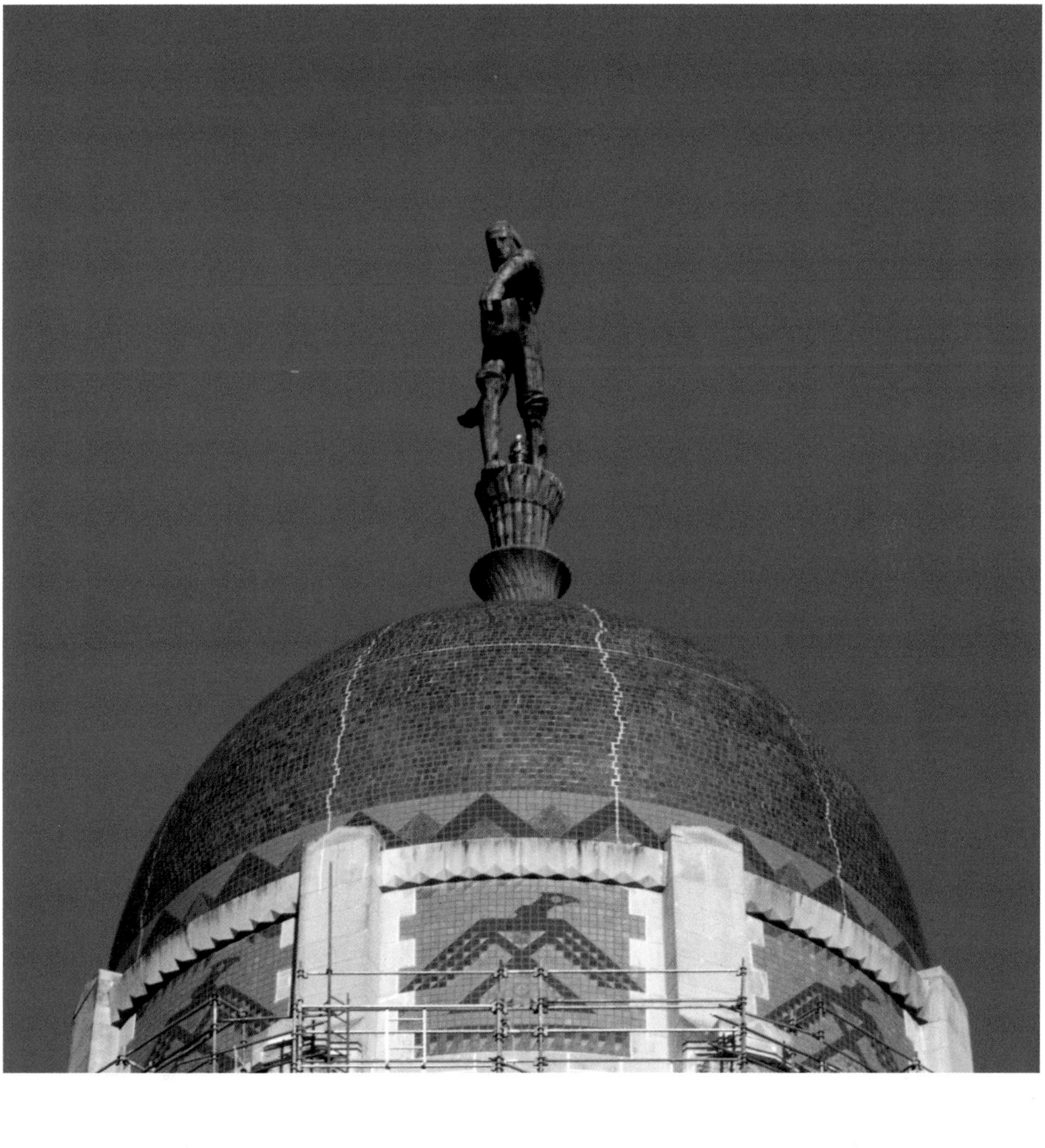

PREVIOUS PAGES: Looking up from the base of the Capitol, which was being refurbished at the time of this photograph. *Right*, standing 19 feet high, the *Sower* casts the seeds of agriculture and noble life. He was designed by Lee Lawrie of New York and is portrayed performing the ancient custom of hand-casting grain. According to state literature, this represents agriculture as the source of all civilization. Barefoot and standing on a pedestal of wheat and corn, the *Sower* was installed in 1930. The Thunderbird, a Native American figure which brought rain to the plains for the first Nebraska farmers, is featured as a repeating mosaic under the *Sower* statue.

ABOVE: The Rotunda floor features Mother Nature in the center with Earth, Air, Fire, and Water symbols revolving around her. The mosaics of the Capitol and other decorative arts were the work of Hildreth Meiere. "Laws And Constitutions Spring From The Moral Dispositions Of The Members Of The State ... Law And Order Deliver The Soul." These words from Plato are inscribed in the Rotunda.

RIGHT: Perspective of the Great Hall and its ceilings.

ABOVE: The former Senate Chamber with the Meiere mosaic in the foreground. When the House of Representatives was abolished in 1934, the Senate moved to that larger chamber. "The building is a monument to those early Nebraskans who came together to build a better life for their families and neighbors. Today, it continues to stand as a symbol of what Nebraskans can achieve with hope and pride in the life we are building on the plains," writes Mike Johanns, Governor of Nebraska, in a greeting to Capitol visitors.

ABOVE: Looking up into the eye of the dome one sees images of
angels. The virtues Charity, Hope, Magnanimity, Justice, Faith,
Wisdom, Temperance, and Courage are represented as winged
figures holding hands. The man responsible for the philosophical
ideals inscribed within and out of the Nebraska Capitol was
Hartley Burr Alexander, Professor of Philosophy at the University of Nebraska and other institutions in the course of his distin-
guished career.

FOLLOWING PAGES: Looking down the Great Hall to the vestibule. The vestibule ceiling mosaic is titled *Gifts of Nature to Man on the Plains*. The sun is represented in the center as well as with the chandelier.

ABOVE: Legislative Chamber. The Nebraska Legislature is unicameral, meaning there is only one lawmaking body. The change was made in 1934. The 49 members are called Senators and are drawn from forty-nine districts in the state. The election of the legislature is non-partisan: no political party names appear next to the candidate's name on the ballot.

Official Name: . . . . State of Kansas

Motto: . . . . Ad Astra per Aspera

Citizen: . . . . Kansan

Capital City: . . . . Topeka, KS

Established: 1854

Joined Union: 1861

Anthem: . . . . "Home on the Range"

Name: . From the Kansas native's tribal word *kanze*, meaning "south wind"

Nickname: . . . . Squatter State; Sunflower State

License Plate Slogan: . . . . N/A

Total Area: . . . . 82,282 sq mi (15)

The State of

Kansas

Ad Astra per Aspera | To the Stars Through Difficulties

A constitution establishes the supreme law by which a body politic is to operate. It sets the domain of the state, the laws it can and cannot make. Constitutions are expressions of the people's sovereign will. In America, constitutions are descended from colonial charters which delineated the power of the people by colony and that of the crown. Charters conveyed, depending on which colony one lived in, the rights of the people to separately make their own laws. When King George III interfered in these and other rights, the colonies declared themselves "Free and Independent States;" each made its own constitution, and then together fought and won the American Revolution.

KANSAS

The Declaration of Independence of 1776 indicted the King for "taking away our Charters, abolishing our most valuable Laws, and altering fundamentally the Forms of our governments: For suspending our own Legislatures, and declaring themselves invested with Power to legislate for us in all Cases whatsoever."

These words expressed the outrage over English interference in what had become the way of Americans since the founding of the House of Burgesses in Virginia in 1619. The people asserted the right to run their individual state as they saw fit, subject to no other power, and successfully fought the American Revolution to secure it.

ABOVE: The columns of the east wing.

OPPOSITE: Views of the Senate Chamber.

PREVIOUS PAGES: The House of Representatives Chamber; *Right*, a perspective of the Kansas Capitol.

And so it seemed to many in 1854 that the way to solve the contentious issue of slavery was to let the people decide for themselves in their state constitutional convention. In the Kansas-Nebraska Act of 1854, the people of the Territory of Kansas were expected to decide for themselves whether to prohibit or permit slavery within its borders. They failed in the task, and civil war in Kansas commenced while the larger War Between the States ensued.

Kansas was the battleground for a dis-United States. The U.S. Constitution and numerous congressional "compromises" not only failed, ultimately, to unite the people from 1789 to the outbreak of war in 1861: some could argue it enabled the separation.

The constitutional clause that recognized slaves as three-fifths of a person for representation purposes empowered the slaveholder. It subsidized the slave interests by giving the slaveholder a disproportionate vote in federal councils. During this period, in the natural evolution of two different economic systems, the one republic became two: the capitalist-industrial system in the north that operated over many state jurisdictions; the agriculture-slave-plantation system in the south in which strong individual states supported the institution of slavery. This was the United States in that day.

A people need to be one, with complementary economic systems, to make a compact with each other, to bring their individual sovereignty together with the others and overwhelmingly agree on a basic law; a code from which all else would come, and by which social issues would be decided. Under this principle each American State since the Revolution constituted itself an independent body politic.

The Union was created when the north and south composed one economic system along the eastern seaboard, mostly of farmers, artisans, traders, and shippers. During the colonial period, northern ships delivered slaves from Africa to the southern states and returned with molasses to make rum in New England. By the U.S. Constitution, all states were obligated to return escaped slaves to their masters. In these ways the northern states were involved in slavery. But any direct northern stake in the institution was subject to congressional prohibition of slave importation after 1808. No similar provision was made for emancipation in the south, though many leaders had urged one.

Kansas was part of the Territory of Missouri until 1821. After Missouri became a state, the region reverted to an unorganized status with the native Kansa, Wichita, Osage, and Pawnee peoples predominating. When it became a territory in 1854 and included the better part of Colorado, only 700 people lived there. But soon tens of thousands arrived. By 1860 the population was over 100,000.

Where did these people come from? The other states, notably from Missouri and New England. Missourians settled Leavenworth and Atchison in 1854. Later that year the Massachusetts Emigrant Aid Society sent settlers who founded Topeka, Lawrence, and other towns. Missourians wanted slavery in Kansas; the New Englanders did not. Now each group, hostile to the other, contended for the right to determine the future of the one Kansas.

Unlike the immigrants from New England, the Missourians brought with them into Kansas "human property." Slavery in the New World had its start in the West Indies in the 1500's when the conquistadors enslaved the native tribesmen. These poor people perished, unable to endure the hard labor of the slave master. In their place were drawn Africans, kidnapped or sold, from the African west coast. These people were strong and well suited to plantation life. The practice of slavery succeeded in places where plantation-style agriculture thrived. It flourished as far north as the State of Delaware.

Kansas seemed an ideal place for it to grow.

On June 10, 1854 pro-slavery citizens met to declare slavery in existence in Kansas. In making this declaration the slaveholders wished to guarantee the transport of slaves across Kansas -- Missouri's western outlet. That October, people in the growing town of Lawrence were attacked by pro-slavery men in an effort to expel those who opposed slavery.

In 1855, the pro-slavery candidate for delegate to Congress won, though it was alleged Missourians crossed the border and voted illegally. When elections to the territorial legislature were held, a pro-slavery slate won amid claims of voter intimidation.

This legislature adopted Missouri's code of laws and named Lecompton the capital. Anti-slavery legislators were refused entry to the House.

That summer the presidentially-appointed governor refused to deal with this legislature and was replaced. Anti-slavery forces, including members of the Free-Soil Party, rebelled against these arbitrary activities and met in their own convention in Topeka. A constitution was drafted that prohibited slavery as well as free Africans from the state. This constitution was approved, and a governor and legislature were elected January 15, 1856.

Kansas now had two state governments. And armed skirmishes between them were frequent.

The Topeka "rebels" were indicted for treason and ultimately were arrested and imprisoned. United States troops prevented the Free-Soil legislature from meeting. But Robert J. Walker, the new territorial governor, brokered a deal among the opposing factions. The Free-Soilers agreed to give up their Topeka regime and submit to the authority of the government in Lecompton in return for amnesty. A constitution for Kansas was then drafted with this clause: "The right of property is before and higher than any constitutional sanction, and the right of the owner of a slave to such slave and its increase is the same, and as inviolable as the right of the owner of any property whatever."

It won approval by all Kansans, mainly because those who opposed slavery stayed away from the referendum. But when the first elections for state offices were held under this constitution, anti-slavery forces voted their candidates into office. They now controlled the legislature.

The end of slavery in Kansas was in sight.

The Kansans, the last people to decide for themselves whether their society would tolerate the morally repugnant slave system, proved a universal truth of sovereignty and rang slavery's death knell.

ABOVE: At the entrance of the Kansas Capitol.

OPPOSITE: The Lincoln statue by Topekan Robert Merrell Gage in front of the Capitol.

Sovereignty is of the people, and in numbers a sovereign people of a state can do as they please in ordering their society. Except, with the addition of the 13th, 14th, and 15th amendments to the U.S.

Constitution, they no longer can enslave people or interfere with their basic rights. Kansans had no such federal prohibition when they voted; but they didn't need one.

Kansas became a member of the United States January 29, 1861 only after slaveholding southern states had left it. In the ensuing War Between the States, more Kansans in proportion to their population served in the Union armies than any other state's people. Right after that great war, in 1866, the Kansas Capitol Commission named Colonel J.G.

Haskell of Lawrence the state architect. Working off a plan by Milwaukee architect E. Townsend Mix, Haskell reworked the plans to the commission's liking, and construction began in 1867. The Kansas Legislature moved into not-yet-completed quarters in the east wing in 1869. The wing was completed in 1872, yet it took 37 years to finally complete the Kansas Capitol. Construction ended in 1903 after some $3,200,588.92 was expended.

The yellow limestone that makes the Capitol unique is native stone from Junction City. The

Kansas Capitol is taller than the U.S. Capitol: the height from the ground floor to the very top is 304 feet. The dome is covered with copper sheets.

Since those controversial days preceding the Civil War, the Kansas Legislature has served the will of the people and does so today in its impressive home. The Kansas Senate is comprised of 40 senators, each elected to a four-year term. Senators represent approximately 61,000 Kansans each. The Kansas House of Representatives has 125 members each representing 19,000 citizens in two-year terms.

ABOVE: The House of Representatives Chamber.

PREVIOUS PAGES: Murals in the House Chamber show the recording of Kansas' History, Justice, and Education. Not far away from the chamber is a copy of the state's handwritten original constitution on display. *Top right*, a relief on one of the pediment's tympanums in the Rotunda has the Great Seal of Kansas.

OPPOSITE: Perspectives of the Senate Chamber. Note the columns made of Italian bronze with cast-iron bases. The chandeliers were installed in the 1970's.

Murals in the Rotunda portray historic events in the life of Kansas. According to Capitol tour literature these include: 1) The explorations of Lewis and Clark in Kansas between 1804-1806; 2) Pioneers enter Kansas; 3) The importance of railroads to state development; 4) A cattle drive along the Chisholm Trail; 5) Francisco Vasquez de Coronado enters the region, 1541; 6) Battle of Beecher's Island, 1868; 7) Battle of Mine Creek, 1864; 8) Settlers cut sod to build homes.

1861

Official Name: . . . . State of Colorado
Motto: . . . . Nil Sine Numine
Citizen: . . . . Coloradan
Capital City: . . . . Denver, CO
Established: 1861
Joined Union: 1876

Anthem: . . . . "Where the Columbines Grow"
Name: . The Spanish word for "red" is *Colorado*, the color of the Colorado River
Nickname: . . . . Centennial State
License Plate Slogan: . . . . N/A
Total Area: . . . . 104,100 sq mi (8)

ABOVE: The dome as seen from the observation deck entrance. The observation deck is open to the public and accessible by taking an elevator to the dome's top.

OPPOSITE: The Colorado House of Representatives Chamber during a period of refurbishment.

Official Name: . . . . State of Idaho

Motto: . . . . Esto Perpetua

Citizen: . . . . Idahoan

Capital City: . . . . Boise, ID

Established: 1863

Joined Union: 1890

Anthem: . . . . "Here We Have Idaho"

Name: . . George Willing made the name up to sound like a native term; it means "Gem of the Mountains"

Nickname: . . . . Gem State

License Plate Slogan: . . . . Famous Potatoes

Total Area: . . . . 83,574 sq mi (14)

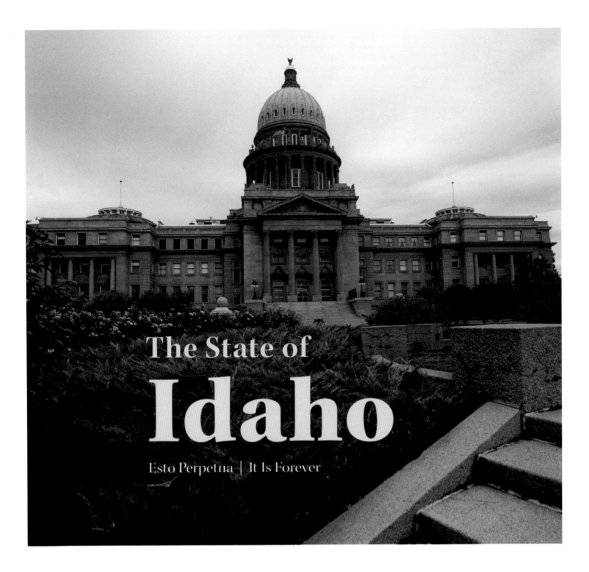

The State of
Idaho

Esto Perpetua | It Is Forever

Meriwether Lewis and William Clark received $2,500 from Congress in 1803 for an expedition to the Pacific Ocean conceived by President Thomas Jefferson. With the Louisiana Purchase being completed, knowledge of the western frontier became a priority of the young republic. On their journey the explorers had to pass over the most treacherous terrain on the continent: the Bitterroot Range of the Rocky Mountains. Sacajawea, their Sioux wilderness guide, saved the expedition by securing horses for the overland passage. From there, with the help of the Nez Perce and Shoshone natives, they navigated the Clearwater and Snake, then Columbia River to reach the sea. Thus Lewis and Clark became the first Americans or Europeans to visit the Idaho region. Little did they know it would be one of the last pieces of frontier in the American West.

IDAHO

Four years after their visit, a fur-trading post was built in the northern part of the panhandle, and in 1855 Mormon settlers in eastern Idaho began farming using irrigation. But not until 1860, with the discovery of gold on Orofino Creek and later in the Boise Basin, did the peopling of Idaho commence. The first permanent settlement was founded by another group of Mormon settlers at Franklin that year. Soon farmers and ranchers followed, including descendants from early-American English, Irish, and Scottish people from the eastern states. Even Basque sheep herders moved from the French and Spanish Pyrenees by the thousands for opportunities in Idaho.

Idaho, as part of the Oregon Country, was claimed by Spain, Russia, Great Britain, and the United States. In 1846 the Treaty of Oregon gave the land to the U.S. Idaho remained a part of this Oregon Territory until 1852, then became part of both the Oregon and Washington territories (1853-59), and then the Washington Territory (1859-63). It was organized as the Idaho Territory by the U.S. Congress in 1863 and included present-day Montana and Wyoming.

Finally, in 1864, Idaho received its current boundaries. Three principal regions coalesced to provide

some of the richest mines, excellent farmland, abundant water supplies, and tremendous forests of Ponderosa Pine, Douglas Fir, and Hemlock. The wildlife is one of the most diverse on the continent: bears, cougars, elk, moose, mountain goats and sheep, pronghorns, beavers, mink, bobcat, and more. Salmon and trout are plentiful as are the number of large and smaller rivers.

This last fragment of the frontier had an indigenous people like those on the earlier frontiers back east. They were the Nez Perce, so-named by the French because some were seen with their noses pierced with ornaments. The Nez Perce were on good terms with the Americans from the start when Lewis and Clark visited their homes. They lived in villages of long houses made of bark during the winter and roamed the surrounding lands in the summer.

In 1831 they requested missionaries from St. Louis to Christianize their fellow tribesmen. One of these, a Presbyterian missionary named Henry Harmon Spalding, taught the Nez Perce how to plant potatoes; this is considered the beginning of the state's famous potato industry. But as settlement picked up with the advent of train transportation, problems loomed.

Chief Joseph became head of the Nez Perce upon the death of his father in 1873. Christianized and educated by the missionaries like his father, Chief Joseph is considered one of the greatest American Native Chiefs. Upon taking leadership of the Wallowa Valley Nez Perce, he refused to honor a treaty made in 1863 that ceded Nez Perce land to the United States. The treaty was never signed by tribal authorities. When the U.S. Army sought to move him to a reservation in 1887, Chief Joseph routed the U.S. forces at White Bird Canyon, in northern Idaho.

OPPOSITE: A corner perspective of the Idaho Capitol.

ABOVE: The monument to Governor Frank Steunenberg who, after putting down an armed revolt against the state by unionizing miners, was assassinated in 1905.

PREVIOUS PAGES: Charles Ostner carved in pine the Washington Equestrian Statue that is now located in the Rotunda. Originally bronzed and set outside on the Capitol grounds, the statue was a gift to the Territory of Idaho in 1869 and remained outside until 1934. The statue was refinished in gold leaf. *Right*, the Idaho Capitol as seen from the Steunenberg Monument.

This great victory and others that followed made him realize, though, the futility of fighting such a great power. So Chief Joseph brilliantly executed a retreat that was of biblical proportions. With U.S. Army units in hot pursuit, he led a group of many women, children, and older men on a 1,000-mile journey to the Canadian border in under 90 days. His orders to the native warriors: do not harm any American civilian not presenting arms against the tribe. This spared the lives of hundreds if not thousands of settlers on the frontier.

In October Chief Joseph and the Nez Perce were surrounded and forced to surrender just forty miles from the Canadian border. Chief Joseph was sent to Fort Leavenworth; the rest of his band were sent to the Indian Territory (Oklahoma). Many perished in the process. Amid cries for justice, the survivors were restored to reservations in Washington and Idaho in 1884.

Five years later the people of the Idaho Territory met in convention in Boise and drafted a constitution. This was adopted and in force for eleven months before Congress, in 1890, passed the act recognizing Idaho as the 43rd member of the Union.

At the same time, the U.S. Census Bureau officially declared that the "American Frontier" no longer existed -- almost four hundred years after Christopher Columbus set foot in the New World. This frontier,

TOP & RIGHT: The House Chamber and its foyer.

ABOVE: *Winged Victory of Samothrace*, a copy of a statue discovered in 1863 on the island of Samothrace in the Aegean Sea. It was given to Idaho from France as a way of thanking the United States for its support in World War II. France organized the "Merci Train" of 49 train cars, packed with presents, one for each state. Idaho distributed the other gifts received to its counties, according to the tour brochure.

OPPOSITE: The Senate Chamber. The Idaho House has 70 members, the Senate has 35, and members of both are elected to two-year terms. Legislative sessions last three months per year.

represented by a line drawn north-south to delineate civilization on the eastern side and the unsettled, wild natural areas to the west, once encompassed most of the continent. Now it was no more.

And with its extinguishment a part of the frontiersman's psyche must have vaporized, collected like a cloud above the continent, and dispersed among all of the people -- the very real "American spirit." But undefined wilderness is needed to have uncertainty. Without it is lost the *obligation* to fearlessly embrace the unknown, the pioneer's companion with each step westward. Such challenges required individuals to possess an independent spirit and be self-reliant, the essence of the settlers of Idaho.

The Idaho Territory's first capital city was Lewiston in 1863, but it became Boise in 1865, and a new Capitol was built there at a cost of $80,000, according to state documents. This Norman-style structure was five stories high and was faced in red brick. It was later destroyed to make way for a new Capitol -- the present east wing today stands where the old building once was.

The Idaho Legislature authorized the new project in 1905, and it took 15 years to complete. J.E. Tourtellotte was named architect and, when the dome and central section were completed in 1912, Boise native Charles Hummel and Tourtellotte began to design the wings. Construction commenced in 1919 and was completed in 1920.

PREVIOUS PAGES: Views of the Rotunda including one look-ing at the eye of the dome. Note the columns in these photo-graphs. An Italian family from New York traveled to Idaho dur-ing construction to oversee the creation of the Capitol's pillars. The reason: they were experts in fabricating scagliola, a faux marble plastering art that mixes gypsum and glue, marble dust and granite to simulate marble. The Italian family knew the art of making scagliola, which originated in Italy during the six-teenth century. The pillars in the Idaho Capitol represent some of the most impressive examples of this art in the world.

ABOVE: The second floor hallway encircles the Rotunda.

OPPOSITE: Perspective of the Idaho Capitol. "The building and its contents reflect the dreams and achievements of many indi-viduals and organizations across the history of Idaho. The archi-tects and designers of the Capitol went to tremendous lengths to assure that the building captures the essence of Idaho and her people," wrote Governor Dirk Kempthorne in the Capitol tour booklet distributed to visitors.

Official Name: . . . . State of Montana
Motto: . . . . Oro y Plata
Citizen: . . . . Montanan
Capital City: . . . . Helena, MT
Established: 1864
Joined Union: 1889

Anthem: . . . . "Montana Melody"
Name: . . *Montana* is Spanish for "mountain," and it
was known as "Land of the Shining Mountains"
Nickname: . . . . Big Sky Country
License Plate Slogan: . . . . Big Sky
Total Area: . . . . 147,046 sq mi (4)

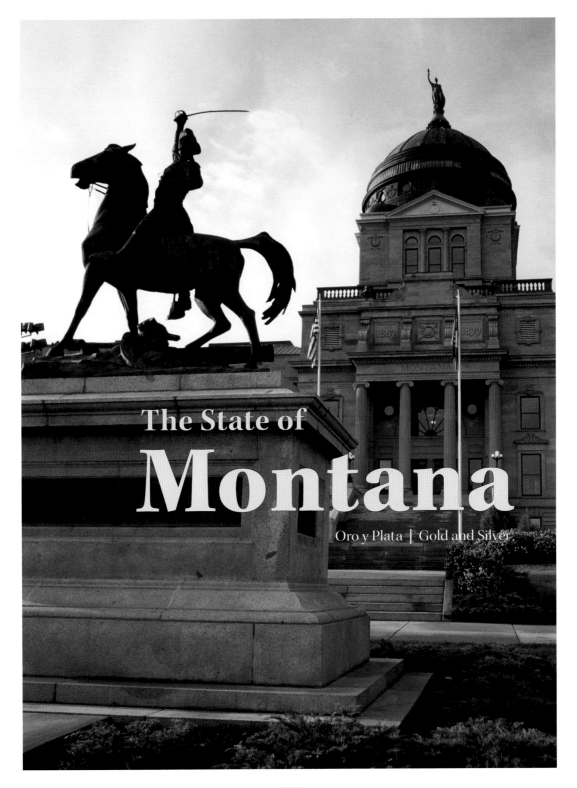

The State of
Montana

Oro y Plata | Gold and Silver

MONTANA

Gold strikes in southwestern Montana lured prospectors into the region in 1862. Soon mining camps sprang up, drawing all sorts of people including some of an unsavory nature. It was an unspoken truth of the American frontier that once a settlement was firmly planted soon an outlaw class followed, there being no local or state authority to arrest criminals or hold court. In these rapidly expanding camps, law and order came by way of what were known as "vigilance committees." Often, as in the Montana camps, the leading men formed themselves into a committee and expelled -- sometimes by deadly force -- those deemed dangerous to the community.

Leaders of the two largest mining camps, Virginia City and Bannack, formed a vigilance committee after it was discovered that one of the biggest outlaws was the sheriff. Virginia City was attracting all sorts among the 10,000 people who came in 1863 when gold was found. The vigilantes rounded up 21 people, including sheriff Henry Plummer, and hanged each one to death in early 1864. Wild rumors about this crude justice now spread throughout the towns.

Some said that the secret symbol 3-7-77 used by the vigilantes related somehow to the secret rituals of the Masonic organization of which they were members. Others said it was used to remind outlaws that a Montana grave measured 3 feet wide by 7 feet deep by 77 inches long.

OPPOSITE: The entablature on the portico has "Montana" chiseled into the frieze.

PREVIOUS PAGES & ABOVE: An equestrian statue of General Thomas Francis Meagher stands in front of the Montana Capitol. Meagher was an Irish revolutionist who escaped capture in Ireland and later served as Montana's territorial governor. Earlier he led the "Irish Brigade" in the War Between the States, which was wiped out by Virginian forces at Chancellorsville. After this event he began his work in Montana.

The Vigilantes of Montana was formally established in 1863, combining the power of the local militia, sheriff, and judge into one group of unelected men. Recognizing the need for civil authority, the U.S. Congress created the Territory of Montana in 1864, and the first Territorial Legislature met in Bannack. The capital became Virginia City.

Meanwhile, Last Chance Gulch was founded in 1864 with the discovery of placer gold. Placer is an ore deposit found with the gravel of a stream. Men known as the "Four Georgians" made the discovery. The earliest prospectors in Montana were ex-Confederate soldiers who found in gold something more important than fighting for state rights. This mining camp didn't dry up when the gold ran out like the others. Instead, the local businessmen worked hard to make it a real community.

Today Last Chance Gulch is the main street of Helena, Montana's capital city.

Virginia City was made the capital of Montana in 1865, six months after territorial status was established. In 1875 Helena became the territorial capital and later, in 1889 with statehood, the permanent capital.

Montana is the fourth largest American State, surpassed in domain only by Alaska, Texas, and California. To gauge how large Montana is, consider that the State of Delaware -- the first state to adopt the U.S. Constitution -- could be multiplied *exactly 59 times* to fit within the 41st state. And of this enormous "Big Sky" country, forty percent is Rocky Mountain range in the west and sixty percent is rolling shortgrass prairie in the east.

Upon seeing the sun reflected off the mountain peaks, early explorers called the region the Land of the Shining Mountains. Little did they know that under the snowy peaks laid the shining metals of gold and silver -- the possession of which served as the driving force of exploration since the landing of Columbus. Other valuable minerals mined were coal, copper, and petroleum. From the land, Montana's 22,000 farms and ranches help make the state a key exporter of beef cattle, wheat, barley, and hay products.

Lewis and Clark traversed the entire length of Montana on their great exploration of the west in 1804-1805. Yet the biggest day in Montana history surely was the extension of the United States to the west coast with the signing of the Treaty of Oregon in 1846. Up until then only eastern Montana had been secured through the Louisiana Purchase in 1803. This treaty guaranteed secured U.S. possession of the mountainous territory in the west and the state's ultimate borders.

Many other important events happened in the state. It was at the Battle of the Little Big Horn in eastern Montana that U.S. Army Lt. Col. George Custer and his 276 men perished before a superior Sioux-Cheyenne force. It was in Montana that Chief Joseph and his band of thousands of Nez Perce were captured close to the Canadian border. And the Blackfeet, Flathead, Crow, Sioux, Cheyenne, and other natives that once reigned in Montana were placed on various-sized reservations in the state -- some later found to hold valuable coal and oil deposits. At the beginning of the 21st century, these lands held 48,000 natives or six percent of the whole state's population.

In 1895 scandal marred the construction of a new Capitol when it was discovered that the building commissioners planned to defraud the state out of a portion of the building funds. No money was lost. Two years later, the Montana Legislature authorized a building at less than half the original price, $485,000. In 1898 Charles E. Bell and John Hackett Kent of Council Bluffs, Iowa were named architects on the condition they become Montanans.

The cornerstone was laid July 4, 1899 and the building dedicated July 4, 1902. It was enlarged with wings in 1909-1912. The architect's neoclassical building was faced in native sandstone from Columbus.

The Rotunda features French Renaissance styling and scagliola (faux marble) columns. The terrazzo tile floor, Tennessee marble wainscoting, and

frescoed dome combine to bring stately taste to the building. The statue of the first woman elected to the U.S. Congress, Jeannette Rankin, stands in the grand stair hall. She has the unique distinction of being the only American to vote against U.S. participation in both World War I (she and 55 others) and World War II (only vote opposing).

"The building design and artwork were the subject of intense consideration -- so Montanans would join the best traditions of the United States and still honor their distinctive heritage," according to the Montana Historical Society's guide, *Montana's Capitol Building*.

ABOVE: Entering the foyer, one is immediately drawn into the regal Rotunda.

OPPOSITE: Looking up into the Rotunda, note the two medallions on the left and right. In each corner of the Rotunda is a medallion painting that tells of four types of the first Montanans. In this picture the *Cowboy* is left and *Native American* is right.

FOLLOWING PAGE: The two other Rotunda medallions are seen in the background; the *Prospector* is left and the *Explorer/Trapper* is right. The medallions were painted by F. Pedretti's Sons and completed in 1902. The Centennial Bell (1889-1989) is in the foreground.

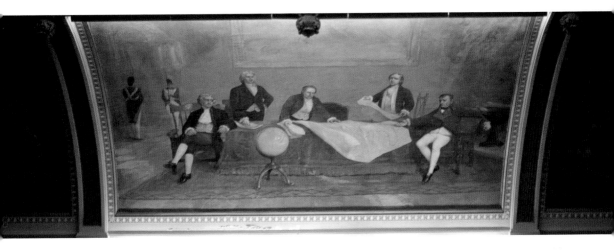

TOP: One of many F. Pedretti's Sons murals in the Senate Chamber, this one titled *Louisiana Purchase*.

ABOVE: The Senate Chamber undergoing restoration. This was originally the House of Representatives Chamber until that body met in its new quarters in 1912.

RIGHT: The House of Representatives Chamber undergoing restoration. The Capitol is the place Montanans make their own laws. The legislature is bicameral. The House of Representatives is comprised of 100 members, serving two-year terms. The Senate is comprised of 50 members, serving four-year terms. The Montana Legislature meets every other year for a ninety-day session.

In a visitor handout the Montana Historical Society reprinted this diary passage from William Clark, he of the Lewis and Clark Expedition. It relates one of the first encounters between Americans and natives in a place that would become Montana. He writes on September 4, 1805: " ... we met a part[y] of the Tushepau [Salish] nation, of 33 Lodges bout 80 men 400 Total and at least 500 horses, those people rec[ei]ved us friendly, threw white robes over our Shoulders & Smoked in the pipes of peace, we Envamped with them and found them friendly, The Chief harangued untill late at night, Smoked in our pipe and appeared Satisfied. I was the first white man who ever wer[e] on the waters of this river."

ABOVE: Ceiling with murals in the old Supreme Court Chamber (1912-1983) and original Senate Chamber. The Pedretti murals include (from top left) *Gates of the Mountains, Wagon Train Under Attack by Indians, Approval of Montana's Constitution, Lewis' First View of the Rocky Mountains, Signing the Enabling Act, Buffalo Chase,* and *The Last of the Buffalo.*

OPPOSITE: Montana's Big Sky country, as seen from the Capitol portico's center window.

FOLLOWING PAGES: The dome is topped with the bronze statue *Liberty* holding a torch and shield. *Right,* a perspective of the Capitol.

Official Name: . . . . State of Wyoming

Motto: . . . . Equal Rights

Citizen: . . . . Wyomingite or Wyomingan

Capital City: . . . . Cheyenne, WY

Established: 1869

Joined Union: 1890

Anthem: . . . . "Wyoming"

Name: . . . . From the Delaware native word
mecheweaming, meaning "big flats"

Nickname: . . . . Equality State; Cowboy State

License Plate Slogan: . . . . N/A

Total Area: . . . . 97,818 sq mi (9)

The State of
Wyoming

Equal Rights

WYOMING

ESTHER HOBART MORRIS

PROPONENT OF THE LEGISLATIVE ACT WHICH
IN 1869 GAVE DISTINCTION TO THE TERRITORY OF

WYOMING

AS THE 1ST GOVERNMENT IN THE WORLD TO GRANT

WOMEN EQUAL RIGHTS

H undreds of thousands of men, women, and children passed through Wyoming in covered wagons on their way westward in the 19th century. They followed the same route across the territory's Great Plains that lie at the foot of the Rocky Mountains, then through the Continental Divide at South Pass. The California Trail, Mormon Trail, and Oregon Trail all traverse Wyoming, uniting at South Pass -- the best natural gap in the Rockies.

Many came, but few stayed. So few, in fact, that at the start of the 21st century Wyoming had the smallest population of the American States (less than 500,000). But Wyoming is huge, twice the size of New York State. It is mountainous, averaging 6,100 feet above sea level, making its lands best suited for cattle grazing. These lands that yield little agriculture give up tremendous minerals including oil, uranium, natural gas, coal, and gold.

Wyoming's people live in scattered small towns separated by an expansive semi-arid terrain. Cheyenne, the capital city named after the people who used to occupy the region, is the state's most populated urban area with some 50,000 citizens.

Wyoming is unique because it was created by all of the four methods territory west of the Mississippi was gained: purchased, negotiated, annexed, or won in war. Most land east of the Continental Divide

ABOVE & OPPOSITE: Esther Hobart Morris greets visitors to the Capitol, symbolizing the fact that Wyoming was the first territory or state to give women the vote.

PREVIOUS PAGES: *The Spirit of Wyoming*, a bronze statue on the Capitol grounds. "Conceived as a symbol to represent Wyoming's people," states the *Wyoming Tour Guide*. It was made by sculptor and artist Edward J. Fraughton; *Right*, early morning sun warms the Capitol.

came from France in the Louisiana Purchase. The northwestern quarter originally was in the Oregon Country. The remaining parts were given by Texas in 1845 and 1850 or were part of the Mexican Cession in 1848. The United States continues to own half of the territory within the state's domain.

Striking, it seems, that this land called Wyoming quickly became one of the most progressive in America. When it became a territory in 1869, the first Wyoming legislature passed a law giving women the vote: the first to do so before any other state, territory, or the federal government. A universal suffrage clause was included in the state's first constitution and approved by the men and women voting on November 5, 1889.

Now Wyoming became the first of the United States to give women the right to vote.

Skeptics say the fact there were six men to every woman in Wyoming at the time had something to do with it, attracting females a priority for the men in the state. In fact, Wyoming's liberality was proven again and again. In 1870 Esther H. Morris of South Pass City became a Justice, the first woman in the U.S. to hold such a post. In 1925 Wyoming elected the first woman governor: Nellie Tayloe Ross.

In other ways this small community in big sky country is progressive. Wyoming does not tax the income of its citizens or its corporations. The state's chief source of revenue is taxes on mineral production and sales taxes. And the Wyoming Legislature is restricted to meeting no more than 40 days a year or 60 days in a two-year period.

In relation to the native peoples, Wyoming escaped the worst violence seen in the west, though there were regular hostilities. When Shoshone aided settlers traveling westward and fought against other tribes hostile to the Americans, the U.S. Government guaranteed Chief Washakie, and later some Arapaho, the Wind River Indian Reservation in the Wind River Basin in 1868.

Cheyenne changed from a small village to a city in a matter of months. The reason: arriving crews of Union Pacific track layers in 1867. Cheyenne was officially made Wyoming's capital in 1869. The Ninth Territorial Legislative Assembly authorized the building of a new Capitol in Cheyenne in 1886 and budgeted $150,000 for the effort. Using a design from the architect firm David W. Gibbs & Co., the Adam Feick & Brothers Co. broke ground September 9, 1886, and the cornerstone was laid May 18, 1887, according to state documents.

Made of native and Colorado sandstone, the Capitol was used by the Tenth Assembly, though it was not yet completed. By 1890, the building was finished. Construction on new legislative chambers began in 1915 and was completed two years later.

PREVIOUS PAGES: A bison stands in the corner of the Rotunda. Raised with the state herd near Thermopolis, this bison weighed 3,000 pounds when living -- the third largest on record. Bison were essential to the native's way of life; with the demise of the bison from over hunting went their society. Below, the elk, or *wapiti* as the Native Americans called the beast, is a popular "big game" animal in a state which remains largely undeveloped. *Left*, a front perspective of the Capitol.

ABOVE & OPPOSITE: Looking up into the dome. The peak of the dome is 146 feet high and the base is 50 feet in diameter. Real gold leaf is used on the dome; it has been gilded six times since 1900. Imported stained glass from England lines the ceiling of the dome. Lights were installed above the glass to give the impression of sun shining through the dome.

OPPOSITE: The House Chamber and, bottom, the Senate Chamber. The House is comprised of 60 representatives, elected to two-year terms. There are 30 senators elected to four-year terms. Wyoming's House of Representatives Chamber features four western paintings by William Gollings. They are titled *Cattlemen, Trappers, Homesteaders,* and *Stagecoach.* In the Senate Chamber there are four murals as well, these by Alan True. They are titled *Indian Chief Cheyenne, Frontier Cavalry Officer, Pony Express Rider,* and *Railroad Builders/Surveyors.*

ABOVE: A perspective of the Rotunda and surrounding floors. The Governor's office is located on the bottom right side.

FOLLOWING PAGES: The stained-glass ceiling in the House Chamber includes the Wyoming Seal; *Right,* a side perspective of the Capitol.

1889

Official Name: . . . . State of North Dakota

Motto: . Liberty and Union Now and Forever, One and Inseparable

Citizen: . . . . North Dakotan

Capital City: . . . . Bismarck, ND

Established: 1889

Joined Union: 1889

Anthem: . . . ."North Dakota Hymn"

Name: From the Dakota natives, meaning "friends, allies;" Dakota is another name for Sioux

Nickname: . . . . Sioux State; Flickertail State; Peace Garden State

License Plate Slogan: . . . . Discover the Spirit

Total Area: . . . . 70,704 sq mi (18)

The State of
North Dakota

Liberty and Union Now and Forever, One and Inseparable

NORTH DAKOTA

I magine a commonwealth where the state owns businesses that compete with private enterprise. A place where the bank itself is state-owned. Where would one find such socialistic principles in action today? Russia? China? Try America. The State of North Dakota to be exact.

North Dakota, a land rich in fertile soil and great mineral deposits including oil, grew rapidly after it was ordained a state in 1889. By 1910 the citizenry had grown to 577,066, most living rural lives as farmers. Soon people became resentful of the growing power out-of-state business interests (mostly from Minnesota) had over their lives, their economy, and state. To combat these influences, the Nonpartisan League was formed. This group argued

ABOVE & OPPOSITE: Two frontal views of the Capitol.

PREVIOUS PAGES: The North Dakota Capitol as seen from the *Cortes Horse* sculpture on the right.

for state ownership of flour mills, grain elevators, and processing plants. It called for banks that made loans at cost (little or no interest).

The result: an Industrial Commission was established by the state legislature to develop and manage its business interests. In 1919 the Bank of North Dakota was established as was the North Dakota Mill and Elevator three years later. Both continue in operation to this day.

Common ownership of property being a distinguishing feature of the Sioux culture, it seems this, too, the North Dakotans inherited from these ancient peoples. Though acquired in the Louisiana Purchase in 1803, it was a grant of land from the

Sioux in 1851 on which the Dakotas (another name for the Sioux people) got their start.

The Dakota Territory was established March 2, 1861 by a Union of States with little more than half its members, the other states having left and formed themselves into a separate republic.

Dakota encompassed the present states of North Dakota and South Dakota and parts of Wyoming and Idaho. As the War Between the States raged, Dakota experienced its own internal conflict. Known as the "Sioux Wars," this conflict also saw native soldiers capitulate to foreign invaders.

At the height of its civilization the Siouan family of tribes (which include the Iowa, Missouri, Kansa, Crow, Winnebago, Omaha, and other native peoples) stretched as far east as Virginia, North Carolina and South Carolina. But as the centuries passed and the populations of the eastern states grew, the Sioux became concentrated west of the Mississippi River.

Final settlement of an issue first raised when natives greeted Columbus in the fifteenth century was at hand. That issue: what was to be the relationship between the European immigrants and the Native American populations? A limitless land rich in natural wealth had delayed its answer. But now the land was becoming limited.

The Sioux embraced American explorers Lewis and Clark, sent by President Jefferson in the early 1800's to explore the northwest. Sacajawea (the Bird Woman), their invaluable westward guide and interpreter, was Sioux. But rising settlement and skirmishes led to hostilities. After Little Crow was defeated in 1867 by Minnesota and federal forces, the Sioux agreed to relocate to the southwest portion of the Dakota Territory by 1876.

But in between those years a young Civil War hero led an expedition that discovered gold in the Black Hills, in the very sacred lands guaranteed the Sioux for their giving up all else. Prospectors rushed in. Survival or extermination now became the issue for the Sioux alone and, with famous chiefs Sitting Bull, Crazy Horse, Red Cloud, and Rain-in-the-Face, hostilities continued for years.

The soldier who helped discover the gold was George Armstrong Custer -- the same man who received General Robert E. Lee's flag of truce and was present at Appomattox where Lee surrendered, ending the Civil War. Successful in helping defeat the Army of Northern Virginia, Custer now confronted the Sioux. In 1876 he marched from Bismarck to attack the natives. At the Battle of the Little Big Horn, in eastern Montana, Custer and his men of the 7th Cavalry, 276 in all, perished before a superior Sioux-Cheyenne force. But the Sioux eventually yielded and accepted smaller reservations.

In 1889 the Dakota Territory was split in two; a constitutional convention met in North Dakota in July and framed the state's government, which was

approved in a referendum. Bismarck was named the capital of the Dakota Territory in 1883 and the first Capitol was built in that year. That building was used six years later to inaugurate the State of North Dakota. It was destroyed by fire in 1930. Oily rags in a janitor's closet were blamed for the loss, according to state documents.

The state moved quickly to build a new Capitol. Governor George F. Shafer appointed commissioners, the legislature approved a $2,000,000 budget, and officials encouraged state citizens to participate in the construction.

North Dakota architects Joseph Bell DeRemer of Grand Forks and W.F. Kurke of Fargo were assisted by Holabird and Root of Chicago, Illinois.

Groundbreaking ceremonies were held August 13, 1932 and the cornerstone was laid September 5, 1933, the 50th anniversary of the dedication of the state's first temple of sovereignty.

Labor troubles plagued construction of the new Capitol. So serious were the problems that Governor William Langer was forced to declare martial law at the building site and backed it up with North Dakota troops to protect the nascent building. The reason for the labor unrest: workers wanted fifty cents an hour, not the thirty cents the state was paying.

In 1935, the building was first occupied. The style is Art Deco, widely used in skyscraper designs of the 1930's and remains as it was built, except for the new judicial wing added in 1981.

OPPOSITE: The Capitol and its unique entrance doors, placed on each side of the glass wall shown above.

ABOVE: The entrance courtyard features a glass wall which, on the inside, serves as the connecting foyer between the legislative chambers and office tower. The modern style was selected, in part, because of the limited budget. The legislative chambers are connected to the 19-story office tower, yet can be sealed off when not in use.

ABOVE: This hallway, connecting with Memorial Hall, separates the chambers which are located on each side. According to state literature, the Capitol is made of Indiana limestone. Inside, Belgium black marble, Montana yellowstone travertine, and Tennessee marble can be seen. Rainforest hardwoods like Honduras mahogany, Burma teak, and east Indian rosewood are used in the paneling. American varieties used include American walnut, California walnut, regional chestnut, and curly maple.

OPPOSITE: North Dakota continues to use its original constitution of 1889 which provides for the two-chamber Legislative Assembly. The House of Representatives Chamber holds 98 members serving two-year terms.

FOLLOWING PAGES: The Senate Chamber in which 49 members meet, representing citizens in districts that the legislature establishes; *Right*, Memorial Hall, the entrance foyer, featuring chandeliers made to resemble North Dakota wheat.

Official Name: .... State of South Dakota

Motto: .... Under God the People Rule

Citizen: .... South Dakotan

Capital City: .... Pierre, SD

Established: 1889

Joined Union: 1889

Anthem: .... "Hail! South Dakota"

Name: .. From the Dakota natives, meaning "friends, allies;" Dakota is another name for Sioux

Nickname: .... Sunshine State; Blizzard State

License Plate Slogan: ..... Great Faces Great Places

Total Area: .... 77,121 sq mi (17)

The State of

South Dakota

Under God the People Rule

The early history of South Dakota is identical with that of North Dakota, both having been part of the Dakota Territory. Established by an Act of Congress in 1861, Dakota also included portions of Wyoming and Montana. Yankton (SD) was made the territorial capital. Twenty-eight years later, it was split into two after repeated requests from those in the territory. The people of Dakota had developed apart, one concentrated in the northern parts and the other in the south. As the railroads ran east-west, there was little to facilitate north-south interaction between them. So, in 1885, the people of the southern region of Dakota met in convention, drafted a constitution, and petitioned for recognition as an independent state.

SOUTH DAKOTA

Two years later, in a plebiscite, all of the people of Dakota voted to split the territory into two independent states. South Dakota became a state with its 1885 constitution intact under the same enabling act that admitted North Dakota, November 2, 1889.

To attain full security, South Dakotans were required, like their northern brethren, to settle the issue of territorial possession with the natives. But the indigenous Arikara and Cheyenne peoples, together with Sioux who were driven from Minnesota, resisted domination from the start. The first clashes between fur traders and natives saw the Sioux joining the Americans against the indigenous village dwellers, the Arikara, in 1823.

Decades later the Sioux fought the Americans and won favorable terms in the Laramie Treaty, successfully creating the Great Sioux Reservation on the lands west of the Missouri River. It was on this "reservation" in the Black Hills where Lt. Colonel George Custer trespassed, illegally searched for, and found gold. Thousands of prospectors rushed in. (To this day the largest gold mine in the Western Hemisphere is the Homestake Mine in Lawrence County.) By 1877 the United States had taken the area and resettled the Sioux elsewhere.

Meanwhile the federal Dawes Act of 1887 sought to individualize native ownership of the reservations. Now each tribe member "owned" land separately, a strange concept for those who for centuries held property in common. This took power away from tribal leaders. It enabled further takeover through the purchase of choice reserved lands from unsophisticated tribesmen.

It was at this time, in the shadows of what seemed to be then a dying people, that a young Paiute dreamed of a messiah who would return the land to its earlier condition before the American invasion. From this dream and other legends came the Ghost Dance religion (so called because of the trance the participants experienced), and it spread among the remaining tribes of the Great Plains. So desperate their situation, many believed the time for the messiah was now.

With an unease settling around South Dakota in its first full year as a state, federal authorities clamped down. Followers of the great Sioux Chief Sitting Bull were massacred by U.S. troops after their leader was murdered in a botched arrest attempt.

Three hundred men, women, and children perished at a camp on Wounded Knee Creek before the guns of the U.S. 7th Cavalry. Was it a coincidence that the 7th Cavalry was Custer's old unit the Sioux destroyed in 1876? *(See North Dakota.)*

This uprising in 1890 would be the last for some eighty years. By now the Sioux's fate on the reduced

PREVIOUS PAGES: The South Dakota Senate Chamber; *Right,* a front perspective of the Capitol.

ABOVE: *Mercy of the Law,* by Charles Holloway, is a painting behind the bench of the South Dakota Supreme Court. It depicts an angel guarding over the legal process.

OPPOSITE: The Rotunda shown with two of its four bronze sculptures created by Dale Lamphere of Sturgis, SD. The sculptures represent Wisdom, Vision, Courage, and Integrity which the artist said represents South Dakotans' strength.

reservations was sealed anyway. There would be no more following of the buffalo. That great beast, a symbol large in their religion and an important source of food, clothing, and shelter, had been over hunted to near extermination by Americans (some shot the animal as sport while sitting aboard a fast-moving train).

Still, the spirit of the Ghost Dance religion lives. The most recent uprising was in 1973 in the South Dakota village of Wounded Knee which was seized by 200 armed natives, acting under the name of the American Indian Movement. A standoff with U.S. authorities ended 71 days later. Only two people were killed in the occupation, three hundred arrested and the authorities promised to investigate the complaints of the rebels.

The first wave of settlers to South Dakota came for the fur trade, establishing Fort Tecumseh in 1817. This would later become Fort Pierre, built by John Jacob Astor's American Fur Company.

Steamboat service to this settlement on the Missouri River began in 1831. Just opposite it is Pierre, which was made the capital city in 1889. It is located in the center of the state.

It would be another twenty years before the Capitol was completed. Modeled after the Montana Capitol, the South Dakota edifice was designed by C.E. Bell and M.S. Detwiler of Minneapolis, Minnesota.

Ground was broken in 1905 and the building completed in 1910 at a cost of just under $1,000,000. Mr.

Bell was one of the architects on the Montana Capitol project. The materials used included native field stone, limestone from Indiana, Vermont marble, and Italian marble. The original structure was 114,000 square feet.

Flags in the Rotunda include the French, Spanish, Dakota Territory, and the U.S. flag; white, red, yellow, and black flags used by Native Americans to indicate direction; and flags from the State of South Dakota, United Sioux Tribes, 50th Anniversary of Mount Rushmore, and a Warrior Eagle Staff. This

staff functioned for the Native Americans much like a flag does today. As people crossed the Great Plains, it was presented as a means of identifying

OPPOSITE: The South Dakota Seal appears on the foyer's ceiling with the Rotunda only steps away.

ABOVE: A view of the third floor after ascending the great staircase of marble. On this floor are the legislative chambers with the House on the east side and the Senate on the west side.

various groups of the Sioux people, according to state literature distributed at the Capitol.

The Capitol's floor is inlaid Italian terrazzo, individually laid by 66 Italian artisans. Legend has it that as a way of "signing" their work, the artisans were given a blue stone to place somewhere in the floor as they determined. To date 55 blue stones have been located. The Rotunda floor also has American-laid prism glass, which helps reflect light from the first floor.

OPPOSITE & ABOVE: Perspectives of the Rotunda. The top of the Rotunda is 96 feet from the floor, and another 65 feet to the top of the dome. The exact center is the brass triangle on the Rotunda floor. All columns are scagliola, a man-made marble, and are not structural components. Below the Rotunda the ground floor (not shown) features the Gallery of Governors, portraits of every governor since the state was born as well as portraits of Supreme Court Justices, and the First Lady Gown Collection.

ABOVE & FOLLOWING PAGE: The Victorian-leaded stained glass that is the Rotunda's ceiling is striking; under it are 16 alcove openings that represent the "Tree of Life," and under these are openings that circle the dome and feature the state flower, the pasque. Acanthus leaves encircle the flower, representing wisdom, and below this is a bottom ring of ribbon designed to symbolize "the ring of eternity." "In each corner of the Rotunda Dome is a large circular mural, each portraying a Greek goddess," states the tour booklet. "Venus with Cupid, Ceres, Minerva, and Europa with Zeus (the bull). The 1910 murals by Edward Simmons were painted to represent the major interests in South Dakota: Love of Family; Love of State; Agriculture; Wisdom, Industry, and Mining; and Livestock. Below each mural are the Seals of Sovereignty or seals of the four white governments which have claimed ownership of what is now called South Dakota. The Seals of France, Spain, South Dakota, and the United States of America are represented."

RIGHT: Front perspective of the Capitol.

ABOVE: Governor's Reception Room which features the original furniture from the Governor's office of 1910.

TOP: *The Peace That Passes Understanding*, by Charles Holloway, is a mural in the central ceiling of the House Chamber. This chamber's chandeliers were removed from the original Federal Court Room in Pierre when the state purchased the building.

ABOVE: The grand staircase of marble. At the top of the stairs is the *The Advent of Commerce*, by Edward Simmons, a painting in the ceiling vault. The scene depicts the first trading between Native Americans and European explorers. The vault itself is made of Victorian-leaded stained glass, with cross members of painted solid oak.

ABOVE: South Dakota's legislature consists of a House of Representatives and Senate. The House has 70 members, the Senate 35. Each state legislator serves a two-year term. The House of Representatives Chamber is shown above.

FOLLOWING PAGES: The Senate Chamber's stained-glass ceiling. House and Senate chambers were restored in the 1980's. *Right*, the Capitol as seen from the park in front of the building. "Sovth Dakota" is spelled on the entablature, a "v" used instead of a "u" to indicate the Greek influence on the building's construction and the state's democratic government.

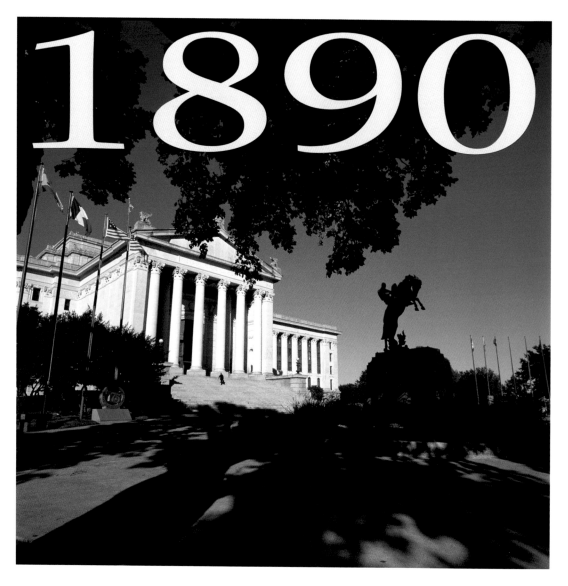

1890

Official Name: . . . . State of Oklahoma	Anthem: . . "Oklahoma" by Rodgers and Hammerstein
Motto: . . . . Labor Omnia Vincit	Name: . . . . Formed from the Choctaw words
Citizen: . . . . Oklahoman	*ukla* "person" and *huma* "red"
Capital City: . . . . Oklahoma City, OK	Nickname: . . . . Sooner State
Established: 1890	License Plate Slogan: . . . . Native America
Joined Union: 1907	Total Area: . . . . 69,903 sq mi (20)

The State of
Oklahoma

Labor Omnia Vincit |
Labor Conquers All Things

OKLAHOMA

Prominently displayed in the Oklahoma Capitol is the state's great seal, recognizing the importance of Native Americans to the state. A five-pointed star in the center gives to one of the Five Civilized Tribes a ray, representing the Chickasaw, Choctaw, Seminole, Creek, and Cherokee. In the center of the star two figures join together with Justice overseeing the union, symbolic of the coming together of the Oklahoma Territory and Indian Territory to form one state.

Oklahoma means "red people." All of it used to be called Indian Territory, and its story begins necessarily with the eastern states from where many of these people came. Georgia did not have but 50,000 citizens in 1776 when it was declared a "free and independent state," and it would be another 25 years before Alabama recorded its first 1,000 citizens. But by 1830 these two states were developing large slave-powered plantations and had over a million souls within their borders -- not to mention tens of thousands of Cherokee.

The Cherokee were a village-based, farming people who took quickly to the ways of the Europeans and later, the Americans. In 1827 they created the Cherokee Nation and formed a constitutionally-based government with an elected chief, a house of representatives, and a senate. The United States recognized the Cherokee Nation and its territorial boundaries in 1791 -- which then encompassed portions of the Carolinas, Tennessee, Alabama, and Georgia -- and guaranteed the natives their land by treaty. Some Cherokee ran large

PREVIOUS PAGES: Two perspectives of the Oklahoma Capitol: on the left, the Constance Whitney Warren *Range Rider* statue and flags of the nations of which Oklahoma was once a part. *Right*, a bronze Native American woman guards the front of the Capitol. *As Long as the Waters Flow* was sculpted by Allan Houser, a Chiricahua Apache artist and state native.

ABOVE & OPPOSITE: Rotunda murals tell the story of Oklahoma. According to the state's tour brochure they include, from left: 1) *Discovery and Exploration*, 1541-1820: images include

Coronado and his men, the Wichita Indians' grass huts, fur trading, Nordic runestones, and a U.S. expedition: 2) *Frontier Trade*, 1790-1830: scenes of early economic and missionary activity including trade with the Osage hunters, schools, salt-making, and trading posts: 3) *Indian Immigration*, 1820-1885: the viewpoint of the western tribes as the eastern tribes are forced into the Plains by the United States Army: 4) *Non-Indian Settlement*, 1870-1906: tells the story of the Land Runs of 1889 through 1893, and the taking of unassigned land by people known as "sooners."

plantations with slave labor, like their southern neighbors, and invested in private enterprises.

But the State of Georgia had other plans. In its cession of western land in 1802 to the United States (which would become Alabama), Georgia added the condition that the U.S. would "extinguish" native land titles in the state through purchase. This the U.S. failed to do, so years later, when the Cherokee formed their nation within the borders of the state, Georgia moved against them. It invalidated their laws and began breaking up their communities and

Georgia humiliated the Supreme Court in 1795 following *Chisolm vs. Georgia*. In that case the court ruled a state could be sued in federal court by an individual. Disagreeing that a sovereign state could be so treated, Georgia led the effort to ratify the 11th Amendment to the U.S. Constitution, which denies such powers to the federal courts.

Its pretensions so easily squashed before, the Supreme Court went to lengths to avoid another confrontation. Now, without Georgia even showing up, the Marshall Court wiggled out of a ruling by declar-

land. Georgia, as an undivided sovereignty, would not permit laws independent of its government.

The Cherokee appealed to President Andrew Jackson for relief. His response: "... the President of the United States has no power to protect them against the laws of Georgia."

They then filed suit in U.S. Supreme Court to stop the state's actions. That court issued a subpoena for the Georgia Governor to appear but he declined, abiding by a mandate from the Georgia Legislature to recognize no federal authority in this matter.

The case was argued without Georgia's participation. And a larger issued loomed: that of the power of the Supreme Court to strike down a state law, which would be required in this case. This power is not granted by the U.S. Constitution to any branch of government. It is given to the court by Congress in statute under section twenty-five of the Judiciary Act of 1789. It remains the source of the court's authority for voiding state laws, though it is subject to simple repeal.

ing the Cherokee Nation not to be a foreign nation, and thus not within the jurisdiction of the court.

With that began the forced deportation of the Cherokee people from their Georgia home to a new Indian Territory created by the Congress in 1830. It was located on the west side of the Mississippi and encompassed most of what today is Oklahoma.

With thousands of Georgia militiamen prodding them along, the Cherokee, their heads bowed, marched to their distant new home under the watchful gaze of U.S. General Winfield Scott. They left their homeland and, at the same time, a gold mine which was "discovered" on their land. Over twenty thousand people were rounded up and placed in stockades, then led on a 1,000 mile trip west to the Indian Territory by the authorities.

Many walked; others rode on horseback through a tough winter. Thousands died. It is solemnly recalled at an annual service as the "Trail of Tears" in Oklahoma to this day. Only a few managed to escape the deportation and settled a reservation in the Smokey Mountains, North Carolina that still exists today.

Oklahoma was part of French Louisiana until that province was sold to the United States in 1803. All of the present-day state, except for the small panhandle, was designated Indian Territory by the U.S. Congress in 1830. Onto these lands the federal government moved many of the native peoples of the east. What was done to the Cherokee was repeated, in varying degrees, to the Creek peoples who lived in Georgia and Alabama; to the Choctaw, who lived in

the southern states, some with slaves on plantations. Each also had its own capital, a place where laws were made. Life in the territory prospered.

After some of the tribes cast their lot with the Confederacy in the Civil War, though, the western portions of the Indian Territory were taken from the natives as punishment by the United States at war's end. In 1889 the U.S. government purchased title from the Creek and Seminole for unoccupied land in their domain. On April 22, 1889 these lands were opened for settlement. The people who cheated and

Mississippi, Louisiana, Georgia, and Alabama; to the Chickasaw, who lived in Tennessee and Mississippi; and to the Seminoles, a Creek people who dominated Florida. Other natives throughout the nineteenth century were also sent there and lands were reserved for future relocations that never occurred.

The people of these five tribes from the east were survivors. They were the remnants of much larger communities which died off from contact with European disease and, later, from colonial wars. Soon they became known as the Five Civilized Tribes. Each had its own constituted government with a governor and legislature. Each had a public school system for children. And they took to the ways of

ABOVE: *Flight of Spirit* by Chickasaw artist Mike Larsen commemorates five world-famous Oklahoma Indian ballerinas.

OPPOSITE: On the Capitol grounds oil is pumped from wells under the building. (The construction next to the oil derrick is unrelated to this.) Oklahoma is a major oil-producing state.

settled the land before this date were called "sooners" because they arrived sooner than allowed by law. The western lands would become the Territory of Oklahoma in 1890, its capital Guthrie. At this time it gained the western panhandle which had been under Texas' jurisdiction. This area was known as "No Man's Land;" outlaws preyed on caravans traveling on the Sante Fe Trail, which cut through it.

A year later the Oklahomans petitioned for statehood but were rebuffed by the U.S. Senate.

The domain of the Five Civilized Tribes was now in doubt. Census figures showed 45,949 native people living among 200,000 "invited" settlers in the Indian Territory. The U.S. government at first used force to keep squatters from the land, some of the most fertile in the region. But then it opted for a more controversial program of Americanizing the people of the Five Civilized Tribes. Federal court jurisdiction was established in the territory. The Dawes Commission was created, and it dismantled the native governments. The commission

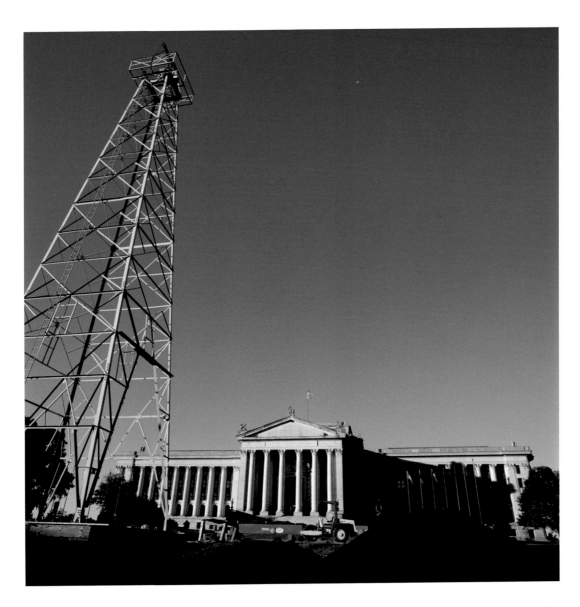

established towns, broke up the tribal holdings in the Indian Territory, and allotted land on an individual basis to the native people. Remaining lands were opened to further settlement, including the Cherokee Outlet. This region saw over 50,000 people claim a piece of its 6.5 million acres in one day in 1889.

In 1905, with approval from the Dawes Commission, the Cherokees-to-be-Americans performed the now familiar ritual of a people constituting a sovereign state. Four of the five tribes, together with non-natives in the territory, called a constitutional convention in Muskogee to adopt a constitution and win its approval from the territory's people.

The Indian Country was to become known as the State of Sequoyah, the constitution stated, in honor of that great Cherokee man who created their language's written alphabet. Congress ignored Sequoyah's petition for statehood; it wanted the Indian Territory and Oklahoma Territory to be combined to form one state, provided the people of each agreed to do so.

In referendums in both lands, the union of the territories was approved. The people there also approved a self-written constitution for the new state, including initiative powers granted to the citizens permitting them to propose law. Congress finally accepted what it considered a radical constitution, and Oklahoma was admitted into the Union in 1907.

The territorial capital of Guthrie lost out when the Oklahoma Legislature declared Oklahoma City the capital city, December 16, 1910. Groundbreaking ceremonies took place July 20, 1914; the cornerstone was tapped into place by Governor Robert C. Williams on Statehood Day, November 16, 1915. Historical documents of the period are deposited in the cornerstone. The Capitol's total cost: $1,515,000.

Designed by Solomon Layton, the principal architect, and Wemyss Smith, the Oklahoma Capitol was completed June 30, 1917 after three years of construction. It is in the neo-classical style. The Capitol is faced in white Indiana limestone.

According to tour information, the base is made of native granites in pink and black, taken from Troy and Coal Springs, respectively. Inside, marble from Alabama is the primary flooring with Georgian marble on the second and fourth floors. Vermont marble is seen in the stairways.

"The Capitol belongs to all citizens of Oklahoma -- it is your palace, your treasure, your inheritance," wrote Governor Frank Keating in a commemorative guide to the Capitol.

OPPOSITE: A perspective of the Capitol's west side.

ABOVE: The Oklahoma Seal appears as a faux eye of the dome. In the Rotunda four famous Oklahomans are honored with portraits, painted by Oklahoma artist Charles Banks Wilson. They include: Will Rogers, who was part Cherokee, a journalist and actor who lifted spirits during the Great Depression; Jim Thorpe, one of the greatest athletes of the 20th century, was a Sac and Fox Indian; Sequoyah, the Cherokee educator; and Robert S. Kerr, former Oklahoma Governor and U.S. Senator.

PREVIOUS PAGE LEFT: Above the grand staircase is the State of Oklahoma's first major art commission: *Pro Patria*, by Gilbert White of Paris, France. It honors Oklahoma soldiers who served in World War I. Murals flanking the painting list the 2,657 Oklahomans who died in the conflict; these murals are now enclosed as part of several conference rooms created in the 1970's. The project was financed by oilman Frank Phillips.

PREVIOUS PAGE RIGHT: The Oklahoma House of Representatives occupies the west wing of the building. The House has 101 members, each elected to a two-year term. Above the Speaker's chair are three pictures: the Governor, the U.S. President, and the Speaker of the House. The Chamber was last renovated in 1967.

ABOVE: The Oklahoma Senate has 48 senators, each elected to a four-year term. Photographs of the Senate President and President Pro Tempore are on the wall in front. The walls of the House and Senate chambers are lined with photographs of every legislator who has served the state.

OPPOSITE: At the steps of the Oklahoma Capitol. The building measures 480 feet long by 340 feet wide. The grand staircase is made of marble taken from Henryetta, OK. A dome was originally intended but never built; funds were scarce after World War I. But the state has never abandoned the idea of someday placing a dome on top of its Capitol.

Official Name: . . . . State of Alaska
Motto: . . . . North to the Future
Citizen: . . . . Alaskan
Capital City: . . . . Juneau, AK
Established: 1912
Joined Union: 1959
Anthem: . . . . "Alaska's Flag"

Name: . . . . . . The name comes from the Aleut word
Alaxxsaq and the Eskimo word *Alaska*, both meaning "the object toward which the action of the sea is directed"
Nickname: . . . . Land of the Midnight Sun
License Plate Slogan: . . . . The Last Frontier
Total Area: . . . . 615,230 sq mi (1)

The State of
Alaska

North to the Future

ALASKA

Russian America was the name of the vast northern terrain bordering western Canada. It would connect to Russia but for the 56-mile-wide Bering Strait the meeting point of the continents of Asia and North America. It is here that scientists believe a great land bridge existed 15,000 years ago which Eurasian immigrants crossed -- the seeds of all future American native peoples, north and south. Russian America is the only part of the continent to which the first explorers (Russian Cossacks) came from the west.

Czar Peter the Great commissioned Vitus Bering, a Danish navigator, to investigate the region. In 1741, on his second voyage, he landed on Kayak Island. The first permanent settlement on Kodiak Island was made by Grigor Shelikov, and from here Russia's rule over Alaska and its natives commenced.

In 1799 the Russian Emperor chartered the Russo-American Company, granting a monopoly over the fur trade. By 1825, a treaty between Russia and Great Britain settled the Canadian border. But in 1861 the company relinquished its monopoly, and the Russian authorities, having failed at numerous development attempts, were looking for quick cash after the costly Crimean War.

Negotiations for the purchase of this vast territory began as early as 1859 with the United States but were delayed with the coming War Between the States. In 1865 the Western Union Telegraph Co. planned a pan-continent cable to connect Europe and North America there, but ceased these efforts with the success of the Atlantic Ocean cable a year later. Not until 1867 did the Russian Minister open formal negotiations to sell her extreme western frontier, a third of which lay above the Arctic Circle.

Representing the United States was William Seward, from Orange County, New York, who was President Lincoln's Secretary of State. The final purchase price was set at $7,200,000 in gold. That figures at about two cents an acre. The Senate ratified the "Treaty of Cession of Russian America to the United States" that year and changed the name of this domain at the insistence of Massachusetts Senator Charles Sumner.

Now it was to be called Alaska (*Aleutian* for great land or mainland).

Critics called it "Icebergia" and "Seward's Folly." Yet the old New Yorker firmly believed the acquisition of this immense territory would be considered his greatest accomplishment. History proved him right: Alaska is twice the size of Texas and packed with vast natural resources not completely known even to this day.

On October 18, 1867 U.S. troops first raised the flag at Sitka. But Congress was slow in providing Alaskans with civil government, and for the next 17 years there was no legal code or courts, and thus no security in property rights. Native customs were the closest to a common law. Most of the Russians returned home. The U.S. Army ruled for a time, but

PREVIOUS PAGES: The Capitol began its service to Alaskans in 1931. *Right*, the *Windfall Fisherman* black bear sculpture was made by Skip Wallen to honor the 25th year of statehood.

OPPOSITE: Sculptures flanking the lobby are *Harvest of the Sea* and *Harvest of the Land*. They were created by Joan Bugbee Jackson. "It is worthy to note," says the Capitol tour brochure, "that Alaskan Eskimos never lived in igloos."

ABOVE: The totem pole *Harnessing the Atom* shows, from the bottom, a raven, a native man standing on the sun, a Russian priest, and eagle. It was made by Amos Wallace.

ABOVE RIGHT: Capitol door handles feature a totemic design.

RIGHT: The Alaska Seal hangs in the Senate Chamber. Made of wood, it is located behind the Senate President's desk.

the last troops were withdrawn in 1877 to help reinforce units fighting Chief Joseph in Idaho. The U.S. Navy and Treasury Department took over until 1884, a warship and revenue cutter being the only "law and order."

In 1880 Joseph Juneau and Richard T. Harris discovered gold in an area they called Juneau, Alaska's future capital. In 1884, at the prodding of Presbyterian Minister Sheldon Jackson, Congress established the Organic Act. Under this ordinance Oregon's laws became Alaska's code and a civil and judicial district was created with a governor and federal court. But the power to make new laws was left to Congress alone. In 1885, Jackson was appointed head of public education for natives and settlers in the territory.

What became known as the Alaska Boundary Controversy with Great Britain, a matter which loomed as large as Alaska's icebergs, now dropped into the open. At issue were interpretations of the 1825 border treaty. Gold had been discovered in the Klondike Region of the Yukon Territory, on the Canada-Alaska border.

OPPOSITE: The columned front of the Alaska Capitol.

ABOVE: The Hall of Governors leads to the executive offices.

To settle the dispute, both nations agreed by treaty to submit to the ruling of the special Alaska Boundary Tribunal. Ultimately, the United States won the present boundaries.

Not until 1912 would Alaskans get the right to elect their own territorial legislature. And months later the Alaska Native Brotherhood was formed, followed by a Native Sisterhood. These groups, and later the Alaska Federation of Natives, fought in the political arena and won voting, education, and land rights for the Intuit and other natives throughout the twentieth century.

According to the tour pamphlet, Congress appropriated monies for a territorial government building in 1911, but World War I postponed construction as did the federal government's refusal to pay the asking price for the land. Juneau residents and businesses raised the money to buy the lots and deeded them to the United States.

Construction did not actually start until 1929. From its first session in 1913 until its new chambers were finished in 1931, the Alaska Legislature met in rented quarters around Juneau.

Groundbreaking ceremonies were held September 19, 1929. The Chicago-based construction company N.P. Severin Co. executed the plans designed by architects in the U.S. Treasury Department. The building is made out of reinforced concrete and faced with brick and the lower facade with limestone.

The four columns of the portico -- the building's dominant feature -- were made from native marble taken from Prince of Wales Island. The building became the property of Alaska when it became a state. The total cost of the building and land was $1,000,000.

The Alaskan Territory would be the only part of the United States occupied in World War II by the enemy, the Japanese holding the islands Kiska and Attu in the Aleutian Archipelago. In 1942 the federal Alaska Highway was built for defense purposes. A year later 152,000 Americans were stationed in Alaska, and the islands were retaken.

From this war would come renewed calls for statehood, the earliest request dating to 1916. Congress made Alaska the 49th American State in 1958.

In 1959 the territorial building Alaskans were so proud of became their Capitol. An event of great consequence happened shortly thereafter that would forever change the goings-on in that building. Atlantic Richfield Company announced one of the biggest oil discoveries in the world at Prudhoe Bay.

Alaskans, who had been able to achieve a harmony between the natives and Americans so elusive in the contiguous states, now equally shared riches never seen before by any people of any state and by very few nations.

In 1976 the Alaska Constitution was amended to create the Permanent Fund in which portions of royalty monies from mineral development were to be placed. High oil prices in the late 1970's led to the abolition of all state income and sales taxes. In 1982 annual dividends from the fund were sent to every state citizen.

At the start of the 21st century, that dividend check was over $2,000 per person. Alaskans of today, it has been said, are more Arab than American when it comes to matters of oil!

TOP LEFT: *Two Alaskan Otters*, by Judd Mullady of Juneau, is sculpted from native marble and placed in the foyer.

ABOVE: Flags fly at the Capitol. A 13-year-old Alaska native, Benny Benson, designed the Alaska flag in 1926.

LEFT: The foyer features ceiling edge designs that symbolize sea life, forests, mining, and the people.

OPPOSITE TOP: The Territorial Senate Chamber is now used by the Speaker of the House of Representatives.

OPPOSITE BOTTOM: The House of Representatives Chamber (left) and Senate Chamber (right). The House has forty members serving two-year terms. The Senate has 20 members serving four-year terms.

UTAH 1849

CALIFORNIA 1849

NEW MEXICO 1850

NEVADA 1861

WEST VIRGINIA 1861

ARIZONA 1863

War
States

"The Mexicans who, in the territories aforesaid, shall not preserve the character of citizens of the Mexican Republic ... shall be incorporated into the Union of the United States, and be admitted at the proper time (to be judged of by the Congress of the United States) to the enjoyment of all the rights of citizens of the United States, according to the principles of the Constitution; and in the mean time shall be maintained and protected in the free enjoyment of their liberty and property, and secured in the free exercise of their religion without restriction."

-- From the Treaty of Guadalupe Hidalgo, made between the United States and Mexico in 1848. This treaty formally ended the Mexican-American War and by its terms the U.S. gained California, Nevada, Utah, Arizona, and New Mexico.

Official Name:................. State of Utah	Name: ..... Named for the Ute, or Utah, natives;
Motto:............................... Industry	the word *yuttahih* means "highlanders,"
Citizen: .... Utahn or Utahan	"mountaintop dwellers"
Capital City:.............. Salt Lake City, UT	Nickname: ... Beehive State; Mormon State; The
Established:............................ 1849	Land of the Saints
Joined Union:.......................... 1896	License Plate Slogan: Ski Utah, Best Snow On Earth
Anthem:............... "Utah, We Love Thee"	Total Area:.................. 84,904 sq mi (13)

The State of
Utah

Industry

The story of Utah begins with that of the Mormons who settled it, built it, and continue to make it prosper. It begins in Vermont and New York when Joseph Smith, born in the former, moved to the latter and founded the Judeo-Christian faith known as the Church of Jesus Christ of Latter-day Saints. In 1819, at the age of 14, Smith began praying to God, asking which of the many Christian denominations offered the way for his salvation. According to Smith's testimony, "a vision of great light" had two spirits come and instruct him to join no church since the Gospel was to be restored by God. In a later vision the angel Moroni directed him to a secret cave in Cumorah Hill, Palmyra, NY where ancient plates of gold told the story of the first peoples of South and North America. The gold plates Smith translated, taking the name "The Book of Mormon" from their title page.

UTAH

The plates tell the story of Israelites who came to South America, landing in Chile. They were one of the lost tribes of the Bible and called Nephites. When a new leader of these people was selected by God, some resisted and were punished. Those punished were called Lamanites and became the ancestors of the North American natives, the plates said. Jesus Christ is reported to have appeared in the Americas after his resurrection, but most Nephites were annihilated in a war with the Lamanites except for a lucky few including Mormon, who wrote the plates, and his son Moroni.

With his translation of the plates completed and published in 1829, Smith founded the Church and began missionary activities. From the start the Mormons were persecuted because of the conflict certain tenets of their faith had with other Christian sects, the most controversial being the acceptance of a man having multiple wives. Smith himself had several wives since polygamy was permitted under ancient Jewish law. Central to Mormon convictions is that their religion was the only true one, a continuation of the Bible, all others not having the authority to officiate in God's name.

Neighbors of these enclaves of Mormons viewed them with suspicion. After violence forced them out of Ohio and Missouri, the prophet Smith and thousands of adherents took over Commerce, IL and created Nauvoo. By the early 1840's, twenty thousand had turned Nauvoo into a booming Mormon haven. A very liberal charter was granted by the Illinois Legislature, making Nauvoo practically an independent state within the state.

When disgruntled citizens published charges in the *Expositor* against Joseph Smith, the executive head of Nauvoo, he had marshalls destroy the

LEFT: Eagle Gate frames the Capitol's dome.

PREVIOUS PAGES: The Utah Constitution is encased just off the Rotunda; *Right*, a front perspective of the Capitol.

OPPOSITE: The Rotunda mural depicting Brigham Young and Mormon pioneers entering the Salt Lake Valley in 1847.

presses. Mobs now rioted over this violation of rights. Smith, whose title included Lt. General of the Nauvoo Legion, called out Mormon troops to maintain order. For this, he was arrested by state authorities and charged with treason against the State of Illinois; he was imprisoned in Carthage. There, a mob of armed men with blackened faces murdered Smith and his brother Hyrum on June 27, 1844.

As Brigham Young was the senior member of the Council of Twelve Apostles, he assumed leadership of the church. A New Yorker who joined Smith in the early years, Young realized the growing Mormon population could not live comfortably next to non-Mormons and conduct their society without outside interference. An agreement with county and state authorities in 1845 forced the Mormons to evacuate their cherished Nauvoo.

But where would they go? Reports of an undesirable piece of desert called the Great Salt Lake Valley reached church authorities. It wasn't even in the United States, being the northern frontier of Mexico. Perhaps there they would be left alone to live as they saw fit.

The story which unfolds could have come, but for the names, from the Old Testament. In 1846 some 15,000 Mormons, 3,000 wagons, and 30,000 head of cattle reached the camps along the Missouri. Not until the long winter of 1846-47 did Young and the Mormons leave camps in Nebraska for the isolated valley in the desert. By January 1, 1848 nearly 1,600 Mormons arrived. One year later, as many as 80,000 more made the one-thousand-mile trip from Nebraska, some even pushing their possessions by hand cart, according to state documents.

Thus the Mormons' new community became the first permanent settlement in Utah.

Up to then the Mormons were theocratic in their community; the state and church were one and the same. The temple, with its hierarchy and structure, was also town hall. Only in New Haven, Connecticut (1639-44) was something similar attempted in North America. But in 1849, under the brilliant leadership of Brigham Young, the Mormons created something grander: the State of Deseret. A provisional government was established with Young as governor, and the people adopted a constitution.

With the United States taking control of the region after defeating Mexico, Young requested that Deseret be permitted to join the American Union of States. Instead, Congress created the Utah Territory in 1850, named after the Ute natives there. Young was made Territorial Governor. And the desert blossomed (Isaiah 35-1). The Mormons used sophisticated irrigation techniques, turning desert into rich farmland. The area grew rapidly.

BRIGHAM YOUNG AND PIONEERS ENTERING THE VALLEY

But the bright dawn now enjoyed would have clouds. The discovery of gold and settlement in the Oregon Country drew growing numbers of non-Mormons through the area. Salt Lake became a key resting point. In 1852 Young affirmed polygamy as church doctrine. Some 20% of Mormons were thought to have practiced it then.

President Buchanan moved to replace Young as Territorial Governor and sent federal troops with his non-Mormon replacement in 1857. The "Mountain Meadows Massacre" of California immigrants traveling through Utah and a rumored rebellion led to the confrontation known as the Mormon War.

Guerrilla tactics delayed the arrival of the federal troops under General Sidney Johnston. In the spring of 1858 the new governor and troops arrived and Young accepted the change in power without opposition, thanks to the peacemaking efforts of Thomas L. Kane. In 1861, the ex-governor sent the first overland telegram to President Lincoln. It stated: "Utah is loyal. Has not seceded from the Union."

For the remainder of his life, Young proselytized and gained many converts to the church. Membership numbered close to five million in 1999. (In Utah that year some 70% of the population was Mormon.)

In 1870 women were given the right to vote, making Utah second only to Wyoming in this regard. Brigham Young died in 1877. He would not live to see Utah become a state. That right would be delayed for twenty more years as the federal government continued to crack down on polygamists in the territory. Finally, in 1894, the Utahns met in convention and drafted a constitution that outlawed polygamy and prohibited church control of the state.

In 1896 Congress ordained the land the State of Utah. The church, meanwhile, did not renounce polygamy but only required the faithful to follow the civil law.

Good fortune continued for these industrious people, even in the gaining of a new Capitol. The story of the current edifice begins with the estate of E.H. Harriman. The railroad magnate's heirs paid a whopping 5% inheritance tax to the state, totaling $798,000, according to the tour pamphlet.

Using this as a down payment, the state selected Richard Kletting's Renaissance Revival plan. On December 26, 1912 ground was broken and the cornerstone was laid April, 1914. On October 9, 1916, the new Capitol was dedicated. Total cost: $2,739,538. It measures 404 feet long by 240 feet wide and 286 feet tall. Fifty-two Corinthian columns wall the exterior of unpolished granite.

The original capital city was Fillmore where part of a new Capitol was built for the territorial legislature. One wing was completed and one session, in 1855, was held. Thereafter, Fillmore was abandoned and the legislature met in various Salt Lake City-area locations.

It took twenty years of statehood before Utahns had a Capitol they could call their own.

TOP: The Utah Capitol photographed in front of Eagle Gate.

OPPOSITE: A copper beehive in front of the Capitol symbolizes industry, the state's motto.

BOTTOM LEFT: A tile mosaic of Utah's Great Seal.

BOTTOM RIGHT: Flags flying at the Capitol.

IN THE YEAR 1857, JAMES BUCHANAN, THEN PRESIDENT OF THE UNITED STATES, BELIEVING CERTAIN UNFOUNDED RUMORS THAT UTAH TERRITORIAL GOVERNOR BRIGHAM YOUNG AND OTHER UTAH TERRITORIAL OFFICERS WERE IN OPEN REBELLION AGAINST FEDERAL AUTHORITY IN UTAH, SENT TO UTAH AN ARMED FORCE OF 25 HUNDRED MEN, KNOWN AS JOHNSTON'S ARMY, TO MAINTAIN FEDERAL AUTHORITY.

ON BEING ADVISED OF THE THREATENED INVASION OF HIS FRIENDS' HOMELAND, THOMAS L. KANE AGAINST THE WISHES OF PRESIDENT BUCHANAN, A FRIEND OF THE KANE FAMILY, AND HIS FATHER, JUDGE JOHN K. KANE, DECIDED TO AGAIN GO TO THE AID OF HIS MORMON FRIENDS. HE SAILED DOWN THE ATLANTIC OCEAN, CROSSED THE ISTHMUS OF PANAMA, SAILED UP THE PACIFIC OCEAN TO SAN FRANCISCO, THEN TRAVELED BY HORSE AND WAGON TO SALT LAKE CITY.

THROUGH HIS EFFORTS PEACE WAS ESTABLISHED IN UTAH AND A GREAT BLESSING BROUGHT THEREBY TO THE PIONEERING PEOPLE OF THIS TERRITORY.

TOP LEFT: A replica statue of Chief Massasoit, the original being in Plymouth, Massachusetts. It was sculpted by Utahn Cyrus Dallin.

TOP RIGHT: The look outside the Capitol from a vestibule.

LEFT: A perspective of the Utah Capitol.

ABOVE: The plaque placed on a statue of General Thomas Kane, who helped maintain peace between Utahns and U.S. troops.

OPPOSITE: The bronze statue of Brigham Young in the Rotunda. Note his finger which many have rubbed for good luck.

OPPOSITE & ABOVE: Reaching 165 feet into the air, the Rotunda features epic murals which tell the story of Utah. According to the state tour booklet, the murals were made during the Great Depression by Lee Greene Richards, Waldo P. Midgley, Gordon Cope, and Harry Rasmussen. Depicted in the four largest murals: 1) The Franciscan friars Dominguez and Escalante visit the area, 1776; 2) American military explorer John Fremont mapping the area, 1843; 3) Peter Skene Ogden and the lucrative fur trade, 1820-50; and 4) Brigham Young and Mormon pioneers entering the Salt Lake Valley in 1847 to begin settlement. The eight higher paintings detail life in Utah. The perspective shown above offers a look directly into the eye of the dome.

ABOVE: Looking across the Rotunda from one chamber to the other. The Utah Legislature consists of the House of Representatives and Senate and meets annually for 45 days, from January to March.

OPPOSITE TOP: The Utah Senate has 29 members, each serving a four-year term. On average each Senator represents 65,000 Utahns. The mural is of Utah Lake near Provo; the walls are made of onyx mined in Utah, according to the tour pamphlet.

OPPOSITE BOTTOM: The Utah House of Representatives is comprised of 75 members elected to two-year terms. Each represents approximately 25,000 Utahns. The dominant painting in the chamber shows Latter Day Saints Church President and first Territorial Governor Brigham Young inspecting granite to be used in building the Mormon Temple.

OPPOSITE: The Capitol as seen from the lower parking lot.

ABOVE: Lunettes on each end of the Great Hall reflect the efforts of the pioneers. On the west end mural shown, the Salt Lake Valley is depicted as the pioneers saw it when they first arrived. On the east end mural is the land one year later after crops were planted. Both murals were painted by Gerald Hale and Gilbert White in 1917.

"WE THE PEOPLE, Grateful to the SUPREME BEING for the blessings hitherto enjoyed, and feeling our dependence on Him for a continuation of these blessings, DO ORDAIN, AND ESTABLISH A FREE AND INDEPENDENT GOVERNMENT, by the name of the STATE OF DESERET ..."

-- Constitution of the State of Deseret, 1849. One year after it was drawn the U.S. Congress created the Utah Territory, replacing Deseret. Nearly fifty years later, Utah became one of the United States.

Official Name: . . . . State of California

Motto: . . . . "Eureka!"

Citizen: . . . . Californian

Capital City: . . . . Sacramento, CA

Established: 1849

Joined Union: 1850

Anthem: . . . . "I Love You, California"

Name: . . . . . The Spanish named the Baja California peninsula after a fictional island republic in *Las Sergas de Esplandian* by Garcia Ordonez de Montalvo

Nickname: . . . . The Golden State

License Plate Slogan: . . . . N/A

Total Area: . . . . 163,707 sq mi (3)

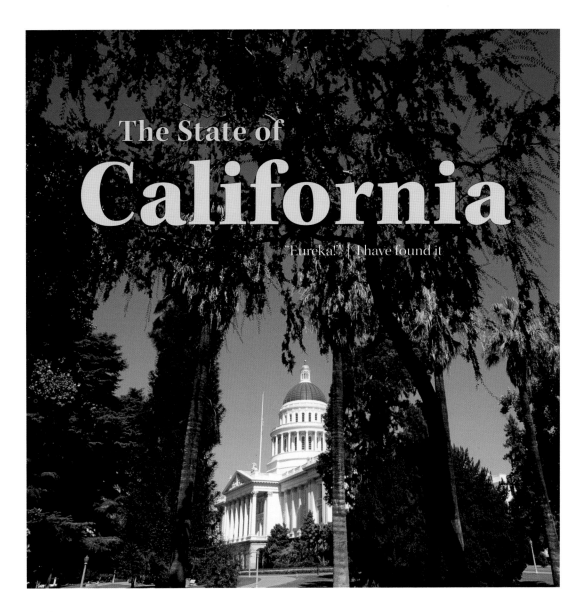

The State of
California

"Eureka!" | I have found it

"California Republic," the state's flag declares to this day. A republic, indeed: with over 32 million citizens living in a domain of over 160,000 square miles, California alone would be a first-rate nation. Its Gross State Product would make it the sixth richest in the world. Cloistered by the Sierra Nevada mountain system and Mojave Desert on its east and the Pacific Ocean on its west, with some of the world's best farmland in between, California's terrain is as varied as her people. Perhaps the state's greatest natural treasure is the giant sequoia, an ancient tree that can weigh hundreds of tons and soar 300 feet in the air -- some alive since the building of the Pyramids 3,000 years ago.

CALIFORNIA

The Spanish legacy is everywhere seen and felt in the words, food, and people of California. The state's name comes from the fictional Spanish romance *Las Sergas de Esplandian*. In the story a democratic island republic called *California* is "very near the Terrestrial Paradise and inhabited by black women without a single man among them and living in the manner of Amazons. They are robust of body, strong and passionate in heart, and of great valor."

California was of two parts under Spanish rule: Baja (Lower) California which is the southern peninsula, and Alta (Upper) California which continues along the coast for 700 miles north. Baja California was discovered in 1533. In 1602 the Monterey region was first explored. Roman Catholic missions led by Franciscan friars began in 1769 with San Diego de Alcala. In 1776 the San Francisco mission was established. Over the next 60 years the friars would establish 23 missions and Christianize over 80,000 people. Mission life meant long hours and hard work for natives who labored on these large estates; some succumbed to disease.

In 1821 Mexico won its independence from Spain, ending Spanish authority in California. Four years later, California became part of the new Mexican republic, but kept its own legislature (the *diputacion*) and militia. It was practically autonomous. Los Angeles, founded in 1781, shared capital city honors with Monterey during the Spanish period. Now Monterey was the provincial capital.

By the early 1830's many Californians tired of the string of poor governors from Mexico, some of whom tried to stop the sale of mission property. The great missions' land and property was being sold off by the defeated Spanish, who claimed the friars never owned it. Vast agricultural holdings known as *ranchos* were sold to *rancheros* and the converted natives who had worked the land. Amidst California's turmoil, U.S. President Andrew Jackson

ABOVE: The Capitol's pediment and dome.

PREVIOUS PAGES: California's Senate Chamber; *Right*, the Capitol framed in redwoods and cypress trees.

offered to buy the northern parts of the province centered around San Francisco. The offer was made in 1835. Mexico refused.

A year later Juan Bautista Alvarado, then head of the *diputacion*, led a revolt against Mexican authority and captured Monterey. The rebels were Californios, Spanish Californians who were taking control of the former mission property by buying titles earlier sold to the converted native laborers. Provincial officials were fired and returned to Mexico City. On November 7, 1836 the rebels declared California to be "a free and sovereign State." Alvarado was named provisional governor, the first civilian governor in California's history. Later his forces took possession of Los Angeles. Alvarado now pushed along privatization of the missions' property.

Bowing to political reality, Mexico offered to make Alvarado governor of California if the rebellion ended immediately. He accepted and, until 1842, governed the autonomous region as part of the Mexican republic.

But peace did not last. Two years later, a new revolt against Mexican authority by the Californios ensued. In 1845 they defeated Mexican forces and took control of California. The governor was deposed. And the rebels returned to the job of creating a new state. Jose Castro was made Military Commandant and based in Monterey. Pio Picos was named governor working from Los Angeles.

But before much progress was made, Ezekiel Merritt and other American settlers staged a revolt with the backing of U.S. Captain John Fremont, who was in California on a military surveying mission. The shadowy Fremont and the soldiers under his command were asked to leave Monterey by California's revolutionary authorities. Fremont refused and ordered the U.S. flag raised in defiance nearby.

Fearing reprisals from the Californios, American settlers captured the northern fort of Sonoma, backed by Fremont. In June, 1846 they raised a banner: a homemade flag for a new republic. This became known as the Bear Flag War because of the banner with the bear, star, and the words "California Republic" which was raised.

The rebels selected William B. Ide as their leader. He in turn proclaimed the creation of the Bear Flag Republic. Shortly thereafter, his forces defeated Commandant Castro's troops and looked to secure their gains when Fremont suddenly reappeared. Fremont knew what no else there did, namely that the United States and Mexico were at war. Ide was forced to transfer command of the California Republic's military forces to Fremont.

Two days later U.S. troops invaded Monterey on July 7, 1846. They then marched to Sonoma, peacefully took the fort where the Bear Flag Republic was born, and lowered that flag for the final time. But it would not come down easily. The man pulling the rope was a U.S. sailor named Joseph W. Revere, the grandson of Massachusetts' revolutionary Paul Revere.

So difficult was the job that eyewitnesses said the Bear Flag came down "growling."

The U.S. Navy's Pacific squadron dominated the coast with Commodore Sloat capturing Monterey and San Francisco and Commodore Stockton taking Los Angeles and San Diego. In a matter of weeks, California was conquered.

The land was made a Territory of the United States on August 15, 1846 in name only, as no territorial government would ever be created for California. John Fremont was made governor. When the Mexican-American War ended in 1848, the United States gained by the Treaty of Guadalupe Hidalgo all of Mexico's northern lands including portions of Colorado, New Mexico, Arizona, Utah, Nevada, and California. For this the United States paid Mexico $18,250,000.

Only one week before the treaty was signed, gold was discovered in California. Lucky John Fremont. It was on his extensive estate that the gold was discovered, as well as the more famous find at Sutter's Mill. California's population exploded from 15,000 people to over 100,000 in a matter of months. Mining towns boomed, including San Francisco and Sacramento. It was the year of the forty-niner.

Meanwhile Californians met in convention in Monterey and drafted a constitution that prohibited slavery and recognized women's property rights. The convention addressed a hard reality of the times: from 1846 with the American takeover until this point in 1849 the territory had no legislature and a general lawlessness prevailed. A year later the U.S. Congress negotiated the Compromise of 1850 by which California became one of the United States.

The California Legislature held a competition for a permanent State House and selected the design of Reuben Clark in 1856. Clark, a Maine carpenter, had worked on the Mississippi Capitol. But in 1860 a new plan, this one by Miner Butler, was selected and Reuben Clark was appointed superintendent of

construction. Work on the foundation began in 1861 as the first shots in the Civil War were fired. That war played havoc with the construction, reportedly driving Clark insane. He died in 1866 and his work was picked up by G.P. Cummings, who pretty much completed the project in 1878.

The original Clark design resembled the Mississippi Capitol he had worked on. The finished California Capitol ended up looking more like the United States Capitol in Washington, DC.

The colors of the Legislative Chambers are borrowed from the British Parliament. The two chairs at the head of each chamber are symbols of the monarchy in England.

"Over the arches, going into the hallways, is the head of the Goddess of Wisdom known as Minerva," states the California State Parks' *Guide to the Capitol.* "She was chosen to be a part of the State Seal because, according to mythology, Minerva was born fully grown from the head of her father, Jupiter. (The Greek name for "Minerva" is "Athena," the daughter of Zeus.) She represents the fact that California, too, was never an infant. California became a state without ever having been a territory."

ABOVE: A side perspective of the Capitol.

TOP & OPPOSITE: Perspectives of the California Capitol as seen from flanking administrative buildings including the State Library & Courts Building and Unruh Office Building. The top of the dome features a ball made of copper and plated in gold.

OPPOSITE: Looking up at *Columbus' Last Appeal* by Larkin Meade. The Vermont native was one of the most prominent sculptors of the 19th century. Working in Florence, Italy he made the statue in 1870. D.O. Mills bought it in 1882 for $30,000 and the Capitol received it on Christmas, 1883, according to state tour information. It shows Columbus convincing Spanish Queen Isabella that the earth is round in an effort to win her support for his westward voyage.

ABOVE: The Rotunda with the Meade statue in the center. Cornucopias encircle the Rotunda, representing agriculture's great impact on the state. California is the number one producer of agricultural commodities of the American States.

ABOVE: The California Seal in a ceramic mosaic near the Rotunda.

RIGHT: The Capitol's foyer as seen from one of the twin stair-case landings.

OPPOSITE: "Bring me men to match my mountains," the frieze on the entablature reads on the State Library & Court Building next to the Capitol.

PREVIOUS PAGE LEFT: Various views of the Senate Chamber. The California Senate holds forty members, each elected to a term of four years; one Senator represents 800,000 citizens. Voting is done by traditional means of roll call, but votes are then recorded electronically on a panel in front of the chamber. "It is the duty of a Senator to protect the liberty of the commonwealth," states the inscription in Latin in front.

PREVIOUS PAGE RIGHT: Assembly Chambers and entrance. The California Assembly has eighty members, each elected to a two-year term. Each member represents about 400,000 citizens. Voting is electronic and done at the desk of the members. "It is the duty of Legislators to make just laws," states the Latin in-scription prominently displayed in front. In these pictures the chamber is being refurbished while students learn how laws are made in California. The original chandeliers in the Legislative Chambers were gas lit; the Capitol was not wired for electricity until 1892.

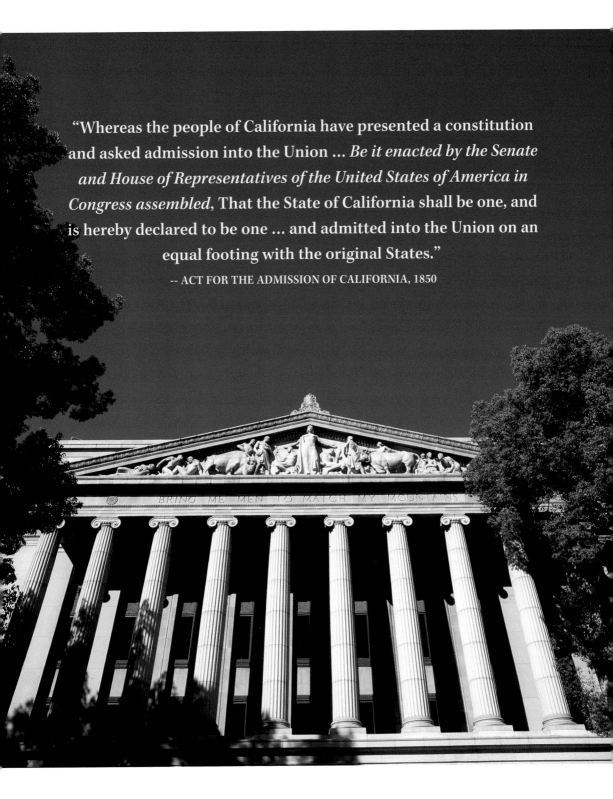

"Whereas the people of California have presented a constitution and asked admission into the Union ... *Be it enacted by the Senate and House of Representatives of the United States of America in Congress assembled,* That the State of California shall be one, and is hereby declared to be one ... and admitted into the Union on an equal footing with the original States."

-- ACT FOR THE ADMISSION OF CALIFORNIA, 1850

1850

Official Name: . . . . State of New Mexico
Motto: . . . . Crescit Eundo
Citizen: . . . . New Mexican
Capital City: . . . . Santa Fe, NM
Established: 1850
Joined Union: 1912

Anthem: . . . . "O, Fair New Mexico"
Name: . . Named *Nuevo Mexico* in the 1500's, from the
Aztec *mexico*, meaning "place of [the god] Mexitli"
Nickname: . . . . Land of Enchantment; Spanish State
License Plate Slogan: . . . . Land of Enchantment
Total Area: . . . . 121,598 sq mi (5)

The State of
New Mexico

Crescit Eundo | It Grows as It Goes

NEW MEXICO

The oldest capitol building in North America is the Palace of the Governors in Santa Fe, built in 1609 and successively occupied by Spanish, Mexican, and American governments. Today it is the State History Museum. But for centuries it stood for law and order over the ancient lands named in the 16th century *Nuevo Mexico*. Back then New Mexico encompassed the present state as well as Texas, Arizona, Utah, Nevada, and California.

Some 30,000 Spanish and native people lived there by the 1700's. Included are descendants of the ancient Anasazi, one of the most advanced native civilizations in North America, and Cliff Dwellers. The earliest inhabitants date to 20,000 B.C.

Santa Fe was founded by the Spanish in 1605 between the Pecos and Rio Grande Rivers. Soon missions were established by Franciscan friars spreading the Roman Catholic faith and educating the natives, despite frequent attacks from roaming Apaches and Navajo.

In 1680 a Pueblo uprising led to the expulsion of thousands of Spanish settlers and friars. Some were killed. The natives resented the slavery-like conditions imposed on them and the attempts by the Franciscans to eliminate all traces of their ancient religious culture. Four hundred settlers, among them priests, died. Spanish troops reasserted control in 1692 and peace was achieved in 1696.

From the beginning Santa Fe was the commercial center of the province, where the southwest native

ABOVE: The New Mexico Seal on the Capitol.

PREVIOUS PAGES: Perspectives of the Capitol's front. The monuments and sculptures on the grounds are displayed for a limited period and then replaced with new art. *To Our Heroes* (left) by Charlene Teters and *Morning Prayer* (right) by Allan Houser are shown. Many of the artists are state citizens.

LEFT: The statue *Earth's Mother* greets visitors near the entrance.

OPPOSITE: The statue *Buffalo Dancer* by Doug Hyde (top) and *Apache Mountain Spirit Dancer* by Craig Dan Goseyun.

executive and sought to establish self-government. The rebellion was put down by Mexican army forces under the command of General Manuel Armijo.

When troops from the Republic of Texas invaded New Mexico in 1841 to take the lands east of the Rio Grande, General Armijo, now the Governor, successfully repelled the Texans. But in 1846, during the Mexican-American War, New Mexico was taken by U.S. soldiers with little resistance.

U.S. Army Commander Stephen Kearny marched into Santa Fe, established a military government for the province, and named Charles Bent civil governor. The New Mexicans knew of Bent: after all, he was the founder of the rival Bent's Fort Trading Post in nearby Colorado. It was on the American side of the Santa Fe Trail.

Bent was the first American governor of New Mexico and the second to be assassinated there, though he kept his head. He was killed in Taos of all places, north of Santa Fe, where Jose Gonzales and the first revolutionary movement began ten years

peoples traded with the Spanish. For two centuries this was a closed market, the Spanish forbidding trade with the Americans. But when Mexico gained her independence from Spain in 1821, the Santa Fe Trail was established. It connected the city with Independence, Missouri and was over 800 miles long.

This trail was in fact a well-worn, two-way highway across which tremendous amounts of goods passed. The New Mexicans traded gold, silver, furs, pots, jewelry, wool, skins for the Americans' hardware, dry goods, and other manufactured items. It was from Santa Fe that Missourians took mules by the thousands for that state's extensive mule trade.

Santa Fe became a key market for American goods and the trail an important link between the east and west. It is believed Coronado used portions of the trail in 1541. Not until the Santa Fe Railroad began service in 1880 did wagon freight cease on it.

After the Texans won their independence from Mexico in 1836, New Mexicans attempted their own revolt. They seized the Palace of Governors and beheaded Governor Albino Perez. The rebels selected a Taos native named Jose Gonzales as their chief

clear up native and Spanish claims with the establishment of a Land Claims Court. New Mexico, after all, is the fifth largest state with only Alaska, Texas, California and Montana larger. The Pueblo people retain to this day vast tracts deeded to them through Spanish royal grants two centuries ago.

Repeated calls for admission went unanswered. In 1901 the U.S. House of Representatives approved an act admitting New Mexico, but it died in the Senate. In 1906 the Congress proposed combining Arizona and New Mexico into one domain, but Arizonans voted against the plan in a referendum.

By 1910 there were 327,301 New Mexicans, yet still the rights and privileges of state citizenship were denied to them. Congress accepted the Arizona results and, after the New Mexican Constitution was drafted and approved by the voters, the State of New Mexico was born, January 6, 1912.

New Mexico has the oldest capital city of all the American States, and the youngest Capitol. The modern structure is of the "New Mexico Territorial Style," a unique combination of native Pueblo adobe architecture and Greek Revival. Designed by W.C. Kruger and built by Robert E. McKee, it was dedicated December 8, 1966. It is the state's fifth Capitol.

The Capitol forms the Zia sun symbol. The Rotunda features the flags of New Mexico's 33 counties, hanging over the inlaid turquoise and brass mosaic of the New Mexico Great Seal and Zia symbol. The marble is native Travertine.

The seal shows the "American bald eagle shielding the smaller Mexican eagle within its wings" symbolizing "New Mexico's change of sovereignty in 1846," according to the Capitol tour pamphlet. "The smaller Mexican brown eagle grasps a snake in its beak and cactus in its talons. This portion of the seal is still the official symbol of Mexico; it illustrates the ancient myth in which the gods ordered the Aztecs to settle where they saw an eagle perched on a cactus devouring a serpent."

New Mexico's Legislature is of two houses, the Senate and House of Representatives. By constitutional mandate, members of the legislature are not paid a salary or any other form of compensation.

Forty-two senators serve four-year terms; 70 members of the House of Representatives serve two-year terms.

before. Bent was implementing what was called "Kearny's Code" of laws. The rebellion began with his murder and was quickly put down, the decisive battle at the church of San Jeronimo at Taos Pueblo ending February 3, 1847. The rebels were taken prisoner and, two weeks later, tried and found guilty of treason. Over twenty New Mexicans were hanged.

The Treaty of Guadalupe Hidalgo provided for the cession of lands in the north to the United States for a price of $18,250,000. The U.S. Congress then established the Territory of New Mexico in 1850 which included Arizona and western Colorado until 1863. Santa Fe was made territorial capital.

In 1850 the United States paid $10,000,000 of Texas' public debt in exchange for that state's renunciation of claims to New Mexican lands east of the Rio Grande. The Gadsden Purchase three years later fixed its boundary with Arizona and Mexico.

But an issue loomed which delayed statehood: the 90,000 people in New Mexico spoke only Spanish. Very few spoke the English of the American States, nor did they speak Mexican-Spanish. Because of the isolation of New Mexico, the early Spanish settlers preserved their language so well it resembled, into the 20th century, that of 16th-century Spain. Not until 1891 did New Mexicans pass a law establishing public schools and the teaching of English.

Another problem: land titles were based on the Spanish land grant system. It would take 40 years to

ABOVE & OPPOSITE: Perspectives of the New Mexico Capitol.

FOLLOWING PAGES: *Eagleman* by New Mexican artist Michael Narayo crouches near the Capitol; *Right*, the Zia symbol on a yellow background makes up the New Mexican flag. Numerous national flags have flown over New Mexico: Spain, Mexico, the Confederate States of America, the United States, and an earlier state flag that had a miniature U.S. flag and state seal.

"I salute the flag of the State of New Mexico and the Zia symbol of perfect friendship among united cultures."

-- Official Pledge
To The State Flag

OPPOSITE: The obelisk monument *To Our Heroes* in front of the Capitol honors the natives of the state.

ABOVE: House of Representatives Chamber. The New Mexico Legislature meets for 30 days in even-numbered years, 60 days in odd-numbered ones.

OPPOSITE: The Capitol Art Foundation was established in 1991 by the New Mexico Legislature. Its purpose: to feature works of art by artists who live and work in New Mexico. By using all four floors of the Capitol, as well as the grounds, the Foundation is able to maintain its mission "to collect, preserve, exhibit, interpret, and promote appreciation of works of art that reflect the rich and diverse history, cultures, and art forms of the people of New Mexico." Shown are a few of the many different works of art in the Capitol.

ABOVE: The Senate Chamber. Senators and representatives had represented counties until, in the 1960's, new legislative districts of equal population were introduced.

ABOVE: The Rotunda features the flags of New Mexico's 33 counties. Instead of a dome the top is made of glass, permitting the sun to light the hall.

OPPOSITE: The Rotunda floor features the New Mexico Great Seal combined with the Zia sun symbol, presented in a turquoise and brass mosaic. The Capitol forms the Zia sun symbol, a cross with a circular sun in the middle and rays pointing north, south, east, and west. It was discovered on a piece of pottery from Zia Pueblo. "To the Zia people, four is a significant number," according to the Capitol tour pamphlet. "It is embodied in the four directions of the earth, the four seasons of the year, the four times of the day (sunrise, noon, evening, night), and in life's four divisions of childhood, youth, adulthood, and old age. Everything is bound together in a circle of life, without beginning, without end. The Zia believe, too, that in this Great Brotherhood of all things, man has four sacred obligations: he must develop a strong body, clear mind, a pure spirit, and a devotion to the welfare of his people."

Official Name: . . . . State of Nevada

Motto: . . . . All For Our Country

Citizen: . . . . Nevadan

Capital City: . . . . Carson City, NV

Established: 1861

Joined Union: 1864

Anthem: . . . . "Home Means Nevada"

Name: . . . . . Shortened version of the Spanish S*ierra Nevada*, meaning "snow-covered" that was given to the California mountain ranges by Spanish sailors

Nickname: . . . . . The Battle Born State; Sage State; Silver State

License Plate Slogan: . . . . The Silver State

Total Area: . . . . 110,567 sq mi (7)

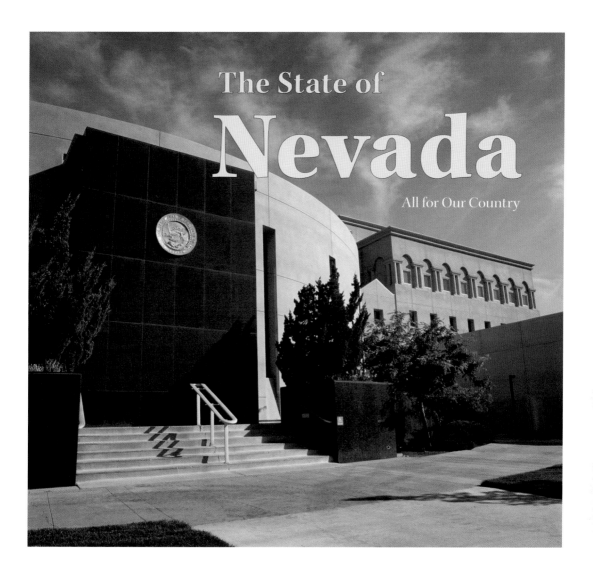

The State of
Nevada

All for Our Country

G old and silver. No state in the Western Hemisphere produces as much gold and silver as Nevada. To this day its mines churn out two-thirds of the United States' gold, and its silver supply seems, though is not, infinite. But that's only half the story. Nevada is the state where the citizens figured out a way to have all that gold and silver return by the billions of dollars, traded for chips and tokens to be gambled away at casinos throughout the land. The tourist and gambling trade is far more valuable than the mining operations, Nevada's first major industry. The state has no income tax, drawing its revenues on sales and gambling taxes (pretty remarkable in a place where 80% of the land is owned by the federal government). As unique as its economy is its social policy: legalized prostitution, a leftover of the wild west era, continues to thrive.

NEVADA

At one time Nevada was part of Mexico, and with California, Utah, most of Arizona, and the western portions of Colorado and New Mexico, it constituted the northern frontier of that nation. When the United States defeated Mexico in the War of 1846-48, it arranged the cession of this territory in the Treaty of Guadalupe Hidalgo. For this, Mexico received $18,250,000.

Henry T.P. Comstock discovered a lode of silver in 1859. This great find which later included gold was named after him, near where Virginia City today stands. He sold his claim for a pittance, not knowing its true worth. Others had a greater appreciation of the value of a stake in Nevada.

At the time of its creation as a state, Nevada's value was not measured in metals mined, but in votes secured. In 1861, the year the Nevada Territory was born, the War Between the States of the Union which created it began. Under the shadow of that great conflict the state was born.

By 1864, it was apparent that the resources of the northern states could outlast those of the south. Now the politicians in Washington considered the ordering of the United States once the southern states surrendered. President Lincoln realized that soon shouts and yells in Congress would replace bullets on the battlefield. He would need votes for his political agenda. With Nevada he would find them.

Nevada's population was not even half the 127,381 residents required before a territory could become a state. As each state was guaranteed one representative in Congress regardless of population, the ratio for the current House of Representatives was one per 127,381 citizens. To admit Nevada would

PREVIOUS PAGES: The Nevada Capitol, including the original building and, right, new legislative chambers. Nevada is one of only four states with a separate legislative building.

LEFT: A monument in the Capitol park dedicated to the miners who produced the first wealth of the state.

OPPOSITE: Symbols of Nevada's sovereignty include the state seal on a government building and entrance foyer flags in the Legislative Building.

technically give Nevadans a greater say in the "people's chamber" than they deserved. In the Senate, in which states are equally represented, they were already guaranteed two votes. Yet the Republicans in Congress, at the prodding of Lincoln, authorized a second constitutional convention. The first had been by Nevadans who, without permission from Congress, drafted a constitution that the voters later rejected in a dispute over the taxing power.

The new convention made the necessary changes and in September, 1864 Nevadans gave their assent. Whereupon the newly ratified Nevada Constitution was cabled to President Lincoln in Washington, DC -- making it the longest and most expensive telegram ever sent (the total cost was $4,303.27, over $60,000 in today's dollars). Time was of the essence.

On October 31, 1864, President Lincoln proclaimed Nevada "admitted into the Union on an equal footing with the original States." That equal footing translated into two votes in the Senate for the Republicans who pushed through amendments to the U.S. Constitution after the war.

These amendments outlawed slavery, guaranteed voting rights, and expressly established a national citizenship with privileges alongside state citizenship for the first time in that document.

Far away from the bickering in Washington, the state's citizens went about their business. Miners in and around Virginia City organized a union in 1867 that established wages at $4 a day. Gambling was first legalized in 1869. Acts to exclude people of Asian descent from settling in the state were passed in 1879. By 1900 the population declined to 42,335 from 62,266 in 1880 as the Comstock and other mines dried up. Ten years later, with the start of copper mining, the state population doubled.

Nevada's first legislature met in the Warm Springs Hotel, Carson City in 1861. Eight years later the legislature authorized construction of a Capitol. Begun April 21, 1870, the new building hosted the fifth session of the Nevada Legislature eight months later, January 2, 1871.

The Capitol was designed by Joseph Gosling of San Francisco and built by Peter Cavanaugh & Son of Carson City. Total cost: $190,000. In 1913 wings were authorized to give the Senate and Assembly new chambers.

But by 1967 it was time to move: the legislature authorized a new building to be located on Legislative Mall just south of the Capitol. The 1969 session was the last to be held in the older building. Dedication ceremonies were held June 9, 1970. Total cost: $3.4 million.

Remodeled in 1996, the Legislative Building features modern chambers. The Nevada Legislature is comprised of a Senate, with 21 senators, and Assembly, with 63 members. Regular sessions of the legislature are held in odd-numbered years and can last only 120 days. Sessions end *sine die* (without a day being set for reconvening).

OPPOSITE MIDDLE: County flags line the hallway into the old Senate chamber, now a museum. The Nevada Senate Chamber is now in the new Legislative Building and its membership is uniquely elected as follows: 11 of the 21 senators represent single districts, and the remaining 10 senators live in two-member districts. Of the 63 members of the Nevada Legislature, 39 represent districts located in Clark County.

ABOVE: The flora of Nevada in a front corner of the Capitol.

OPPOSITE TOP: Nevada Attorney General's building sits parallel to the Capitol across the street.

OPPOSITE BOTTOM: The Capitol's silver dome.

ABOVE: The preamble of the Nevada Constitution, etched into sidewalk stone near the Supreme Court, reads: "We the people of the State of Nevada grateful to God for our freedom, in order to secure its blessings, insure domestic tranquility, and form a more perfect government, do establish this Constitution."

TOP: Assembly Chamber wing entrance.

OPPOSITE: Nevada Senate Chamber.

LEFT & ABOVE: Nevada Assembly Chamber.

FOLLOWING PAGES: The Nevada Supreme Court is located between the Capitol, where the governor conducts his duties, and the Legislative Building. It is shown with the Capitol fence in the foreground which was installed in 1875 to keep livestock off the grounds. According to tour literature, the modern Legislative Building was remodeled for the 1997 session.

Official Name: . . . . State of West Virginia
Motto: . . . . Montani Semper Liberi
Citizen: . . . . West Virginian
Capital City: . . . . Charleston, WV
Established: 1861
Joined Union: 1863
Anthem: . . "This Is My West Virginia"; "West Virginia
My Home Sweet Home"; "The West Virginia Hills"

Name: . . Virginia was named in honor of the "Virgin
Queen" Elizabeth I of England; the name was
retained by the western counties when they seceded
from the Commonwealth of Virginia
Nickname: . . . . Mountain State; Panhandle State
License Plate Slogan: . . . . Wild, Wonderful
Total Area: . . . . 24,231 sq mi (41)

The State of
West Virginia

Montani Semper Liberi | Mountaineers Are Always Free

Virginians almost seem genetically disposed to rebellion; their history is replete with revolts against authority including Bacon's Rebellion (1676), the American Revolution (1776), and the War Between the States (1861). Only in that last conflict, though, did Virginians revolt against Virginians and establish a separate commonwealth. This is the story of West Virginia where "mountaineers are always free."

WEST VIRGINIA

The western portions of the Commonwealth of Virginia were some of the most rugged, mountainous areas in the Appalachian Mountain Range, where the Alleghenies are the principal elevation. Very little of it was flat. Where the Shenandoah Valley ends the Allegheny Mountains begin, and in a district of some 24,000 square miles of hills, mountains, and steep valleys grew a unique breed of Virginians.

The first to explore this remote region were Thomas Batts, Robert Fallam, and Abraham Wood who crossed the Alleghenies in 1671. They found these native border lands unoccupied after centuries of wars between the Cherokee, Iroquois, and Shawnee. Virginia Governor Spotswood visited the west in 1716 and later promoted its settlement.

Morgan Morgan was the first settler, building his house at Mill Creek in 1726. The first permanent settlement west of the Alleghenies was Marlinton, Pocahontas County, in 1749. Thereafter Virginia concluded the Fort Stanwix Treaty with the Six Nation Confederacy, clearing the way for full incorporation of these lands under its domain. In 1774 in Lord Dunmore's War, Virginians routed the natives at Point Pleasant located on the Ohio River.

OPPOSITE: Ground floor perspective of the Rotunda.

ABOVE: The statue titled *Lincoln Walks At Midnight* stands in front of the Capitol, a copy of Fred Torrey's original.

PREVIOUS PAGES: The entrance and dome of the West Virginia Capitol. The 293-foot gold dome is five feet higher than the dome of the U.S. Capitol, according to state literature. It is gilded in 14-karat gold leaf through application of 3-3/8" gold squares to the copper surface. The unique dome is composed of the ribs, tower, lantern, staff, and eagle.

Some of the first settlers arrived by way of Pennsylvania or Maryland and included Scotch-Irish, Welsh, and Germanic peoples. Soon an enclave encompassing the northwest of Virginia and extreme west of Pennsylvania developed, due in part to a colonial map maker's error. While drawing the western limits of William Penn's Pennsylvania for the British King, cartographers ended Pennsylvania's border miles short of the Ohio River, creating the small northern strip of West Virginia in which Wheeling is located.

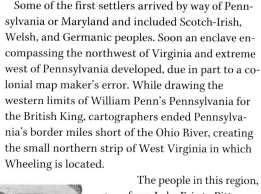

The people in this region, from Lake Erie to Pittsburgh to Point Pleasant, began to assert themselves during the Revolutionary War. Being a part of two different states, the situation was analogous to Vermont. So, the people petitioned the Continental Congress to be recognized as the State of Westylvania. Nothing came of it.

Instead, in 1794, some settlers in western Pennsylvania felt the sting of federal authority when President Washington ordered 13,000 militia there to enforce the collection of duties from whiskey producers and end armed rebellion.

By that year the population of the western Virginia counties was nearing 60,000 and growing. The National Road, which ran along Virginia's jumbled northern border, brought more settlers when opened in 1818. The Baltimore & Ohio Railroad, laid next to the National Road, connected Wheeling with Baltimore in 1852.

With the introduction of steamboats on the Ohio River, it became easier for a Virginian in the west to get to New Orleans than to Richmond, the capital. The result: western Virginia's economic life was tied to the mid-west, not the east. Westerners regularly complained of poor representation in the General

Assembly and lack of investment in their region. At the Virginia Constitutional Convention of 1829-30, delegates from the western counties made their first call for separation from the Commonwealth.

The Constitution of 1851 granted some political concessions, but differences endured: westerners tended not to be slaveholders and resented slaves being taxed at a lower rate than other property.

When the abolitionist John Brown seized the arsenal at Harper's Ferry, VA (now WV) in 1859, he was captured by General Robert E. Lee, who was commanding a company of U.S. Marines. Brown was put on trial in a Virginia court and charged with treason against the commonwealth. Less than two months later, he was hanged. The War Between the States loomed.

Virginia remained in the Union when the six lower southern states followed South Carolina's lead and left the United States. Most prayed that compromise could be found in peace talks. But when President Abraham Lincoln called for troops, April 15, 1861, Virginians met two days later in convention and voted to leave the United States in the same manner they had joined.

That action, in turn, caused a reaction and thereafter the Commonwealth of Virginia, like the United States of America it helped to create, split in two.

Some westerners, including the likes of General Stonewall Jackson, dedicated themselves to supporting Virginia. Others, who always wanted independence for their region, saw an opportunity. Meeting in Wheeling in May, the rebel westerners who opposed leaving the Union joined with those who wanted to be free from Virginia. In a revolutionary convention, they created the Reorganized Government of Virginia, acted as if it were the rightful government of all Virginia, and filled it with officers. Wheeling was made the capital and support for the United States pledged -- all of this happening under the protection of federal troops.

Only then was another convention prepared, in August, 1861, for the authorization to create a new state called Kanawha, after the river and valley in the southwest. By February, 1862 a constitution was drawn for this new state and the name was officially changed to West Virginia. Application was made to become one of the United States.

The U.S. Congress required the state to provide for the emancipation of slaves; West Virginians, however, wanted only to prohibit slaves from being brought into the state for permanent residence. After West Virginia conformed to the congressional requirement, President Lincoln proclaimed its admission on June 20, 1863.

These machinations were undertaken to get around that part of the U.S. Constitution that prohibits part of a state from becoming a state without consent. "New States may be admitted by the Congress into this Union," Article IV, Section 3 states, "but no new State shall be formed or erected within the Jurisdiction of any other State; nor any State be formed by the Junction of two or more States, or Parts of States, without the Consent of the Legislatures of the States concerned as well as of the Congress."

The extra-legality of these proceedings aside, that many West Virginians yearned for self-government cannot be denied. But they were not to live in a secure, free state just yet. The Commonwealth of Virginia's civil war was just as dramatic as the War Between the States. Some 652 battles occurred in West Virginia, many pitting neighbors and family members against each other. Who was loyal and who was disloyal had multiple answers. Some of the great hillbilly feuds, including the Hatfields and McCoys, have their origin in conditions created at this time.

When the war ended in 1865, the Commonwealth of Virginia lay in ruin, defeated by overwhelming enemy forces. No further effort was made to regain the seceded western counties. In 1915 West Virginia's share of the old state debt incurred before the war was finally adjusted to $12,393,929, with interest at $8,178,000.

Wheeling served as the capital until 1870; then it was moved south to Charleston until 1875, when it was moved back to Wheeling. In a referendum the people voted to make Charleston the permanent capital, where it has remained since 1885.

When the Capitol burned in 1921, state authorities selected the master Cass Gilbert to be architect. Gilbert is best known for designing the Woolworth Building in New York, the first skyscraper in America. He also designed the New York Life Insurance Building and was a consulting architect on the George Washington Bridge. He also designed Minnesota's Capitol, the Arkansas Capitol, and the U.S. Supreme Court Building.

The impressive West Virginia Capitol was constructed in three stages: the west wing was built in 1924-25; the east wing was constructed in 1926-27;

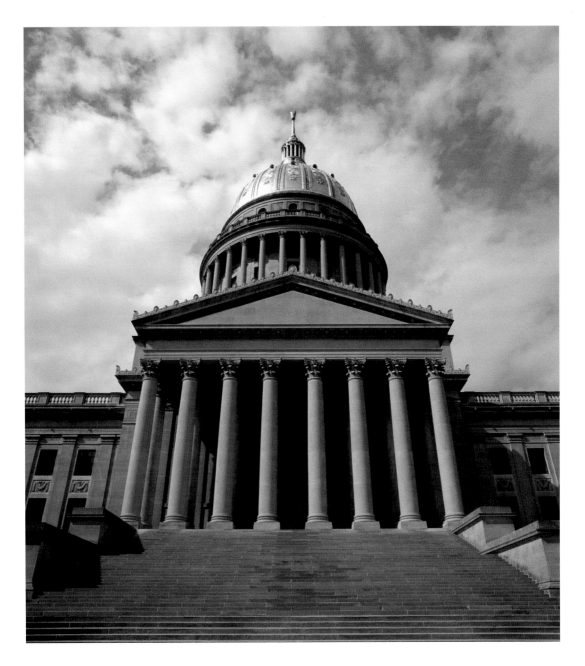

and the Rotunda area connecting east and west was completed in 1930-32. Sixty-nine years after becoming a state, the Capitol was dedicated June 20, 1932. Total cost: $10 million.

Interestingly in the Rotunda are busts of two great West Virginians: Cleveland M. Bailey and Stonewall Jackson. Bailey was a popular representative of the people, serving in the U.S. Congress for 16 years. Jackson, on the other hand, commanded Virginian forces defending the commonwealth against northern invasion and was beloved for his courage, honor, and valor.

Traits the rebel gained, no doubt, growing up in Clarksburg, just outside of Wheeling.

PREVIOUS PAGES: Perspectives of the West Virginia Capitol.

ABOVE: The House of Delegates Chamber foyer (like the Senate) features columns made of solid marble weighing 34 tons each, according to the tour information. The Capitol's interior is predominantly marble and of four kinds: Italian Travertine, Imperial Danby, white Vermont, and Tennessee marble. Some 700 train carloads of Indiana limestone were used for the exterior.

The West Virginia Legislature is comprised of a Senate (34 senators) and House of Delegates (100 delegates). Maintaining the rights of its legislature was the basis for this addition to the state's constitution in 1872: "The State of West Virginia is, and shall remain, one of the United States of America. The Constitution of the United States of America, and the laws and treaties made in pursuance thereof, shall be the supreme law of the land ... The Government of the United States is a government of enumerated powers, and all powers not delegated to it nor inhibited to the States are reserved to the States or to the people thereof. Among the powers so reserved by the States is the exclusive regulation of their own internal government and police, and it is the high and solemn duty of the several departments of government created by this constitution to guard and protect the people of this State from all encroachments upon the rights so reserved."

ABOVE: The Rotunda chandelier hangs on a 54-foot chain, 180 feet from the floor. It weighs 4,000 pounds and is eight feet in diameter. The chandelier is made of Czechoslovakian crystal, 10,000 pieces in all.

The Rotunda has many blank walls and places for paintings and sculptures to honor future West Virginians. Various spots were set aside in the original plans for "sculpture and mural decorations" but to date have gone unfilled.

RIGHT: A corner perspective of the Capitol.

OPPOSITE: The Senate Chamber and its chandelier.

ABOVE: The House of Delegates Chamber. According to tour literature, the legislative chambers are identical, though the architect built in differences to distinguish the rank of the lawmaking bodies. For instance, the ceiling of the Senate (or Upper House) is domed and the House of Delegates (or Lower House) is flat. Another example: the carved eagles in the House have their wings closed; in the Senate the eagle's wings are spread. Yet both chambers have the same replica of the Great Seal of West Virginia carved in cherry.

Official Name: . . . . State of Arizona
Motto: . . . . Ditat Deus
Citizen: . . . . Arizonan
Capital City: . . . . Phoenix, AZ
Established: 1863
Joined Union: 1912
Anthem: . . . . "Arizona March Song"

Name: . . . The Papago word *aleh-zon*, meaning "little spring," was given to a spring in the southern part of the Arizona territory that remained a part of Mexico after the Mexican-American War
Nickname: . . . . . . Grand Canyon State; Apache State
License Plate Slogan: . . . . Grand Canyon State
Total Area: . . . . 114,006 sq mi (6)

The State of

Arizona

Ditat Deus | God Enriches

ARIZONA

Arizona is the oldest, continuously settled area in North America. The Hopi people have lived at Oraibi since the 1100's and have enjoyed a prosperous farming village life to this day. The Hohokam farming communities in the 500's introduced irrigation and cotton farming to Arizona, which means "arid zone." These are but two of various ancient civilizations evidenced in the considerable Pueblo ruins in the Gila, Colorado, and Salt River valleys.

Soon stories of the "Seven Cities of Cibola" and their fantastic wealth made their way to Spanish authorities in Mexico. These fabled lands in the north were called Cibola and overflowed in jewels, silver and gold, the Spanish were told. In 1539 a Franciscan friar named Marcos de Niza became the first European in the Arizona region searching for these cities. He didn't find them.

Francisco Vasquez de Coronado was selected by Mexican Viceroy Antonio de Mendoza to find the mythical land where vast and incredible riches lay. Outfitted with 300 mounted lancers and 700 infantry, he traveled throughout the southwest and even, some believe, into Kansas. (The route he took for a good part of

the journey is Arizona's Route 191.) Coronado's men visited as far north as the Grand Canyon. The 1540 expedition was a failure.

It wasn't until outsiders came around this time that the Hopi found their way of life in jeopardy. The invaders were not Europeans. They were Navaho and Apache peoples who arrived just before the Spanish, and for the remaining centuries of the second millennium the relationship between them and the Hopi remained tenuous.

The San Xavier Mission was founded near present-day Tucson in 1700 by Father Kino. In 1776 Tucson was made a presidio (Spanish fort) with thick adobe walls built for protection against Apache attack. When Spain lost in the Mexican Revolution in 1821, this northern frontier came under Mexican jurisdiction as part of New Mexico. Mexico was defeated in the war with the United States and sold, by the Treaty of 1848, her northern frontier.

Arizona north of the Gila River was part of the bargain. The land south of Gila to the Mexican border was purchased in 1853 for $10,000,000 and became known as the Gadsden Purchase. James Gadsden, then Minister to Mexico, negotiated the deal as part of a strategy to link all the southern states with the west via a railroad. The most

practical route was through these purchased lands in Arizona and New Mexico. The War Between the States ended these plans.

Lawlessness on the border by Sonora, Mexico cowboys and other outlaws thrived in the absence of legal authority. A convention meeting in Tucson in 1856 petitioned Congress for territorial status without result. In 1862 a delegate was sent to the Confederate Congress as many Arizonans supported the south. A year later, after a southern force sent to take Arizona was defeated, Arizona became a territory of the United States. But not until 1912 would it become the 48th American State.

One reason for the delay was the terror campaign of the famous Geronimo, chief of the Chiricahua Apache, who together with other natives raided Arizonan and New Mexican ranches and settlements for nearly three decades. Geronimo was captured in 1886 and died at Fort Sill, Oklahoma in 1909.

Another reason was that the U.S. Senate disagreed with portions of the Arizona Constitution of 1891, which her people ratified. Of particular concern were clauses that seemed to establish two money systems and permitted the repudiation of some contracts. When neither the Senate nor Arizona would budge on the matter, Congress proposed that Arizona rejoin New Mexico to form one state. A vote of the Arizona people rejected the scheme.

OPPOSITE: The House Chamber.

ABOVE: A mosaic of the state seal under the Rotunda.

Arizonans wanted their own commonwealth.

In 1910 they held a constitutional convention, revised their constitution, and again won citizen approval. This was submitted to the U.S. Congress but members there, along with President Taft, objected to a "radical" provision that provided for popular recall of judges. An act making Arizona a state was passed on condition that the recall clause be stricken. To this, the people agreed and the state constitution was amended. President Taft proclaimed Arizona a state on February 14, 1912.

No sooner did Taft speak than the Arizonans reinstated the recall of judges, made all elected offices subject to popular recall, and extended the right of suffrage to women. They understood well how democracy works, these Arizonans. And the federal government could do nothing about it.

These bold expressions of state sovereignty all happened in the Arizona Capitol. Built in 1899 to house the territorial government, it served as home to the constitutional convention in 1910 and both chambers of the Arizona Legislature from 1912 until 1974. Adjoining buildings were then added: on the right the Senate, and on the left the House of Representatives. Today the original building is known as the Arizona State Capitol Museum.

The Arizona Senate has 30 members serving two-year terms; the House has 60 members serving two-year terms. With the original Capitol's courtyard separating them, the new Senate and House chambers provide for the growth in state government and needs of the public to interact with it.

ABOVE: The Arizona Senate Chamber.

OPPOSITE: Perspective of the House Chamber from the gallery.

FOLLOWING PAGES: Views of the Capitol and courtyard. A replica Liberty Bell is featured in front. Arizona, along with the other American States, received the bell as part of a promotion for U.S. Savings Bonds after World War II.

ACKNOWLEDGEMENTS

My tendencies toward journalistic pursuits began when I was a boy. They were encouraged by my father, a successful author, and supported by my mother, whom I remember buying my first camera with a week's worth of earnings. It was through that camera's lens that I spotted my wife, Marcy, and it is with her that the acknowledgements for this work should begin. Without her assistance, this book would not have been published. She suffered to read it several times, collected and ordered capitol information, and drove the RV at least half as much as myself, though perhaps not as safely. Most of all, her counsel on the myriad issues raised was immeasurable. Our capitol trip will remain one of my fondest memories.

Likewise the Excelsior publishing team has been outstanding. This work benefits greatly from the hand of a master grammarian in Timothy Ruggiero. He edited, proofed, and indexed its contents. Allen Curtiss headed up vital fact verification and context accuracy. Kim Hyzer performed logistical and operations support. Susan Reinshagen acted as project liason with the states once the trip was concluded. And while on the road Frederic Wolff and Lance Humphries helped with my other responsibilities.

These Americans I can name. Unfortunately there were hundreds of people encountered during the course of the trip I cannot name but who, in some way, aided in the completion of this project. The cleaning personnel in Olympia, WA who opened the chambers when no one else was around. The Hawaiian policeman who let down his guard and talked freely about his state. The film processors in Minneapolis who pushed through rolls of film in hours, then gave me a Minnesota Viking flag when they found out I was a fan. (It remains in the back window of the RV.) The expedition in and out of the American States seemed like an elaborate relay race for us -- a person always around the corner ready to hand us not a baton but a burrito, as we set off for the next state.

Looking back, I am amazed at how pleasant the whole experience was. How kind and generous the Americans we met were who lived in and between the capital cities. Like Rhode Island Governor Lincoln Almond who, while I was lying on my back shooting straight up into the eye of the Rotunda, leaned over and looked into my lens, startling me. He laughed, introduced himself, and then chatted for twenty minutes on various topics. The state leaders we bumped into went out of their way to be helpful. The retired medical doctor turned senator in North Carolina, the retired school teacher turned representative in New Hampshire -- and countless others like them who gave a little of their time to help with this project.

Much assistance was received by the people who work at their State Capitol: the state police, building managers, administrators, secretaries, janitors, security personnel, and tour guides. The people who turn on the lights, polish the wood, answer the questions, and guard the property every day were indispensable in assisting the photographic aspects of the project. In terms of writing the book, the most important state employees were the archivists, curators, and historians who substantiated facts and provided necessary documentation when needed. To acknowledge all of the state employees' assistance, the publisher is providing to their superiors or leaders listed below a copy of this book so that it may be shared by all in the years to come.

ALABAMA

Governor: *Don Siegelman*
Speaker of the House: *Seth Hammett*
President of the Senate and the
Lieutenant Governor: *Steve Windom*
Clerk of the House: *Greg Pappas*
Secretary of the Senate: *Charles McDowell Lee*
Secretary of State: *Jim Bennett*

ALASKA

Governor: *Tony Knowles*
Speaker of the House: *Brian Porter*
President of the Senate: *Rick Halford*
Chief Clerk of the House: *Suzi Lowell*
Senate Secretary: *Heidi Vogel*

ARIZONA

Governor: *Jane Dee Hill*
Speaker of the House: *Jim Weiers*
President of the Senate: *Randall Gnant*
Clerk of the House: *Norman Moore*
Secretary of the Senate: *Charmion Billington*
Secretary of State: *Betsey Bayless*

ARKANSAS

Governor: *Mike Huckabee*
Speaker of the House: *Shane Broadway*
President of the Senate: *Mike Beebe*
Chief Clerk of the House: *Ms. Jo Renshaw*
Secretary of the Senate: *Ann Cornwell*
Secretary of State: *Sharon Proest*

CALIFORNIA

Governor: *Gray Davis*
Speaker of the House: *Herb Wesson*
President of the Senate (President Pro Tempore): *John Burton*
Chief Clerk of the House: *E. Dotson Wilson*
Secretary of the Senate: *Greg Schmidt*
Secretary of State: *Bill Jones*

COLORADO

Governor: *Bill Owens*
Speaker of the House: *Doug Dean*
President of the Senate: *Stan Matsunaka*
Clerk of the House: *J.R. Rodrigue*
Secretary of the Senate: *Karen Goldman*
Secretary of State: *Donetta Davidson*

CONNECTICUT

Governor: *John G. Rowlands*
Speaker of the House: *Moira K. Lyons*
President of the Senate (Pres. Pro Tempore): *Kevin B. Sullivan*
Clerk of the House: *Garey E. Coleman*
Clerk of the Senate: *Thomas P. Cohen*
Secretary of State: *Susan Bysiewicz*

DELAWARE

Governor: *Ruth Ann Minner*
Speaker of the House: *Terry Spence*
President of the Senate and Lieutenant Governor: *John Carney*
Clerk of the House: *Joanne Hedrick*
Clerk of the Senate: *Bernad Brady*
Secretary of State: *Harriet Winslow*

FLORIDA

Governor: *Jeb Bush*
Speaker of the House: *Ton Feeney*
President of the Senate: *John McKay*
Clerk of the House: *John B. Phelps*
Secretary of the Senate: *Faye Blanton*
Secretary of State: *Katherine Harris*

GEORGIA

Governor: *Roy E. Barnes*
Speaker of the House: *Thomas B. Murphy*
President of the Senate (Pres. Pro Tempore): *Terrell Starr*
Clerk of the House: *Robert E. Rivers*
Secretary of the Senate: *Frank Eldridge Jr.*
Secretary of State: *Cathy Cox*

HAWAI'I

Governor: *Benjamin Cayetano*
Speaker of the House: *Calvin Say*
President of the Senate: *Robert Bunda*
Chief Clerk of the House: *Patricia Mau - Shimizu*
Chief Clerk of the Senate: *Paul Kawaguchi*

IDAHO

Governor: *Dirk Kempthorne*
Speaker of the House: *Bruce Newcomb*
President of the Senate (Pres. Pro Tempore): *Robert L. Geddes*
Clerk of the House: *Pamela Juker*
Secretary of the Senate: *Jeannine Wood*
Secretary of State: *Pete T. Cenarrusa*

ILLINOIS

Governor: *George H. Ryan*
Speaker of the House: *Michael Madigan*
President of the Senate: *James "Pate" Philip*
Clerk of the House: *Tony Rossi*
Clerk of the Senate: *Linda Hawker*
Secretary of State: *Jesse White*

INDIANA

Governor: *Frank O'Bannon*
Speaker of the House: *John R. Gregg*
President of the Senate (Pres. Pro Tempore): *Bob Garton*
Principal Clerk of the House: *Lee A. Smith*
Secretary of the Senate: *Mary Mendel*
Secretary of State: *Sue Anne Gilroy*

IOWA

Governor: *Tom Vilsack*
Speaker of the House: *Brent Siegrist*
President of the Senate: *Mary Kramer*
Chief Clerk of the House: *Margaret Thomson*
Secretary of the Senate: *Michael E. Marshall*
Secretary of State: *Hon. Chet Culver*

KANSAS

Governor: *Bill Graves*
Speaker of the House: *Kent Glasscock*
President of the Senate: *Dave Kerr*
Chief Clerk of the House: *Janet E. Jones*
Clerk of the Senate: *Pat Saville*
Secretary of State: *Ron Thornburgh*

KENTUCKY

Governor: *Paul E. Patton*
Speaker of the House: *Jody Richards*
President of the Senate: *David L. Williams*
Clerk of the House: *Lois Pullam*
Clerk of the Senate: *Barbara Ferguson*
Secretary of State: *John Y. Brown III*

LOUISIANA

Governor: *M.J. "Mike" Foster Jr.*
Speaker of the House: *Charlie Dewitt*
President of the Senate: *John Hainkel*
Clerk of the House: *Alfred W. Speer*
Secretary of the Senate: *Michael Baer*
Secretary of State: *W. Fox McKeithen*

MAINE

Governor: *Angus S. King Jr.*
Speaker for the House: *Michael Saxl*
President of the Senate: *Richard A. Bennett*
Clerk of the House: *Honorable Millicent M. MacFarland*
Secretary of the Senate: *Pamela L. Cahill*
Secretary of State: *Dan A. Gwadosky*

MARYLAND

Governor: *Parris N. Gendening*
Speaker of the House: *Casper R. Taylor, Jr.*
President of the Senate: *Thomas V. Mike Miller, Jr.*
Chief Clerk of the House: *Mary Monahan*
Secretary of the Senate: *William Addison*
Secretary of State: *John T. Willis*

MASSACHUSETTS

Governor: *Jane Swift*
Speaker of the House: *Thomas M. Finneran*
President of the Senate: *Thomas F. Birmingham*
Clerk of the House: *Steven T. James*
Clerk of the Senate: *Patrick Scanlan*
Secretary of the Commonwealth: *William Francis Galvin*

MICHIGAN

Governor: *John Engler*
Speaker of the House: *Rick Johnson*
President of the Senate: *Dick Posthumus*
Clerk of the House: *Gary Randall*
Secretary of the Senate: *Carol Morey Vwenti J.D.*
Secretary of State: *Candice Miller*

MINNESOTA

Governor: *Jesse Vuntura*
Speaker of the House: *Steve Sviggum*
President of the Senate: *Don Samuelson*
Clerk of the House: *Ed Burdick*
Secretary of the Senate: *Patrick Flahaven*
Secretary of State: *Mary Kiffmeyer*

MISSISSIPPI

Governor: *Ronnie Musgrove*
Speaker of the House: *Timothy Ford*
President of the Senate (Pres. Pro Tempore): *Travis L. Little*
Clerk of the House: *Ed Terry*
Clerk of the Senate: *John Gilbert*
Secretary of State: *Eric Clark*

MISSOURI

Governor: *Bob Holden*
Speaker of the House: *Jim Kreider*
President of the Senate (Pres. Pro Tempore): *Peter Kinder*
Clerk of the House: *Ted Wedel*
Secretary of the Senate: *Terry Spieler*
Secretary of State: *Matt Blunt*

MONTANA

Governor: *Judy Martz*
Speaker of the House: *Dan McGee*
President of the Senate: *Tom Beck*
Chief Clerk of the House: *Marilyn Miller*
Secretary of the Senate: *Rosana Skelton*
Secretary of State: *Bob Brown*

NEBRASKA

Governor: *Mike Johanns*
Speaker of the Legislature: *Doug Kristensen*
Clerk of the Legislature: *Patrick J. O'Donnell*
Secretary of State: *John A. Gale*

NEVADA

Governor: *Kenny Guinn*
Speaker of the House: *Richard Perkins*
President of the Senate and the Lieutenant Governor: *Lorraine T. Hunt*
Chief Clerk of the House: *Jacqueline Sneddon*
Secretary of the Senate: *Claire J. Clift*
Secretary of State: *Dean Heller*

NEW HAMPSHIRE

Governor: *Jeanne Shaheen*
Speaker of the House: *Gene Chandler*
President of the Senate: *Arthur P. Klemm, Jr.*
Clerk of the House: *Karen O. Wadsworth*
Clerk of the Senate: *Tammy L. Wright*
Secretary of State: *William M. Gardner*

NEW JERSEY

Governor: *James E. McCreevey*
Speaker of the House: *Albio Sires*
President of the Senate: *Richard J. Codey*
Clerk of the House: *Christine Reibe*
Secretary of the Senate: *Donna A. Phelps*
Secretary of State: *Regina L. Thomas*

NEW MEXICO

Governor: *Gary E. Johnson*
Speaker of the House: *Ben Lujan*
President of the Senate (Pres. Pro Tempore): *Richard Romero*
Clerk of the House: *Steven R. Arias*
Chief Clerk of the Senate: *Margaret Larragoite*
Secretary of State: *Rebecca Vigil-Giron*

NEW YORK

Governor: *George E. Pataki*
Speaker of the Assembly: *Sheldon Silver*
President of the Senate (Pres. Pro Tempore): *Joseph L. Bruno*
Acting Clerk of the House: *Karen L. McCann*
Clerk of the Senate: *Steven Boggess*
Secretary of State: *Randy A. Daniels*

NORTH CAROLINA

Governor: *Michael F. Easley*
Speaker of the House: *James B. Black*
President of the Senate and the Lieutenant Governor: *Beverly Perdue*
Clerk of the House: *Denise Weeks*
Clerk of the Senate: *Janet Pruitt*
Secretary of State: *Elaine Marshall*

NORTH DAKOTA

Governor: *John Hoeven*
Speaker of the House: *LeRoy G. Bernstein*
President of the Senate and the Lieutenant Governor: *Jack Casselton Dalrymple*
Clerk of the House: *Mark Johnson*
Secretary of the Senate: *Bill Horton*
Secretary of State: *Alvin A. Jaeger*

OHIO

Governor: *Bob Taft*
Speaker of the House: *Larry Householder*
President of the Senate: *Richard H. Finan*
Clerk of the House: *Laura Clemens*
Clerk of the Senate: *Matt Schuler*
Secretary of State: *J. Kenneth Blackwell*

OKLAHOMA

Governor: *Frank Keating*
Speaker of the House: *Larry E. Adair*
President of the Senate (Pres. Pro Tempore): *Stratton Taylor*
Chief Clerk of the House: *Larry Warden*
Clerk of the Senate: *Debbie North*
Secretary of State: *Mike Hunter*

OREGON

Governor: *John A. Kitzhaber*
Speaker of the House: *Mark Simmons*
President of the Senate: *Gene Derfler*
Chief Clerk of the House: *Ramona Kenady*
Secretary of the Senate: *Judy Hall*
Secretary of the State: *Bill Bradbury*

PENNSYLVANIA

Governor: *Mark Schweiker*
Speaker of the House: *Matthew J. Ryan*
President of the Senate: *Robert C. Jubelirer*
Clerk of the House: *Ted Mazia*
Chief Clerk of the Senate: *W. Russell Faber*
Secretary of the Commonwealth: *C. Michael Weaver*

RHODE ISLAND

Governor: *Lincoln Almond*
Speaker of the House: *John B. Harwood*
Majority Leader of the Senate: *William V. Irons*
Clerk of the House: *Lou D' Antouno*
Secretary of the Senate: *Raymond Hoyas*
Secretary of State: *Edward Inman III*

SOUTH CAROLINA

Governor: *Jim Hodges*
Speaker of the House: *David Wilkins*
President of the Senate and the Lieutenant Governor: *Robert Peeler*
Clerk of the House: *Sandra McKinney*
Clerk of the Senate: *Jeffrey S. Gossett*
Secretary of State: *James M. Miles*

SOUTH DAKOTA

Governor: *William (Bill) Janklow*
Speaker of the House: *Scott Eccarius*
President of the Senate (Pres. Pro Tempore): *Arnold Brown*
Clerk of the House: *Karen Gerdes*
Secretary of the Senate: *Patricia Adam*
Secretary of State: *Joyce Hazeltine*

TENNESSEE

Governor: *Don Sundquist*
Speaker of the House: *James O. Naifeh*
President of the Senate: *John Wilder*
Clerk of the House: *Burney Durham*
Chief Clerk of the Senate: *Russell Humphrey*
Secretary of State: *Riley Darnell*

TEXAS

Governor: *Rick Perry*
Speaker of the House: *James Laney*
President of the Senate and the Lieutenant Governor: *Bill Ratliff*
Chief Clerk of the House: *Sharon Carter*
Secretary of the Senate: *Patsy Spaw*
Secretary of State: *Gwyn Shea*

UTAH

Governor: *Mike Leavitt*
Speaker of the House: *Martin Stephens*
President of the Senate: *L. Alma "Al" Mansell*
Chief Clerk of the House: *Carole Peterson*
Secretary of the Senate: *Annette Moore*

VERMONT

Governor: *Howard Dean, M.D.*
Speaker of the House: *Walter E. Freed*
President of the Senate and the Lieutenant Governor: *Douglas Racine*
Clerk of the House: *Donald Milne*
Secretary of the Senate: *David Gibson*
Secretary of State: *Deborah L. Markowitz*

VIRGINIA

Governor: *Mark Warner*
Speaker of the House: *S. Vance Wilkins, Jr.*
President of the Senate (Pres. Pro Tempore): *John H. Chichester*
Clerk of the House: *Bruce Jamerson*
Clerk of the Senate: *Susan Clarke Schaar*
Secretary of the Commonwealth: *Anita A. Rimler*

WASHINGTON

Governor: *Gary Locke*
Speaker of the House: *Frank Chopp*
President of the Senate and the Lieutenant Governor: *Brad Owen*
Chief Clerk of the House: *Cindy Zehnder*
Secretary of the Senate: *Tony Cook*
Secretary of State: *Sam Reed*

WEST VIRGINIA

Governor: *Scott McCallum*
Speaker of the House: *Robert S. Kiss*
President of the Senate and the Lieutenant Governor: *Earl Ray Tomblin*
Clerk of the House: *Gregory M. Gray*
Clerk of the Senate: *Darrell Holmes*
Secretary of State: *Joe Manchin III*

WISCONSIN

Governor: *Scott McCallum*
Speaker of the House: *Scott Jensen*
President of the Senate: *Fred Risser*
Chief Clerk of the House: *Donald J. Schneider*
Secretary of State: *Douglas Lafollett*

WYOMING

Governor: *Jim Geringer*
Speaker of the House: *Rick Tempest*
President of the Senate: *Henry "Hank" H. R. Coe*
Clerk of the House: *Marvin Helart*
Clerk of the Senate: *Diane Harvey*
Secretary of State: *Joseph Meyer*

SOURCES & NOTES

Great effort was made to quote and name the source of information in the body of each state article and introductory chapters. When this is done, it is not repeated here unless it is a capitol brochure or informational document supplied by the state. See the General Bibliography for common sources of information {ex: all of the state constitutions quoted appear in a book of them listed under the "State and Federal Constitutions" heading}.

Important statements of fact in this book were verified in interviews with state authorities or historical groups and through various references, including:

The World Almanac And Book Of Facts 2000, Primedia Reference Inc., Collector's Edition published by Easton Press, Norwalk, CT: 1999

The Almanac of American History, Arthur M. Schlesinger, Jr., General Editor, G.P. Putnam's Sons, New York: 1983

The Concise Columbia Encyclopedia, Edited by Judith S. Levey and Agnes Greenhall, with the Reference Staff of Columbia University Press, Avon Books, New York: 1983

Facts About The States, 2nd Edition, editors Joseph Nathan Kane, Janet Podell, and Steven Anzovin, The H.W. Wilson Company, New York: 1993

History of the United States In Chronological Order, From A.D. 432 to the Present Time, Robert James Belford, The World, New York: 1886

These grammar and style references were consulted during the writing of this book:

Webster's Third New International Dictionary of the English Language Unabridged, Philip Babcock Gove, Ph. D., Editor In Chief, G & C Merriam Co., Springfield, MA: 1961

Associated Press Stylebook, Eileen Alt Powell and Howard Angione, Editors, New York: 1980

The Elements of Rhetoric, Vincent Ryan Ruggiero, Prentice-Hall, Englewood Cliffs, New Jersey: 1971

ON-SITE INTERVIEWS, FACT COLLECTION

Sources of information for each state include on-site interviews made at the time each Capitol was photographed, memorials and plaques found there, and follow-up phone conversations and research. Some of these may be noted below under the heading "Special Thanks."

ALABAMA

A Self-Guided Tour Of The Alabama State Capitol, National Park Service, U.S. Department of the Interior, Alabama Historical Commission: 1992

Capitals of Alabama, Alabama Department of Archives and History, Montgomery, AL

ALASKA

Alaska's State Capitol, Juneau, Alaska, Legislative Affairs Agency, Juneau, AK

Alaska State Capitol Self-Guided Tour, Legislative Affairs Agency, Juneau, AK: 1997

[SPECIAL THANKS to the State of Alaska Libraries, Archives and Museums.]

ARIZONA

Arizona State Capitol Museum, Arizona State Library, Archives and Public Records, Phoenix, AZ

Arizona Blue Book, Millennium Edition, State of Arizona

The Howell Code, Adopted by The First Legislative Assembly of the Territory of Arizona, Prescott: Office of the Arizona Miner, provided by the State Library of Arizona

Named Campaigns - Indian Wars of the United States Army, 1790-1891, reference document iwcmp, U.S. Army, Washington, DC: 2000

The History of Arizona, Thomas E. Farish, Phoenix, AZ: 1915 from a copy provided by the Arizona State Archives, State of Arizona

ARKANSAS

Welcome to the Arkansas State Capitol, Sharon Priest, Secretary of State, Arkansas State Capitol, Little Rock, AR

Old State House Museum, The Old State House Museum, Department of Arkansas Heritage

Arkansas Odyssey, Michael B. Dougan, Ross Publishing Co., Little Rock, AR: 1994

Arkansas, A Bicentennial History, Harry S. Ashmore, W.W. Norton, New York: 1978

CALIFORNIA

The California State Capitol Self-Guided Tour, State Capitol Museum, Sacramento, CA

California State Parks Kids' Guide To The California State Capitol, California State Parks

The Capital That Couldn't Stay Put: The Complete Book of California's Capitols, by June Oxford, James Stevenson Publisher, Fairfield, CA: 1983

Records of the Constitutional Convention of 1849, and other documents and histories related to the beginning of California, California State Archives, and the Golden State Museum, State of California, Sacramento, CA

The Vallejo Family: A Military History of Early California, Lt. Col. Ira Lee Plummer, California Military Museum, California State Military Department

Page 583: An excellent account of the Bear Flag revolt is found in *Sonoma Barracks*, by Col. Herbert M. Hart, USMC (Retired), California Military Museum, California State Military Department. The "growling" quote comes from a letter eyewitness Midshipman John Montgomery wrote to his mother, according to the Sonoma Bear Flag Sesquicentennial Committee.

The History of Arizona, Chapter 8 Conquest of California by Fremont and Sloat, Thomas E. Farish, Phoenix, AZ: 1915

COLORADO

Visitor's Guide To Colorado's Capitol, Colorado General Assembly, Colorado Legislative Council

A Colorado History, Carl Ubbelohde, Maxine Benson, Duane Smith, Pruett Publishing, Boulder, CO: 7th Edition

The Growth Of The American Republic, S.E. Morison and H.S. Commager, Oxford University Press, New York: 1962

[SPECIAL THANKS to the Colorado State Archives for a plethora of information, State of Colorado, Denver, CO.]

CONNECTICUT

Soldiers and Sailors Memorial Arch-Bushnell Park, Bushnell Park Foundation: 1997

Connecticut State Capitol Self-Guided Tour, The League of Women Voters of Connecticut/Education Fund, Capitol and Tours, State Capitol, Harford, CT

Connecticut State Capitol Statuary, The League of Women Voters of Connecticut/Education Fund, Capitol Information and Tours, State Capitol, CT

Page 75-76: The Charter Oak story is told in various ways and certain aspects have been challenged. This version of the legend is taken from the *2001 State of Connecticut Register & Manual*, issued by the Secretary of State and was provided by the Connecticut State Library.

[SPECIAL THANKS to Capitol Police Chief Bill Morgan for his assistance in the shoot.]

DELAWARE

Guide to Legislative Hall, State of Delaware: 1999

Letters to and from Caesar Rodney, 1756-1784, Edited by Herbert Ryden, PhD., University of Pennsylvania Press, Philadelphia: 1933

[SPECIAL THANKS to Ms. Sylvia Short, Cindy Snyder, State of Delaware, Department of State, Division of Historical and Cultural Affairs, Delaware State Museums, New Castle, DE; and Cliff Parker, Delaware Public Archives, Dover, DE.]

FLORIDA

The Old Capitol, Museum of Florida History, Division of Historical Resources Florida Department of State, Katherine Harris, Secretary of State

The Constitution of the West Florida Republic, Edited by James A. Padgett, The Louisiana Historical Quarterly, October, 1937, as provided by the Secretary of State, Baton Rouge, LA

Page 402: An excellent early history of state and U.S. money appears in *Warman's Coins & Currency*, A.G. Berman and A.G. Malloy, Wallace-Homestead, Radnor, PA: 1995.

Named Campaigns - Indian Wars of the United States Army, 1790-1891, U.S. Army, Washington, DC: 2000

[SPECIAL THANKS to the Bureau of Library and Network Services, Florida Department of State.]

GEORGIA

Welcome to the Georgia Capitol, *Self-Guided Tour*, Office of Secretary of State Cathy Cox

Georgia House of Representatives, with excerpts from the *Handbook for Georgia Legislators*, published by the Georgia House of Representatives

[SPECIAL THANKS to the Georgia Capitol Museum.]

HAWAI'I

Names and Insignia of Hawai'i, Hawai'i State Public Library System: 1993

Hawai'i's Story By Hawai'i's Queen, by Queen Liliuokalani, Mutual Publishing, Honolulu: 1990

The State of Hawai'i, from the GTE Hawaiian Telephone Company, Inc., Honolulu: 1995

Hawai'i State Capitol, State of Hawai'i, Honolulu

Sugar Yields Sweet Deal For 'Big Five' Firms, Richard Borreca, Honolulu Star-Bulletin, 7/12/99

A Compilation Of The Messages And Papers Of The Presidents 1789-1908, by J. D. Richardson, 11 vols., United States Bureau Of National Literature And Art, Washington: 1909

United States Public Law 103-150, (The Apology Resolution), signed by President Clinton, Washington: 1993

Hawai'i's Sugar Industry, Hawai'i Agriculture Research Center, Aiea, HI: 2001

Page 348: The quote on the missionaries doing very well was heard by the author, and appears in the article *Waving Fields of Cane*, by Wayne Smith, Alexander & Baldwin Sugar Museum. This is an excellent, frank account of the history of sugar on Maui up to the present.

IDAHO

Welcome To Idaho's State Capitol, Idaho State Historical Society, Museum and Historic Sites Division, Boise, ID

History of Idaho, Hiram T. French, Vol. 1, Lewis Publishing, Chicago: 1914

Named Campaigns - Indian Wars of the United States Army, 1790-1891, reference document iwcmp, U.S. Army, Washington, DC: 2000

Brief History of the Idaho Potato Industry, Idaho Potato Commission, State of Idaho, Boise, ID: 2001

[SPECIAL THANKS to Kathy Hodges, Idaho State Historical Society, Library & Archives, Boise, ID.]

ILLINOIS

Illinois State Capitol, Jesse White, Secretary of State, State of Illinois, Springfield, IL: 2000

Illinois Blue Book, 1979-1980, Edited by Alan J. Dixon, Secretary of State, Springfield, IL: 1980

Records of the Illinois Territory, Record Group 100, Illinois State Archives, Springfield, IL: 2001

Patrick Henry's Instructions to George Rogers Clark, The Library of Virginia, Richmond, VA

The Memoir of George Rogers Clark, The Library of Virginia, Richmond, VA

General George Rogers Clark's Conquest Of The Illinois, by H.W. Beckwith, from the *Collections of the Illinois State Historical Library*, edited by the same man, Vol. 1, pgs. 213-214, Springfield, IL: 1903

INDIANA

Your Indiana General Assembly, State of Indiana

Some Indiana Facts, State Information Center, Indianapolis, IN

A Self-Guided Tour, State of Indiana

The Memoir of George Rogers Clark, The Library of Virginia, Richmond, VA

The Indiana Statehouse, Kathleen A. Thompson, Indiana Department of Administration

Page 239: The account of Tecumseh and the Prophet is partially drawn from the excellent rendition in R. Hildreth's *The History of the United State of America*, volume six, pages 251-256, 339, 438, 446. See General Bibliography.

Named Campaigns - Indian Wars of the United States Army, 1790-1891, U.S. Army, Washington, DC: 2000

IOWA

The Iowa Capitol, Iowa General Assembly, Legislative Information Office, State Capitol, Des Moines, IA

The Iowa State Capitol: A Self-Guided Tour, State of Iowa

History of Bee Trace and Grand Divide, U.S. Army Corp of Engineers, Kansas City, MO

Schuyler County, profile with information on the Honey War and Bee Trace from the Audobon Society of Missouri

Page 412: For a detailed account of the "Honey War" and the use of honey on the frontier see *War Was Never So Sweet* by Joel M. Vance, Iowa Counties Historical Information.

KANSAS

Enjoying History & Heritage at the Kansas State Capitol, A Self-Guided Tour, Kansas Department of Commerce and Housing, Travel & Tourism Division, Topeka, KS

Welcome To The House, Janet E. Jones, Chief Clerk, Kansas House of Representatives, Topeka, KS

Page 467: If you want to know what it was like to be living freely in Africa one moment and then suddenly kidnapped into slavery the next, read the chilling *An Account of the Slave Trade*, Alexander Falconbridge, 1788. It appears in *Living Documents In American History*, Edited by John A. Scott, Washington Square Press, NY: 1964.

[SPECIAL THANKS to the staff at the Kansas State Historical Society for their assistance.]

KENTUCKY

A Self-Guided Tour of the Kentucky State Capitol, Division of Historic Properties, Frankort, KY

The Growth Of The American Republic, S.E. Morison and H.S. Commager, Oxford University Press, New York: 1962

[SPECIAL THANKS to Mike Hudson of the Kentucky History Center for information relating to the disinterment of Daniel Boone's remains and reburial in Frankfort, KY. The plaster cast of Boone's head is at the location where he works.]

LOUISIANA

The Louisiana State Capitol, State of Louisiana booklet, Baton Rouge: 1999

Louisiana History, Louisiana Department of Economic Development: 1994

Supreme Court of Louisiana Historical Development, Supreme Court of Louisiana, Baton Rouge, LA: 2001

The Cabildo, Colonial Louisiana, State of Louisiana, Baton Rouge: 2001

The People and Culture of New Orleans, by Arnold Hirsch and Joseph Logsdon, Dept. Of History, University of New Orleans, New Orleans Online: 2001

The Constitution of the West Florida Republic, Edited by James A. Padgett, Louisiana Historical Quarterly, October, 1937, as provided by the Secretary of State, Baton Rouge, LA

The Story of How 'Bloody' O'Reilly Got His Nickname, by George Avery, Alexandria Daily Town Talk, 10/15/67

The Louisiana Governors, Edited by Joseph G. Dawson III, Louisiana State University, Baton Rouge, LA: 1990

Page 364: The account of Josiah Quincy is drawn from R. Hildreth's excellent report in the *History of the United States*, vol vi, 226-228.

[SPECIAL THANKS to the Louisiana Department of State, Division of Archives, Records Management, and History; the Louisiana Old State Capitol Center for Political and Governmental History; and the State Library of Louisiana.]

MAINE

Maine State House and Maine Senate Chamber, State of Maine, Augusta

Women In The Maine Senate, Joy J. O'Brien, Secretary of the Senate, Judith DelFranco, Asst. Secretary: Rev. 10/99

Constitution of Maine, Laws of the State of Maine, Etc., Annotated, Maine State Archives, Augusta, ME

The Maine Book, Henry E. Dunnack, pp. 110-113, Augusta, ME: 1920 as reprinted by the Waterloo Public Library

Saint Croix Island International Historic Site, National Park Service, www.nps.gov, 2001

MARYLAND

Maryland State House, Maryland Dept. of Business and Economic Development and Maryland State Archives: 1999

Welcome to the Maryland State House, Maryland General Assembly

MASSACHUSETTS

The Massachusetts State House, A guide to a walking tour and a short but interesting history of the building, William Francis Galvin, Secretary of the Commonwealth, State House Tours and Government Education Division: 2000

Welcome to the Massachusetts State House, William Francis , Secretary of the Commonwealth

Page 83: The information about Plymouth Rock was garnered from documents supplied by the Pilgrim Hall Museum, Plymouth, MA.

[SPECIAL THANKS to the delightful Paul Lynch, Sergeant-At-Arms, Massachusetts Senate for his enlightening conversation enjoyed while shooting the Senate Chamber.]

MICHIGAN

Your State Capitol, A Walking Tour Capitol Tour and Information Service, State of Michigan

Michigan In Brief, Facts, Symbols, And Dates In Michigan History, State of Michigan Library, Lansing, MI: 2001

Political Revolution and Reformers, State of Michigan Archives, Lansing, MI: 2001

The War Between Michigan And Ohio, from detroitnews.com, editorial and production by Larry Wright and Alex Vida, The Detroit News, Detroit, MI

The Michigan Constitutional Conventions of 1835-36, Edited by Harold M. Dorr, University of Michigan Press, Ann Arbor, MI: 1940

MINNESOTA

Art Treasures in the Minnesota State Capitol, Minnesota Historical Society, St. Paul: 1998

Minnesota State Capitol Self-Guided Tour, Minnesota Historical Society

Minnesota State Capitol Mall, A Walking Tour of Memorials and Remembrances, Minnesota State Capitol Historic Site, Minnesota Historical Society

North Star Statehouse, An Armchair Guide To The Minnesota State Capitol, Thomas O'Sullivan, Pogo Press: 1994

Named Campaigns - Indian Wars of the United States Army, 1790-1891, reference document iwcmp, U.S. Army, Washington, DC: 2000

The Sioux Uprising of 1862, Kenneth Carley, Minnesota Historical Society, pages 59-62, St. Paul, MN: 1976

MISSISSIPPI

Mississippi New State Capitol 1901-1903, Jackson, Mississippi, State of Mississippi

"Chimneyville" Was Jackson's Legacy In The Civil War, Clarion-Ledger, 7/20/89; and *Revisit The Town That Was Chimneyville*, Jackson Daily News, 12/6/76

MISSOURI

Souvenir Guide To Missouri's Capitol, Missouri Department of Natural Resources

Welcome To The Missouri State Capitol, State of Missouri, Jefferson City, MO: 2000

Self-Guided Outdoor Walk of the Capitol, Missouri Department of Natural Resources

Missouri State Capitol Center Of State Government, Missouri Dept. of Natural Resources, Jefferson City, MO: 2000

Missouri and Missourians, F.C. Shoemaker, LL.D, five volumes, Lewis Publishing, Chicago: 1943

Journal and Proceedings of the Missouri State Convention, March, 1861, George Knapp & Co., St. Louis, MO: 1861

Pages 376-377: This quote is taken from a letter Thomas Jefferson wrote to William Short in 1820.

[SPECIAL THANKS to David E. Snead at the Missouri State Archives for his extra assistance.]

MONTANA

A Short History & Self-Guided Tour of Montana's Capitol Building, Montana Historical Society

Named Campaigns - Indian Wars of the United States Army, 1790-1891, reference document iwcmp, U.S. Army, Washington, DC: 2000

[SPECIAL THANKS to the staff at the Montana Historical Society, State of Montana, Helena, MT.]

NEBRASKA

Guide To Exterior Art And Symbolism, Nebraska State Capitol, State of Nebraska Department of Administrative Services, Lincoln, NE: 1995

Tower On The Plains, The Nebraska State Capitol, *NEBRASKAland* Magazine, Nebraska Game and Parks Commission, and the Department of Administrative Services

A Harmony Of The Arts, The Nebraska State Capitol, Frederick C. Luebke

Nebraska Capitol Masonry Restoration Project 2000, Department of Administrative Services, State Building Division, Nebraska Capitol Collection

The Sower, a page discussing the figure atop the Nebraska Capitol, by Pam Roberts-Gentry

Welcome to the Nebraska State Capitol and the Governor's Greeting, Governor Mike Johanns

Inscriptions On The Nebraska State Capitol, State of Nebraska, Lincoln, NE

[SPECIAL THANKS to the Nebraska State Historical Society, Lincoln, NE.]

NEVADA

Nevada's State Capitol, Monument to Democracy, Barb Prudic and Ron James, State Historic Preservation Office

1999-2000 Guide to the Nevada State Legislature, Research Division, Legislative Counsel Bureau, 12th edition

Political History of Nevada, Nevada State Archives and Records Management, State of Nevada, Carson City, NV

NEW HAMPSHIRE

State House Park, New Hampshire General Court, New Hampshire State House Visitors' Center, Concord, NH

State of New Hampshire, Hall of Flags, a self-guided tour of the Hall of Flags, New Hampshire State House Visitors' Center, Concord, NJ

Self-Guided Tour of New Hampshire's State House, NH General Court, Visitors' Center, State House, Concord, NH

[SPECIAL THANKS to Karen O. Wadsworth, Clerk of the House, New Hampshire House of Representatives for her assistance; to Rep. Francis W. "Frank" Davis, Clerk, Election Law Committee for sharing his insights on what it means to be from New Hampshire.]

NEW JERSEY

Visit the New Jersey State House, New Jersey State House Tour Office, Office of the Legislative Services, Trenton, NJ

Visiting the New Jersey State House, A Walk Through History, Office of Legislative Service, Office of Public Information, Trenton, NJ

The State House Through the Years/The State House Today, Office of Legislative Services, Office of Public Information, Trenton, NJ

The New Jersey State House, Information for Visitors with Special Needs, Office of Legislative Services, Office of Public Information, Trenton, NJ

Your State Capitol, A student guide to the New Jersey State House, Office of Public Information, Office of Legislative Services, Trenton, NJ

NEW MEXICO

New Mexico State Capitol, New Mexico State Legislature, Santa Fe, New Mexico

New Mexico -- A History, Bluebook of the State of New Mexico, New Mexico State Records Center & Archives, Santa Fe, NM

The Growth Of The American Republic, S.E. Morison and H.S. Commager, Oxford University Press, New York: 1962

The Oxford History of the American People, Samuel Eliot Morison, Oxford University Press, New York: 1965

NEW YORK

Visitor's Guide to the New York State Capitol, The New York State Office of General Services and The State Commission on the Restoration of the Capitol, Albany, NY: 1998

The New York State Senate Chamber, New York State Senate brochure, Albany, NY

The Great Seal of the State of New York, Senator Joseph L. Bruno, President Pro Tem - Majority Leader, Albany, NY

The William Dodge Murals, The Governor's Reception Room, New York State Capitol, Albany, NYS Office of General Services, George E. Pataki, Governor, New York State

The Decline of Authority, Public Economic Policy and Political Development in New York State, 1800-1860, L. Ray Gunn, Cornell University Press, Ithaca: 1988

Page 125: The state seal quote comes from *Historical Essays* of Henry A. Holmes, L.L.D., N.Y.S. Library

NORTH CAROLINA

What Is A Tar Heel?, a state handout based on an article by William S. Powell, UNC-CH History professor, *Tar Heel* magazine: March 1982

North Carolina State Legislative Building, State of North Carolina, Raleigh, NC

Heroes & Heroines On Union Square, The Statues and Monuments on Union (Capitol) Square at Raleigh, North Carolina, The State Capitol Foundation Inc.

The Great Seal Of The State of North Carolina, by the State of North Carolina

The North Carolina State Capitol, State Capitol Foundation, Inc., North Carolina State Capitol, Raleigh, NC

NORTH DAKOTA

North Dakota State Capitol Bismark, Facility Management, Capitol Custodian

North Dakota State Capitol Self-Guided Walking Tour, State Historical Society of North Dakota

State Capitol And Grounds, With A Welcome From The Governor, State of North Dakota

North Dakota Centennial Blue Book 1889-1989, Secretary of State, State of North Dakota

The Dakota or Sioux Tribe, James Henri Howard, Museum News (Vermillion, SD), May-June 1966

Named Campaigns - Indian Wars of the United States Army, 1790-1891, reference document iwcmp, U.S. Army, Washington, DC: 2000

[SPECIAL THANKS to Susan Dingle, State Historical Society of North Dakota.]

OHIO

The Ohio Statehouse, Completed In 1861-Restored In 1996, State of Ohio, Columbus, OH

The Ohio Senate, The 123rd General Assembly, Richard H., Finan Senate President, Columbus, OH

The Ohio House of Representatives, The 123rd General Assembly, Jo Ann Davidson, Speaker

The Delaware Indians, Richard C. Adams, Hope Farm Press, Saugerties, NY: 1995

Named Campaigns - Indian Wars of the United States Army, 1790-1891, reference document iwcmp, U.S. Army, Washington, DC: 2000

[SPECIAL THANKS to Edward Schirtzinger, Sergeant-At-Arms, Ohio Senate for sharing his insights on the Ohio Statehouse.]

OKLAHOMA

Oklahoma State Capitol, A Commemorative Guide, Oklahoma Today Magazine

A Self-Guided Tour of the State Capitol Of Oklahoma, The Oklahoma Tourism and Recreation Department Travel and Tourism Division

Dedicated & Historic Trees & Monuments, State Capitol Park, Oklahoma City, OK, Oklahoma Department of Tourism and Recreation: 1997

Oklahoma City National Memorial, Oklahoma City National Memorial, Oklahoma City, OK

Oklahoma Almanac, 47th Edition, Ann Hamilton, Editor, The Oklahoma Dept. Of Libraries, Oklahoma City, OK: 1999

A History of the State of Oklahoma, Luther B. Hill, Volume 1, Lewis Publishing, Chicago: 1909

Oklahoma's History, as written by the State of Oklahoma, Oklahoma City, OK: 2000

Named Campaigns - Indian Wars of the United States Army, 1790-1891, U.S. Army, Washington, DC: 2000

[SPECIAL THANKS to Oklahoma State Archives and Records Management, State of Oklahoma.]

OREGON

Oregon State Capitol, Tour Oregon's Past, Present, and Future, Visitor Services, Oregon State Capitol, Salem, OR

A Walking Tour, State Of Oregon Capitol Grounds, Dept. of Administrative Services, Facilities Division Landscape

Guide to Provisional and Territorial Records, Oregon State Archives, State of Oregon, Salem, OR: Revised 2000

PENNSYLVANIA

The Pennsylvania Capitol and General Assembly, Commonwealth of Pennsylvania, Harrisburg, PA

At the Dawn of the Millennium ... Pennsylvania's Capitol: A Building for All Time, Pennsylvania House of Representatives, Harrisburg, PA

The Pennsylvania Capitol, A Self-Guided Tour, Welcome Center, Harrisburg, PA

The Supreme Court of Pennsylvania, with an introduction from the Chief Justice John P. Flaherty, Commonwealth of Pennsylvania

The Story of a Commonwealth, by Robert Fortenbaugh, Ph.D., Adeline Sager, Professor of History, Gettysburg College, and H. James Tarman, M.Ed., Teacher of Social Studies Edison Junior High School, Harrisburg, PA: 1940

RHODE ISLAND & PROVIDENCE PLANTATIONS

Rhode Island State House Guide, Office of the Secretary of State, James R. Langevin, Secretary of State, State of Rhode Island and Providence Plantations, Providence, RI

Welcome to the Rhode Island State House, The Publications Division of The Office of the Secretary of State, James R. Langevin, Secretary of State, Providence, RI

The State House Centennial Ball, The Rhode Island State House Restoration Society, Providence, RI: 2000

Page 95: The Dorr Rebellion history is contained neatly in documents exchanged between the federal government and the parties involved. *Messages and Papers of the Presidents,* pages 2136-2160 (see General Bibliography).

SOUTH CAROLINA

South Carolina, State Symbols and Emblems, Sandra K. McKinney, Clerk, House of Representatives, Columbia, SC

2000 Millennium Edition, South Carolina Legislative Manual, Sandra K. McKinney, Clerk, House of Representatives, Columbia, SC: 2000

[SPECIAL THANKS to James R. Melton, Sergeant-at-Arms, South Carolina Senate.]

SOUTH DAKOTA

Self-Guided Tour Script Of South Dakota State Capitol Building, Bureau of Administration, Pierre, SD: 2000

History Of The South Dakota State Flag, Bureau of Administration, Division of Central Services, Pierre, SD

The Capitol Grounds and Hilgers Gulch Governors Grove, Arboretum Trails, Bureau of Administration: 2000

The Dakota or Sioux Tribe, James Henri Howard, Museum News (Vermillion, SD), May-June 1966

Named Campaigns - Indian Wars of the United States Army, 1790-1891, reference document iwcmp, U.S. Army, Washington, DC: 2000

[SPECIAL THANKS to Ken Kredit, a candidate for the South Dakota Legislature, for his insights on the state's governmental processes.]

TENNESSEE

The Tennessee State Capitol, A Self-Guided Walking Tour, Tennessee State Museum, Nashville, TN: 1998

The Watauga Petition To North Carolina, July 5, 1776, North Carolina State Archives, Raleigh

Page 190: A great, short account of the State of "Franklinland" appears in *The History of the United States of America* by R. Hildreth, Vol. 3, pages 469-471, 539-540 (see General Bibliography); it was a source for related paragraphs.

TEXAS

Lone Star Treasure, The Texas Capitol Complex, State Preservation Board, Austin, TX: 1998

The Texas Capitol, A Self-Guided Tour, State Preservation Board, Austin, TX: 1998

The Texas Capitol Grounds, A Self-Guided Tour, State Preservation Board, Austin, TX: 1998

The Texas Almanac, Sesquicentennial Edition, Mike Kingston, Editor; Ruth Harris, Associate Editor, The Dallas Morning News, Dallas, TX: 1986

UTAH

Welcome to the Utah State Capitol Building, Utah Travel Council and Salt Lake Convention & Visitors Bureau, Salt Lake City, UT

Constitution of the State of Deseret, Utah History Information Center, Utah State Historical Society, Salt Lake City, UT

Utah Since Statehood, Noble Warrum, Editor, Vol. 1, S.J. Clarke Publishing, Chicago, IL: 1919

[SPECIAL THANKS to the Utah State Historical Society, State of Utah, Salt Lake City, UT.]

VERMONT

Welcome To Vermont's Historic State House!, State of Vermont, Montpelier, VT

Vermont: The State with the Storybook Past, Cora Cheney, The New England Press, Shelburne, VT: 1986

VIRGINIA

The Virginia State Capitol, Douglas W. Price, Office of Graphic Communications, Division of Purchases & Supply, Department of General Services, Richmond, VA

Notes On The State Of Virginia, by Thomas Jefferson, introduction by Thomas Perkins, Harper Torchbooks, The University Library, Harper & Row, New York: 1964

Page 54: John Greenleaf Whittier's words are taken from his poem *The Vow of Washington*, Stanza 14.

[SPECIAL THANKS to Mrs. Charlotte Troxell, Supervisor, Capitol Hostess, Commonwealth of Virginia who provided key background information for this article. She retired April, 2002 after serving at the Capitol for 26 years.]

WASHINGTON

Welcome To The Washington State Capitol, Washington State Legislature and Washington State Senate Graphics Department

In Memory, Washington State Veterans Monuments, State of Washington, Olympia, WA: 2000

History of the Washington Legislature 1854-1963, by Don Brazier, 2000

[SPECIAL THANKS to the Washington State Historical Center, WSHS Research Center, Tacoma, WA and the Washington State Capitol Museum, Olympia, WA; and Crystal Lentz, Washington State Library.]

WEST VIRGINIA

A Capitol Idea, The West Virginia State Capitol Complex, WV Division of Tourism, Charleston, WV

Clarksburg Convention and *Proceedings of the First Wheeling Convention*, Wheeling Intelligencer 4/25/1861 and 5/14/1861, provided with other documents by the West Virginia State Archives, Charleston, WV

WISCONSIN

Wisconsin State Capitol, State Historical Society of Wisconsin, Madison, WI: 2000

State Capitol, Tour Narration, English, Wisconsin Department of Administration, Madison, WI: 1999

American National Biography, J.A. Garraty and M.C. Carnes, General Editors, Volume I, John Jacob Astor pages 696-699, Oxford University Press, New York: 1999

Page 290: The fur trade is well documented in *The American Fur Trade*, by H.M. Chittenden, 3 vols., Harper, New York: 1902

WYOMING

Wyoming Capitol Tour Guide, State of Wyoming

[SPECIAL THANKS to the Wyoming State Archives, Cheyenne, WY.]

General Bibliography

STATE CAPITOLS

Executive Mansions and Capitols Of America, by Jean Houston Daniel and Price Daniel, published by Country Beautiful, Waukesha, WI: MCMLXIX

America's Heritage: Capitols of the United States, Willis J. Ehlert, Sixth Edition Rev, State House Publishing, Madison, WI: 1999

State Capitals, Thomas G. Aylesworth, W.H. Smith Publishers, The Image Bank, New York: 1990

Temples Of Democracy: The State Capitols Of The U.S.A., Henry-Russell Hitchcock and William Seale, Harcourt Brace Jovanovich, New York: 1976

National Geographic Picture Atlas of Our Fifty States, published by The National Geographic Society, The Book Division: 1991

STATE & FEDERAL CONSTITUTIONS

A Defence of the Constitutions of Government of the United States of America, Against the Attack Of M.Turgot In His Letter To Dr. Price, by John Adams, LL.D. President Of The United States. In Three Volumes. The Third Edition, Printed by Budd And Bartram, Philadelphia: 1797. This edition reprinted by The Lawbook Exchange, Ltd., Union, NJ: 2001

The Constitution of the United States Of America Analysis And Interpretation, Annotations Of Cases Decided By The Supreme Court Of The United States To June 29, 1992, Prepared by the Congressional Research Service Library of Congress, Johnny H. Killian, George A. Costello Co-Editors, U.S. Government Printing Office, Washington, DC: 1996

The Federal And State Constitutions, Colonial Charters, And Other Organic Laws Of The United States. In Two Parts. Compiled under an order of the U.S. Senate, by Ben. Perley Poore, Clerk of Printing Records, Second Edition. Washington, DC: 1878. This edition reprinted by The Lawbook Exchange, Ltd., Union, NJ: 2001

The Debates In The Several State Conventions, On The Adoption Of The Federal Constitution, As Recommended By The General Convention At Philadelphia, In 1787. In Five Volumes. Second Edition, by Jonathan Elliot, J.B. Lippincott Co., Philadelphia: 1891. This edition was reprinted by William S. Hein & Co., Inc., Buffalo, NY: 1996

[SPECIAL NOTE: Originally published in 1836, "Elliot's Debates" is one of the most important sources for understanding Revolutionary America and the legal environment in which the Articles of Confederation and the United States Constitution were made.]

The Northwest Ordinance of 1787, from a copy supplied by the National Archives, Washington, DC

[SPECIAL NOTE: The Northwest Ordinance concludes thusly: "Done by the United States, in congress assembled, the 13th day of July, in the year of our Lord 1787, and of their sovereignty and independence the twelfth.]

Contract Between the King and the Thirteen United States of North America, and related treaties between France and the United States, The Avalon Project at the Yale Law School, New Haven, CT

The Louisiana Purchase, Transcriptions, Treaty Between the United States of America And The French Republic, National Archives and Records Administration, Washington, DC

A Brief Enquiry Into The True Nature And Character Of Our Federal Government, Abel P. Upshur, (the C. Chauncey Burr Edition), Van Evrie, Horton & Co., New York: 1868

[SPECIAL NOTE: Abel Upshur became Secretary of State in 1843 after Daniel Webster resigned. He was killed a year later in the *USS Princeton* accident. Schooled at Yale and Princeton, he wrote this compelling treatise in response to Judge Joseph Story's *Commentaries on the Constitution of the United States.*]

History of the Constitution of the United States, George Bancroft, D. Appleton & Company, New York: 1885

Leading Constitutional Decisions, 13th edition, Robert E. Cushman in collaboration with Robert F. Cushman, Appleton-Century-Crofts, division of Meredith Publishing Company, New York: 1966

The Law of the American Constitution, Charles K. Burdick, G.P. Putnam's Sons, New York: 1922

AMERICAN HISTORY

Biographical Sketches Of The Signers Of The Declaration Of American Independence: The Declaration Historically Considered; And A Sketch Of The Leading Events Connected With The Adoption Of The Articles Of Confederation. And Of The Federal Constitution by B.J. Lossing, New York: Derby & Jackson: 1858

A Compilation Of The Messages And Papers Of The Presidents 1789-1908, by James D. Richardson, a Representative from the State of Tennessee (with Revisions), in eleven volumes with index, Published by United States Bureau Of National Literature And Art, Washington: 1909

American Historical Documents 1000-1904, The Harvard Classics, Edited by Charles W. Eliot LL.D., P F Collier & Son Company, New York: 1910

Named Campaigns - Indian Wars of the United States Army, 1790-1891, reference document iwcmp, U.S. Army, Washington, DC: 2000

The History Of The United States Of America, by Richard Hildreth, revised edition, 6 vols., New York, Harper & Brothers, Franklin Square: 1880

Journals Of The Continental Congress 1774-1789, Library Of Congress, edited from the original records in the Library Of Congress by Worthington Chauncey Ford, Chief, Division of Manuscripts, U.S. Government Printing Office, Washington, DC: 1904

Living Documents in American History, edited and with Introductions by John A. Scott, Washington Square Press, Inc., New York: 1963

A Universal History of the United States of America, C.B. Taylor, Published by Ezra Strong, New York: 1838

A Political and Civil History of the United States of America, Timothy Pitkin, Hezekiah Howe, New Haven: 1828

Beginnings of the American People, Carl Becker, Houghton Mifflin Co., Boston and New York: 1915

The Cambridge Modern History, Volume VII, The United States, Lord Acton LL.D., Cambridge University Press: 1905

The Formation of the Union (Original Documents pictured and described including the Declaration of Independence, the Articles of Confederation, and the U.S. Constitution), National Archives Publication number 70-13, Richard Nixon, President of the United States, Washington, DC

A People's History of the United States, Howard Zinn, Longman, London: 1980

Pictorial Field Book of the Revolution, B.J. Lossing, in two volumes, Harper Brothers, New York: 1859

The Formation of the American Republic 1776-1790, Forrest McDonald, Penguin Books, Baltimore, MD: 1965

[SPECIAL NOTE: If you want to understand the political and legal issues involved in the formation of the United States, this work is a must. Well-written, objective, and provocative -- what more would you want from a history book?]

The Articles of Confederation, Merrill Jensen, University of Wisconsin Press, Madison, WI: 1940

Notes on the Iroquois; or Contributions to American History, Antiquities, And General Ethnology, H.R. Schoolcraft, with color plates, Erastus H. Pease & Co., Albany: 1847

SOVEREIGNTY

The Supreme Court In United States History, Charles Warren, in two volumes, revised edition, Little Brown, And Company, Boston: 1926

[SPECIAL NOTE: A profound work for which Mr. Warren won the Pulitzer Prize for History, this book provides extensive insights into the nature of the federal government, the states, and the arbiter between them, the U.S. Supreme Court.]

New Views Of The Constitution Of The United States, John Taylor of Caroline, Virginia, Washington City: 1823. This edition by The Lawbook Exchange, Union, NJ: 2002

Commentaries On The Constitution 1790-1860, by Elizabeth Kelley Bauer, Ph.D., Columbia University Press, New York: 1952. This edition reprinted by The Lawbook Exchange, Ltd., Union, NJ: 1999

The Law of Nations; Or, Principles of the Law of Nature Applied to the Conduct of Nations and Sovereigns, M. De Vattel, translated from the French, Luke White, Dublin: 1738

The Status Of Federalism In America, A Report Of The Working Group On Federalism Of The Domestic Policy Council, Charles J. Cooper, Chairman, Executive Branch, U.S. Government, Washington, DC: 1986

Pennsylvania's Concepts Of The Commonwealth And The Keystone, by Louis Waddell, Bureau of Archives and History, Pennsylvania Historical and Museum Commission, a paper presented at the 65th Annual Meeting of the Pennsylvania Historical Association: 1996

Six Books Of The Commonwealth, Jean Bodin, translated by M.J. Tooley, Alden Press, Oxford, England

[SPECIAL NOTE: To Jean Bodin (1530-1596) we are eternally indebted. This great Frenchman pioneered the study of sovereignty and wrote extensively on the subject.]

INDEX

Nelson, Thomas, 52, 58

"A man of sovereign parts he is esteem'd;
Well fitted in arts, glorious in arms:
Nothing becomes him ill that he would well.."

-- WILLIAM SHAKESPEARE, *Love's Labour's Lost*, Act II, Sc. 1, Line 44

"To the States or any one of them, or any city of the States,
Resist much, obey little,
Once unquestioning obedience, once fully enslaved,
Once fully enslaved, no nation, state, city of this earth,
ever afterward resumes its liberty."

-- WALT WHITMAN, *To The States*, appearing in *Leaves of Grass*